Kuczynski

D0669509

The New Foreign Policy

The New Foreign Policy

The New Foreign Policy

U.S. and Comparative Foreign Policy in the 21st Century

Laura Neack

ROWMAN & LITTLEFIELD PUBLISHERS, INC.
Lanham • Boulder • New York • Oxford

ROWMAN & LITTLEFIELD PUBLISHERS, INC.

Published in the United States of America
by Rowman & Littlefield Publishers, Inc.
A Member of the Rowman & Littlefield Publishing Group
4720 Boston Way, Lanham, Maryland 20706
www.rowmanlittlefield.com

12 Hid's Copse Road, Cumnor Hill, Oxford OX2 9JJ, England

Copyright © 2003 by Rowman & Littlefield Publishers, Inc.

All rights reserved. No part of this publication may be reproduced,
stored in a retrieval system, or transmitted in any form or by any
means, electronic, mechanical, photocopying, recording, or otherwise,
without the prior permission of the publisher.

British Library Cataloguing in Publication Information Available

Library of Congress Cataloging-in-Publication Data

Neack, Laura.
   The new foreign policy / Laura Neack.
      p. cm.
   ISBN 0-7425-0146-9 (alk. paper)—ISBN 0-7425-0147-7 (pbk. : alk. paper)
   1. United States—Foreign relations—2001– 2. September 11 Terrorist
Attacks, 2001. 3. Globalization—Political aspects. 4. United States—Foreign
relations—1989– 5. United States—Foreign relations—Philosophy. I. Title.
E895 .N43 2003
327.73'009'049—dc21

                                                                    2002002373

Printed in the United States of America

⊗™The paper used in this publication meets the minimum requirements
of American National Standard for Information Sciences—Permanence of
Paper for Printed Library Materials, ANSI/NISO Z39.48-1992.

In loving memory of
Charles William Neack
1923–2001

Contents

Illustrations

Figures

Table

Boxes

Preface

On September 11, 2001, terrorists hijacked four commercial airplanes in the United States and turned three of them into weapons of mass destruction. Two planes were flown into the towers of the World Trade Center in New York City and a third was flown into the side of the Pentagon in Washington, D.C. The fourth hijacked plane went down in a field in rural Pennsylvania as the passengers and crew fought the hijackers to regain control of the plane. The people on that flight used cell phones to communicate with their families after the plane was hijacked. These heroes knew the fate of the other hijacked planes and were determined not to let a fourth plane wreak such death and destruction.

September 11, 2001, will be one of those days that we'll never forget; we will always remember where we were and what we were doing when we heard the incredible news. On that morning, I was working on the book you are holding now, at home in southwestern Ohio. My husband called from a classroom at Miami University right before ten o'clock to say he had heard something about a plane hitting one of the World Trade Center towers, and to ask what I had heard. Then my father called and said, "Are you watching the news, someone has *attacked* the World Trade Center and the Pentagon; turn on your TV." I asked him to repeat what he said; it seemed incredible. I turned on the television and watched the live pictures of the WTC towers billowing smoke. Then one of the towers collapsed. I had trouble understanding that what I was watching was not some imagined reality but *was* reality. Within moments of the collapse of the second tower, my son called from school—was I watching and could I believe it? As so many people did that day—even people who were claimed ultimately as victims of the attacks—we were reaching out to loved ones to try to make some sense of what we were watching and hearing.

My father was a World War II vet—Dad served in the Marine Corps in the South Pacific. When I called him back that dreadful September morning, Dad said this was just like Pearl Harbor, but so much worse. He was in shock, like me, like so many others. Later that day, as my teenage son and I were watching nonstop television coverage of the attacks, we heard former U.S. Secretary of State Henry Kissinger use the same analogy Dad had—that this attack was another Pearl Harbor. Kissinger said that once we learned who perpetrated this attack we should do to them what we did to the Japanese. My son looked at me with wide, horrified eyes and said, "Kissinger thinks we should *nuke* them?" We knew that an American response was in order, but *what kind*? As I write this preface, the American response continues to unfold. The readers of this book will have the advantage of some time and distance with which to assess the response and (some) of its aftermath.

September 11, 2001, *was* like December 7, 1941, in that the United States, a country that luxuriated in its geographical isolation, found it was not so isolated after all. But September 11, 2001, was more *unlike* December 7, 1941, than it was like it. On September 11 (1) the continental United States was attacked; (2) the perpetrators used commercial aircraft as their weapons of choice, taking charge of those aircraft by wielding cardboard cutters and no "typical" weapons; and (3) the perpetrators *represented no government* and did on a grand scale what no country had dared since December 7, 1941. The political "game" or landscape *seemed* to have shifted dramatically in September 2001.

We should keep in mind, though, that a far less "successful" attack occurred in 1993 when persons alleged to be affiliated with the September 11 hijackers bombed the World Trade Center. Had Americans been paying closer attention, we might have been aware that a new "game" had been upon us for a number of years.

The New Foreign Policy presents the tools and lessons developed by scholars over the last half of the twentieth century, honed to the shifting landscape of the twenty-first century and new millennium. The events and aftermath of September 11 appear in these pages, but two larger—meta-level—phenomena have had more shaping impact on what is written in this book than the terrorist attacks: globalization and the predominance of the American superpower. But, as I discuss in chapter 5, these meta-level phenomena may have generated the anger behind the attacks of September 11.

Within this framework of globalization and American predominance, *The New Foreign Policy* rests on the assumption that foreign policy is best understood as a "nested game" in which national leaders attempt to "play" the two games of domestic and international politics to their advantage. Foreign policy *analysis*, then, is best undertaken as a study of this nested game, or, as a multilevel study.

This book begins with a case study on Tibet, the United States, and China—on Buddhism, human rights, and opening the Chinese market—

that demonstrates the complexity of foreign policy. Such complexity requires complex analysis. But if we try to do too much in any single study, we might be overwhelmed by the details and might never arrive at any worthwhile and useful conclusions. And so, also in chapter 1, I explain that foreign policy scholars make use of approaches and theories to narrow and make more manageable their subject of study. Chapter 1 also provides readers with a refresher course on the dominant international relations worldviews that shape foreign policy study and with a brief history of the *study* of foreign policy.

Chapters 2, 3, and 4 present a survey of the scholarship on foreign policy using the individual, state, and system levels of analysis, respectively. I have tried to be inclusive, but could not possibly be exhaustive, in my selection. My approach blends cases with scholarship. I hope that the cases provided in each chapter (some short, some quite detailed) generate that "aha!" that comes when students are shown the practical uses of scholarship. Even with the cases provided, though, I encourage teachers and students to use this book as a guide that prompts further investigation. Chapters 2, 3, and 4 are devoted to separate levels of analysis, but the reader is reminded throughout that a multilevel approach gives the most complete understanding of any foreign policy puzzle.

Chapter 5 returns us to the nested game with another case study, this one on the tangled tale of a Spanish judge, a former Chilean dictator, human rights groups, and the British home secretary. Chapter 5 asserts that one of the lessons of September 11 is that states would be foolish to ever again underestimate or dismiss the role of *nonstate* actors in shaping world politics and foreign policies.

I wish to thank Professors Ole Holsti and Robert J. Beck for their supportive, constructive, and thorough reviews of the first draft of this book. Every author should be so lucky as to get such feedback. Thanks to Lindsay Mosser for constructing the glossary for this book. Thanks, too, to the New Millennium Books in International Studies editorial board who were from the start enthusiastic about and protective of this project. Special thanks are due to NMB series editor Deborah Gerner—although it was a daunting task to write a foreign policy book for a renowned foreign policy scholar. At Rowman & Littlefield, thanks go to Renee Legatt, who took charge of bringing this book to print with great competence and cheer. I am at a loss to describe adequately the encouragement and insight and direction and patience given me by Jennifer Knerr, executive editor of political science at Rowman & Littlefield. I never doubted that Jennifer was in my corner, but that feeling was confirmed when she told me she had dreamed about ways to improve the book. Thank you, Jennifer. May you always have sweet(er) dreams!

Finally, many, many thanks go to my guys—to my husband, Roger Knudson, for the standard love and support through not-so-standard times, and to my son, Harry Neack, for the support given from one writer to another. The year 2001 was marked by an enormous personal loss when my father, Charles Neack, passed away at the end of the year. This book is dedicated to you, Dad. I wish you would call and ask once more how the book is going.

1

Introduction: A New Approach to Foreign Policy

In This Chapter

- A Tangled Tale of Tibet
- The New Foreign Policy
- Selecting Entrance Points: Levels of Analysis
- Worldviews and Theories
  - *Realism*
  - *Liberalism*
  - *Marxism*
- Time to Back Up and Consider the Subject: Foreign Policy
- The Bridge between International and Comparative Politics
- A New Millennium
- A Road Map of *The New Foreign Policy*
- Review: Important Observations about Foreign Policy
- For Further Study

A Tangled Tale of Tibet

Let's go back to 1989 and up to the top of the world—Tibet. In 1989, the Tenth Panchen Lama, one of two of the highest leaders of Tibetan Buddhism, died under mysterious circumstances in his monastery. By Buddhist tradition, the soul of the Panchen Lama would be reincarnated, returning to earth to teach others the path to enlightenment. Also according to Buddhist tradition, the former friends and teachers of the late Panchen Lama would begin a series of divinations designed to determine where he would be reincarnated so they could locate the living Buddha and ensure his proper religious training and preparation.

What does this have to do with *The New Foreign Policy*? This is one entrance into a tangled tale that involves many countries strong and weak, key international figures, transnational human rights and religious groups, the **United Nations,** and even Hollywood. We could open the tale years earlier—decades and centuries earlier—or in the year 2000. Changing the starting point would change the issues somewhat, but the tangled nature of the tale would not change, nor would its entanglement in the foreign relations of some powerful states. Indeed, the fate of Tibetan Buddhism is inextricably enmeshed in the foreign policy choices of several important countries, and presents us with a perfect case study on *The New Foreign Policy*.

So back to our tale.

In early 1995, the Panchen Lama search party narrowed their search to a short list of boys, in and outside Tibet, and assembled photos and evidence to present to the highest holy figure in Tibetan Buddhism, the Dalai Lama. The search party would offer its opinion on which boy was most likely to be the reincarnate lama. The Dalai Lama would make the final decision regarding the recognition of the Eleventh Panchen Lama, taking into account the evidence and opinion of the search party, as well as the information gathered through his own divinations. For many centuries, the Dalai and Panchen Lamas served as each other's teacher and helped identify reincarnates of each other.

So here's where we'll bring foreign policy in—the Dalai Lama is the spiritual and temporal leader of the government of Tibet *in exile*. The Dalai Lama and his government reside in Dharamsala in northern India, where they sought refuge from the Chinese occupation of Tibet. The Chinese army asserted its control of Tibet—invaded Tibet—in 1950 in order to incorporate it into the new communist **regime.** This incorporation required eliminating the independence-minded Tibetan government led by the young Dalai Lama. By 1959, brutal Chinese efforts to eradicate Buddhism and the culture of the Tibetan people led the Dalai Lama to flee Tibet in the hope of maintaining some semblance of the true Tibet in sanctuary. The Dalai Lama and his supporters would maintain a government in exile until the world (or powerful actors in the world) ended the Chinese occupation and/or oppression. Of course, this is not the story the Chinese government told—then or now.

Regardless of whether one takes the position that Tibet was part of China for centuries or that Tibet was independent until 1950, since 1950 Tibet has been part of the territory called the People's Republic of China. Ever since he fled Tibet, the Dalai Lama has frustrated and angered the

Chinese government because of his persistent work for the liberation of his people and culture. Since his flight from Tibet, the Dalai Lama has been accorded head of **state** treatment by governments around the world, including the executive and legislative branches of the U.S. government, and been praised and supported by international human rights and religious freedom groups, and even Hollywood movie stars. As an advocate of nonviolence, the Dalai Lama was awarded the Nobel Peace Prize in 1989. The Dalai Lama constantly reminded the world that his people, culture, and religion were being decimated by the Chinese government in clear violation of international human rights and religious freedom standards. He was but a single individual who caused the Chinese government considerable consternation and bad international publicity. Further, the Dalai Lama's government in exile was/is located in the territory of one of China's most hostile, long-standing enemies—India.

The Panchen Lama chose to be reincarnated inside Tibet, it turned out. The Dalai Lama, worried about the reaction of the Chinese authorities, carefully weighed the options about announcing who the reincarnate lama was. In April 1995, the Dalai Lama decided to name the boy to start the process of his training and preempt any efforts by the Chinese to thwart the process. The Chinese government responded by arresting the boy, his family, and the monk who headed the Panchen Lama search team. A new naming team was quickly assembled by Chinese authorities. This team chose a different boy as the reincarnation, and in December, the Chinese government (which is officially atheist) staged a grand ceremony at which its designate assumed the position of the Eleventh Panchen Lama. The Dalai Lama's choice, Gedhun Choekyi Nyima, and his family disappeared into Chinese custody and have not been seen since the spring of 1995. The Dalai Lama, human rights groups such as Amnesty International, and religious groups declared the boy to be the world's youngest political prisoner. The Chinese government, when its spokespersons even acknowledged Gedhun Choekyi Nyima's existence, only said that he "is where he is supposed to be."[1]

How does this tale become a foreign policy issue? The Chinese government has declared many times that this tale or any tale about Tibet should *never* be a foreign policy issue, since it involves the *domestic* affairs of China. As a foreign ministry spokesperson said in 1993 regarding Tibet, "The business of the United States should be addressed by the American people, and the business of the Chinese people should be handled by the Chinese people."[2] But the domestic affairs of any country are often a source of contention with other countries. How and to what extent the tale of the Panchen Lama gets entwined in foreign policy depends on the decisions and actions taken and the "power" held by various interested actors in various countries. Let's switch sites and see how this plays out.

In 1992 in the United States, Democratic presidential candidate Bill Clinton focused his campaign efforts on U.S. domestic issues. "It's the economy, stupid," was a statement prominent in his campaign offices. President George H. W. Bush (Bush 1) had declared himself the "foreign policy president," setting himself up for criticism on domestic issues. The Clinton campaign also found opportunities to criticize Bush on foreign policy, most prominently on U.S. inaction in the Bosnian war and U.S.-Chinese relations post–Tiananmen Square.

Since the Chinese government's violent crackdown on the prodemocracy demonstrators in Tiananmen Square on June 3, 1989, the Bush 1 administration had been open to criticism for his policy toward China. (A few months prior to Tiananmen, the Chinese had used violence to break an uprising in Lhasa, Tibet.) President Bush's view was that the best way to influence China, avoid future Tiananmens, and end other alleged human rights violations was to remain "constructively engaged" with China, offering incentives rather than disincentives to change. Since 1990, Chinese and American officials had begun a series of talks on human rights that were not fruitful but were seen by the Bush 1 administration as keeping the door to China open.

A majority in Congress disagreed with **constructive engagement,** as did human rights and religious interest groups. When an attempt by Congress to pass a tough sanctions bill to punish China was defeated by presidential veto, congressional critics decided to place human rights conditions on the yearly renewal of China's **most favored nation (MFN)** trading status.[3] Constructive engagement remained U.S. policy during the remainder of the Bush 1 administration, but the 1992 presidential elections would keep a prosanctions coalition alive and hopeful.

Signaling disagreement with the Bush China policy, the Democratic-dominated Senate Foreign Relations Committee held its first ever hearing on the Chinese occupation of Tibet in July 1992. A special envoy of the Dalai Lama and the movie actor Richard Gere (a Buddhist) testified about Chinese "systematic genocide" in Tibet.[4] A deputy assistant secretary of state, representing the Bush 1 administration, denied any human rights abuses in Tibet by China and testified that the official U.S. position was that Tibet was part of China. Democratic Senator Daniel Patrick Moynihan disagreed with this statement of U.S. policy, recollecting that during the 1950s the United States had been in favor of Tibetan **self-determination.** Committee Chairman Democrat Claiborne Pell reportedly remarked, "American policy has not been true to the Tibetans. . . . Once having supported Tibetan independence, State Department officials now say that Tibet is part of China."[5] With this tone established by the Senate Democrats, the Clinton campaign adopted a clear pro-Tibet, tough-on-China line.

After meeting with members of Congress and leaders of various interest groups opposed to the Bush 1 policy, Democratic presidential candidate Bill Clinton came out in favor of attaching human rights conditions to any future granting of MFN status to China. Clinton announced his position: "I do not want to isolate China . . . but I believe our nation has a higher purpose than to coddle dictators and stand aside from the global movement toward democracy."[6] This statement was repeated many times by Clinton on the campaign trail. Upon Clinton's election, Chinese authorities signaled their unhappiness with the results of the U.S. election by suspending further human rights talks. The complexities of the China policy were becoming more clear to President-elect Clinton, who announced a moderated view in late November 1992: "We have a big stake in not isolating China, in seeing that China continues to develop a market economy. . . . But we also have to insist, I believe, on progress in human rights and human decency."[7]

Before his inauguration, Clinton hosted several conferences in his hometown of Little Rock, Arkansas, to clarify key issues for the new administration. At the economic conference, the chief operating officer of toy manufacturer Mattel raised worries about Mattel's ability to stay on top of the world toy market if human rights conditions were attached to renewing China's MFN status. Voices within the United States—such as the aircraft and wheat industries—and voices outside the United States—such as the governments of Japan and Hong Kong—were similarly urging Clinton to back away from his campaign stand on China.[8] Despite these voices, Clinton appointed prohuman rights advocates to key foreign policy positions. Some of these appointees met regularly with interest groups who advocated linking U.S. trade policy toward China with measurable improvements in China's human rights record. Yet Clinton, like Bush before him, found that those who disagreed with him on China policy—in Congress, among members of the Democratic Party, business interests and even foreign interests—were willing to continue to push to (re)define the ultimate policy of the new administration.

Right before the Clinton inauguration, two different groups of Democratic senators visited China and Tibet in December 1992 and January 1993, *at the invitation of the Chinese government.* This Chinese effort to influence the domestic political debate within the United States—and thereby shape U.S. foreign policy in the new administration—reaped some benefits, as several of the senators declared that it would be shortsighted to link trade and human rights.

A new U.S. policy on China was formulated in 1993 by the new administration in which the president, acting under executive orders authority, attached some pro–human rights conditions to the U.S.-Chinese relationship, *but not on trade issues.* This compromise policy was hammered out by talks on many levels between administration officials and various members of Congress, and with their respective domestic groups engaged behind the scenes. The compromise allowed voices on both sides to be partially satisfied and partially dissatisfied. Farm and business groups and their supporters in Congress were glad to keep trade off this particular table, human rights groups and their Congressional supporters were glad to see some official pronouncement privileging human rights and **democracy**. Even in this age of **globalization** where market forces seemed to drive so much international activity, it appeared that key noneconomic values would remain central to U.S. foreign policy. At the signing ceremony for the executive order, leaders of human rights groups, business leaders, prodemocracy Chinese students, and members of the Tibetan government in exile stood behind President Clinton.[9] The president warned that the *next* year's renewal of MFN status would be subject to human rights conditions and conditions designed to curtail Chinese weapons sales (an increasingly troublesome issue). Concurrently, demonstrations in Lhasa, Tibet were being ended with force.[10]

There were others in the Clinton administration and Congress who favored a tough China policy for reasons other than Tibet or the treatment of prodemocracy advocates. Chinese weapons sales to "rogue" states were causing worries among some **security** analysts. Adding to these worries, in October 1993, the Chinese conducted an underground nuclear weapon test. In response, Clinton ordered the Department of Energy to prepare for its own test.[11]

The compromise China policy would not last and the threat about *next year* would not be carried out. Internal divisions within the Clinton administration—reflecting divisions in American society—led to a reevaluation of policy over the year to follow. "On the one side were the economic agencies, Treasury, Commerce, and the National Economic Council (NEC), who favored developing ties with China and pursuing human rights concerns only secondarily. . . . On the other side were State Department officials . . . who favored continuing a tough stance on human rights."[12] The economic agencies gained the upper hand on the issue, with support from corporate leaders and increasing numbers of members of Congress, all of whom were interested in tapping into China's enormous potential market. This coalition was able to change the Clinton policy and avoid future annual threats to link MFN status with human rights issues. As Clinton explained the change in policy in May 1994, "**linkage** has been constructive during the last year, but . . . we have reached the end of the usefulness of that policy."[13] Human rights groups went along with this delinking in order not to lose their potential **leverage** on the rest of the China policy.[14]

In the next year, 1995, the controversy over the reincarnation of the Panchen Lama came to a climax of sorts with the naming of the two competing "soul boys." That December, as the Chinese-favored Panchen Lama was ceremoniously installed, the Chinese government also sentenced a prominent democracy advocate to fourteen years in prison. These events caused some members of Congress and human rights groups to attempt to force a Clinton policy reassessment on trade with China. Yet even in the face of this pressure, Deputy U.S. Trade Representative Charlene Barshefsky reassured all that the President's previous decision to delink MFN status and human rights "remains fixed and unchanged."[15] Although human rights problems in China might temper the climate of talks somewhat, the president was committed to helping China gain entry into the World Trade Organization. *Unless,* Barshefsky warned, the Chinese leaders continued to make no progress on *opening their markets.*

As already mentioned, some important international and domestic actors were attempting to change the Clinton policy. In early December, representatives of the Dalai Lama called on the Geneva-based U.N. International Human Rights Commission to demand that Chinese officials disclose the location and condition of Gedhun Choekyi Nyima (the Dalai Lama's choice as the Eleventh Panchen Lama).[16] In midmonth, *Agence France Presse* reported,

The U.S. Senate unanimously passed a resolution urging China to support the Dalai Lama's choice of a new Panchen Lama—the second-highest leader of Tibetan Buddhism—rather than the boy Beijing has enthroned.

In a resolution approved late Wednesday, Senators called on the Clinton administration to press Beijing to support the exiled spiritual leader's choice of a new Panchen Lama and to ensure his safety.[17]

The Senate resolution was designed to assist the efforts of the Tibetan government in exile by requiring the administration to press the issue of the Panchen Lama's whereabouts in March at the meetings of the U.N. Human Rights Commission. The point of this resolution, declared a spokeswoman for the NGO International Campaign for Tibet, was to send a "very important message to the Chinese that Congress is paying very close attention to what they are doing."[18] The Chinese government responded by loudly protesting U.S. interference in its internal affairs.[19]

The Clinton White House hosted the Dalai Lama on several occasions in the following years to indicate its ongoing support for the cause of the people of Tibet and for the peaceful efforts of the Dalai Lama. At the same time, the administration made it clear that Tibet was an internal problem of China's that could not be productively linked to trade. In June 1998 while on a state visit to China, President Clinton urged the Chinese government to hold talks with the Dalai Lama in a speech broadcast live on Chinese television. Five months later, the Dalai Lama visited the White House again, drawing condemnations from the Chinese government and a warning that such meetings could harm U.S.-Chinese relations.[20]

In January 2000, during the early U.S. presidential primary season, various pro-Tibet American groups—including Amnesty International, New Hampshire Friends of Tibet, Concord High School's Children of Peace, Hanover's Students for a Free Tibet, and the American Friends Service Committee—followed the presidential hopefuls attempting to get commitments in support of Tibet. Most responded "favorably" regarding meeting the Dalai Lama, although none would commit to altering U.S. trade policy because of Tibet.[21] The power of the domestic coalition supporting the linking of human rights with trade was far less than it had been in the 1992 presidential campaign.

In late spring 2000, when the granting of permanent normal trade relations (PNTR) with China was set for a vote in the U.S. Senate, human rights groups were far-off voices. At a pro-PNTR joint appearance featuring President Clinton, former Presidents Jimmy Carter and Gerald Ford, Vice President Al Gore, Secretary of State Madeleine Albright, and former Secretaries of State Henry Kissinger and James Baker, the vice president acknowledged the existence of dissenting opinions regarding China, mentioning Tibet last in a line of American concerns:

> There are those who disagree with us on this issue. I respect their views, and I understand their impatience with the pace of change in China. I share it, as do most people in this room. We have to continue to press China on issues like human rights and workers' rights, environmental protection, religious freedom, and treatment of Tibet.[22]

The Senate voted to give China PNTR, which was hailed as a significant foreign policy victory for the lame-duck Clinton administration. To get back almost to where we started, the U.S. Senate vote also could be seen as a significant foreign policy victory *for the Chinese government*—a government that had long insisted that Tibet was no one's business but China's.

The New Foreign Policy

This saga demonstrates several important observations about foreign policy that will be explored in detail in this book:

- Foreign policy is made and conducted in complex domestic and international environments.
- Foreign policy results from coalitions of interested domestic and international actors and groups.
- Foreign policy issues are often linked and delinked, reflecting the strength of various parties and their particular concerns.
- The *stuff* of foreign policy derives from issues of domestic politics as well as foreign relations.

• Foreign policy analysis needs to be multilevel and multifaceted in order to confront the complicated sources and nature of foreign policy.

How each of these key features pertains to the tangled tale of Tibet is summarized below.

Foreign policy is made and conducted in complex domestic and international environments. The "tangled tale of Tibet" illustrates that decision makers—here, Bill Clinton and the members of his administration in charge of China policy—operate in at least two different environments, domestic and international. Bill Clinton the candidate was focused primarily on the domestic environment, with very little attention paid to the international environment. Bill Clinton the newly elected president had to give attention to both the domestic and international environments, as the U.S. president plays important roles and has important responsibilities in both. We might say that Clinton the candidate had more flexibility than Clinton the president, because (1) he was not yet the person making U.S. policy nor dealing with the consequences of that policy and (2) he was free to worry about the domestic situation alone since American voters tend to vote on domestic and not foreign policy issues. Once he became president, Bill Clinton had to divide his attention between the two environments, which had an impact on the ultimate shape of his China policy.

Political scientist Robert Putnam has described this situation that national leaders find themselves in as a **"two-level"** or **nested game.**[23] Leaders cannot afford to focus exclusively on one level but must try to play both to some advantage. Sometimes issues on one level will cause a leader to put greater emphasis there, and sometimes leaders will use issues in one level to pursue goals in the other, but no leader can afford to ignore the reality of this nested game.

Foreign policy results from coalitions of interested domestic and international actors and groups. Coalitions are, by nature, in constant change. The coalition of interests and groups that might get a politician elected is not necessarily the coalition that will get that leader's programs legislated or executed. Leaders come to power "owing" some groups yet often intent on "wooing" others. As the environments shift, the issues shift and the nature of **coalition building** shifts. Leaders often need to pay more attention to those who form the opposition—trying to entice them into forming **policy coalitions** to get favored programs passed—than to their loyal constituents. The human rights and religious groups *inside* the United States and human rights and democracy advocates *outside* the United States (such as the Tibetan government in exile, Chinese students studying in the United States, and the governments of other countries) could not pose any significant threat to the Clinton presidency if Clinton were to "water down" his China policy somewhat. Indeed, we might say that these groups needed the Clinton presidency more than the Clinton presidency needed them—especially the coalition of non-U.S.

actors who were not very "powerful" international actors. In order to pursue his broader list of goals—both domestic and international—Clinton
needed to garner key support from groups that *opposed* linking trade with
human rights. In this way, these groups might support other Clinton policies as a quid pro quo. Without currying the favor of these groups, Clinton
might have trouble getting any policies approved, his presidency under
constant attack from the opposition.

*Foreign policy issues are often linked and delinked, reflecting the strength of
various parties and their particular concerns.* Because of the "nested game"
leaders play and the necessity of building various policy coalitions, issues cannot help but be linked and delinked. Politics is a game of bargaining and compromising, and this involves trade-offs. The politics of
foreign policy making is no different. Although the Chinese government
insisted that human rights should not be linked to trade issues, by this
very demand China made it clear that the United States could not hope
to achieve its goals vis-à-vis China unless it quit talking about human
rights. That is, the Chinese linked favorable relations with the United
States on a broad array of issues to the requirement that human rights
stay off the table. The Chinese government and the U.S. domestic interests that wanted entrance into the potential Chinese market commanded
the greatest influence over the Clinton policy, and this informal "coalition" was able to win the day and get trade policy delinked from human
rights. The domestic and international groups in favor of using trade as
a way to compel China to follow a better human rights standard found
themselves with less leverage, perhaps because their issues were more
narrowly focused, and so they could not link their desired China policy
to other issues over which they had control.

*The stuff of foreign policy derives from issues of domestic politics as well as for-
eign relations.* Despite Chinese insistence that domestic politics was off-lim-
its to outsiders, the line between domestic politics and international politics
is blurry. Issues go across national borders, and coalitions supporting or opposing certain policies on those issues also form across national borders.
Some have called this blurring of the distinction between international and
domestic politics "intermestic," combining the words to indicate the combining of issues and interests. Others prefer to use the terms **transnational
actors** and transnational forces to indicate the linking of interests and actions across national lines. Since the mid-1990s, most observers have suggested that the line between domestic and international politics is not just
blurry but is quickly disappearing because of globalization. Globalization is
a term that refers to "the increasing internationalization of culture and economics."[24] As national markets are increasingly opened to the global market, national cultures similarly are opened to the global culture. National
sovereignty is eroded in terms of both control of the national economy
and—perhaps more importantly—preservation of national culture. When

the Clinton administration took human rights conditions off its China trade policy, the justification was that opening up China for trade would open up China for other influences, ultimately changing the behavior of the Chinese government in the way that human rights and democracy groups wanted. Put another way, the Clinton policy was based on the idea that, ultimately, the forces of globalization would compel changes in Chinese human rights behavior, and U.S. policy should facilitate those forces.

Further emphasizing this "intermestic" quality of politics, leaders have been known to use foreign policies to promote domestic agendas, and vice versa. In the U.S. presidential election of 1992, President Bush (Bush 1) attempted to convince American voters to reelect him—a domestic agenda—by pointing to his foreign policy accomplishments. This can be turned around the other way—sometimes domestic credentials are used to promote foreign policy goals. The Chinese government has released political prisoners from time to time as a demonstration of its cooperative nature in order to garner greater U.S. investment, U.S. support for Chinese membership in the World Trade Organization, and international support for hosting the 2008 Olympic Games in Beijing.

Selecting Entrance Points: Levels of Analysis

This book rests on the assertion that studying foreign policy is a complicated undertaking requiring multilevel, multifaceted research. This is not meant to imply, though, that we need to study every foreign policy case in all of its varied aspects. Indeed, this quickly could become an unmanageable task. Instead, foreign policy analysts disaggregate or break down each case into different component parts in order to study and understand select aspects. The knowledge generated by many such studies—studies conducted in the same way, asking the same questions, in similar *and* different contexts and cases—begins to accumulate and form a body of knowledge.

As the case of the tangled tale of Tibet demonstrates, we can enter a case and study it at many different points. For example, we might want to study the change that occurred in Bill Clinton's stance from the perspective of Bill Clinton the individual decision maker. Was Bill Clinton inclined to see the world through a particular "lens" that somehow altered what he saw to fit what he believed? Did he hold some weakly held beliefs about the Chinese, allowing him to be open to new thinking about China policy? Were there key advisers whose opinions shaped his, or did his opinion or preferences shape the views of his closest advisers? Were there some group dynamics at play that gave the economics-focused Cabinet members greater leverage over those who privileged human rights, thus leading to an imbalanced consideration of the policy and, therefore, a policy recommendation that did not leave Clinton much room for choice? We could conduct a study of this case using any of these questions to guide our research. Each of these is posed at what scholars call the *individual level of analysis*—a focus on individual decision makers, the roles they play, the perceptions they hold, the ways key decision makers interact in small, top-level groups.

We might, instead, decide to explore the involvement of interest groups and Congress in the changing nature of the Clinton China policy. We could explore the lobbying of Congress and the Executive branch by groups on the pro–human rights and protrade sides. We could explore the "turf" problems between the Executive and Legislative branches on the defining of the U.S. China policy. We could ask whether the Pentagon, worried about potential Chinese military threats, lobbied the White House and Congress for a certain stand against the Chinese. We could investigate the rise and fall of the fortunes of the pro–human rights groups and the rise of the protrade groups, charting their different strategies, arguments, and overall effectiveness. Entering the case in this way involves study at the *state level of analysis*. In the state level, we examine those societal and governmental factors that contribute to the making of foreign policy in a particular state.

If we expanded our focus, we could investigate the following questions. Did changes in the overall balance of power between countries in the Asia Pacific region convince American leaders that accommodating China was the most prudent way to have some influence over China? Were there some international mechanisms—such as through various U.N. organs—for pursuing human rights separately from trade, thus allowing the United States to delink the issues and still pursue both? Was there some consensus among key allies that China would need to be enticed into being a "good international citizen" rather than bullied into such a role? These questions about state versus state, or geostrategic concerns about regional power tilts, or states acting through **international organizations,** are all posed at the *system level of analysis*. The system level explores **bilateral** (state-to-state) relations, regional issues and interactions, and global issues and **multilateral** interactions between states. At this level we also consider the role played by regional and international organizations and by **nonstate actors** such as transnational **nongovernmental organizations (NGOs)** that have a direct influence or impact on the foreign policies of states.

The levels of analysis are tools—heuristic devices—that help us study our subject. All disciplines employ levels of analysis, although the levels vary depending on the discipline. The levels might be understood easiest by thinking about the lens on a camera and the detail you desire in your subject. If you are photographing flowers, you might use a zoom lens to take a detailed photograph of a single bud. This close-up shot lets you see the variations in color in the single bud, the degree to which it is opened, and even the stray spider or aphid. This is analogous to the individual level of analysis.

You might decide that the best way to capture the essence of that flower is to photograph it as part of the entire bush on which it grows. In this picture shot with a normal camera lens, you frame the bud in its relationship to other buds and opened flowers on the same plant, as well as the leaves and stems. Using this camera lens, you learn about the bud by looking at the elements of the entire plant, just as we might examine a foreign policy pronouncement in the context of all the voices in the domestic political arena who had a say in its formulation. This is analogous to the state level of analysis.

Of course, the bud and the plant on which it grows do not exist in a vacuum. Both are part of a larger ecosystem we call the garden. Using a panoramic lens on our camera, we can put to film where the plant sits in the garden, what plants compete with it for water and sunlight, and what smaller plants *it* shelters—or robs—of water and sunlight. We can also see whether the garden sits by any large structures such as buildings. The panoramic lens gives us a picture of the plant at the system level of analysis, we might say. We might not be able to see the single bud anymore, nor many of the other buds and flowers on the plant. Instead, the plant's component parts blend together because of the distance we've created using the panoramic lens. We can understand why the plant looks so strong and healthy when we see that it holds a premier position in the garden, standing in full sunlight, towering over the smaller plants below it.

At each level of analysis, we gain a particular understanding of our subject. Our understanding may be quite thorough for that level but will necessarily exclude information that can only be attained using one of the other levels of analysis. When we pose our questions at a single level, we acknowledge that our understanding will be limited. Recall that the case study detailed above revealed complexities across the levels of analysis. One level of understanding will not yield a complete picture. Yet we take such a risk and emphasize a single level because we are curious about questions at that level and, perhaps, we are convinced that one level gives a better explanation than the others. It is also true that choosing to frame our study at a single level helps us better manage what we study.

This book is organized by the three levels of analysis. Just as these can help us make a single research project more manageable, the levels are useful ways to divide the study of foreign policy. We could divide our subject using more levels of analysis. One of the "pioneers" of foreign policy study, James Rosenau, suggests five levels or sources of foreign policy making: individual, role, governmental, societal, and systemic.[25] The levels used in this book encapsulate these five. Another important international relations scholar, J. David Singer, describes two broad levels: system and subsystem. This scheme collapses our individual and state levels into the subsystem category.[26] It is important to reiterate that we'll use a levels-of-analysis approach in this book *as a way to manage the study* of foreign policy. It is, though, impossible to truly isolate one level from the other levels, as we'll see when we discuss each. Not only is it analytically impossible to isolate one level from another, it would also be foolhardy to make pronouncements or policy decisions using but a single-level analysis in an era of globalization.

Worldviews and Theories

In some important ways, the number of levels described is related to what the individual scholar thinks is important. Every one of us holds a view of "how things work" or "human nature." These views might be very elaborate or very simple, but they predetermine how we act in the world. These "worldviews" don't have to apply to politics; generally a personal worldview can be used to explain why your best friend won't talk to you today, how to play the stock market or pick lottery numbers (or whether to bother playing the market or picking lottery numbers), or why countries choose peace over war.

The study of foreign policy derives, in large part, from the discipline called international relations. There are three worldviews or grand theories that dominate the study of international relations: realism,[27] liberalism,[28] and Marxism.[29] Although there are variants and even disagreements *within* each of these worldviews, these offer three fairly straightforward explanations of "how things work" in the world. Scholars and foreign policy makers all have an identifiable worldview, although from time to time, individuals may use one or the other or borrow key concepts to fit particular circumstances.

An explanation of how something works is also known as a *theory*. We can call realism, liberalism, and Marxism worldviews, traditions, or theories. At their most fundamental level, each offers what we call a *grand theory* of how the world of politics works. A grand theory purports to explain how things are the way they are—or, how things *might be*. In this latter sense, theories can be *prescriptions* for action to achieve the desired endpoint.

Theories are also used to help us tell the future, or predict. An explanation of a single incident in the past might be interesting, but it cannot tell us anything about the future. This is a problem for scholars, but even more so for foreign policy makers. Foreign policy makers need to be able to confront new circumstances with decisive, effective responses, and they need to be able to be proactive when planning the course for their countries. Theories about how the world works can help policy makers generalize from the past to new experiences, thereby helping them know which policy to undertake and which to avoid.

When analysts apply their theories about the world to the study of particular aspects of foreign policy—such as why countries form

---

A GAP BETWEEN THE WORLD OF THEORY AND THE WORLD OF PRACTICAL POLITICS?

How often do policy makers avail themselves of scholarship in order to formulate better policy responses? Alexander George has spent some time pondering this question in order to find a "bridge" across the "gap" between theory (the scholarly world) and practice (the policy-making world). George utilizes case studies of recent U.S. foreign policy events to determine what kind of scholarly knowledge was fundamental to the decisions made by policy makers, as well as what kind of scholarly knowledge *not used* would have contributed to sounder policies. Acknowledging that policy makers often are constrained by the time pressures of the real world and thus cannot be expected to engage in extensive study of scholarship prior to making a decision, George nonetheless believes that they could and should make better use of scholarly knowledge on a regular basis.

Not all scholarly knowledge is useful to policy makers, nor should it be, George cautions. Policy makers have the greatest need for general or generic knowledge on substantive themes such as deterrence, crisis management, and détente, and knowledge on "how to structure and manage the policy-making process in ways that will improve information processing and foster sound judgments" (p. xxii). Scholars who wish their work to have some relevancy in the real world will seek to produce such research, especially that which is attentive to the real-world limitations and opportunities faced by policy makers (p. 140).

References

George, Alexander L. *Bridging the Gap: Theory and Practice in Foreign Policy.* Washington, D.C.: U.S. Institute of Peace, 1993.

---

alliances, why countries enter into trade agreements, why countries ban land mines or why they don't—they offer something of use to policy makers. The explanations of the world that result from these particularized studies are called *midrange theories*. These midrange theories don't claim to explain everything, just selected parts of world politics. In fact, midrange theories tend to do a better job explaining parts of the world than the grand theories do in explaining all of the world. This should make sense on an intuitive level.

Theories explain the past and help predict the future. With predictive ca-

"International Politics Is Not Foreign Policy"

The eminent scholar Kenneth N. Waltz might take exception to the assertion that midrange theories do a better job explaining parts of the world than do grand theories. Waltz, a neorealist or structural realist, is the author of the definitive *Theory of International Politics*. In *Theory*, Waltz says he describes the conditions present in the international system that permit states to take some foreign policy actions and not others: "the *interaction* of states generates a structure that then constrains them [states] from taking certain actions and disposes them toward taking others" ("International Politics Is Not Foreign Policy," 54). In one sense, then, *Theory* offers an explanation of foreign policy situated at the system level of analysis. Yet Waltz is not comfortable with this and insists that a firm line exists between international politics and foreign policy. *Theory of International Politics* explains

> how variations in conditions external to states push or pull them in various directions. The theory explains why states similarly placed behave similarly despite their internal differences . . . In contrast, a theory of foreign policy would explain why states similarly placed in a system behave in different ways. Differences in behavior arise from differences of internal composition. Foreign policies are governmental products. ("International Politics Is Not Foreign Policy," 54–55)

Waltz contends that theories of international politics focus on factors external to states that tend to make the *behavior of all states more or less uniform*. Foreign policy theories focus inward to explain why states do *not* behave in the uniform manner predicted by realists.

Waltz did not always draw such a firm line between theories of international politics and foreign policy. Two decades before *Theory of International Politics*, Waltz presented a picture of how the grand

pability, policy makers can plan their own actions. Theories are of no use to analysts or policy makers if they are too particular, or overly specified. For instance, a poorly constructed "theory" might read: *Whenever interests within the U.S. government and private sector wish to increase American business opportunities within China, issues of self-determination and human rights in Chinese-occupied Tibet will be put aside or delinked from all trade discussions.*

The limits of such a "theory" should be clear: it could only apply to par-

theories of international politics can be reconciled with midrange theories derived from an internal focus on different states. In *Man, the State, and War,* Waltz suggested that a comprehensive understanding of why states go to war (a foreign policy behavior) should include an understanding of the dynamics of the international system, the internal characteristics of the state, and its leadership. Focusing on the dynamics of the international system helps us understand the *conditions* under which we can expect *any* state to undertake or not undertake war. Focusing on the internal characteristics of a *particular* state and its leadership helps us to understand the *immediate* reasons why war is undertaken or not. He called each level of analysis an "image"—the first image is the individual level, the second image is the state level, and the third is the international system level of analysis. Waltz's conclusion in *Man, the State, and War* was this:

> The third image describes the framework of world politics, but without the first and second images there can be no knowledge of the forces that determine policy; the first and second images describe the forces in world politics, but without the third image, it is impossible to assess their importance or predict their results. (*MSW,* 238)

In *Man, the State, and War,* Waltz advocated a multilevel approach to understanding foreign policy phenomenon—much the same as the one offered in this book. In this multilevel approach, we study foreign policy from the vantage of external conditions and internal characteristics, constrained only by our particular worldview.

References

Waltz, Kenneth N. "International Politics Is Not Foreign Policy." *Security Studies* 6, no. 1 (1996).

———. *Man, the State, and War.* New York: Columbia University Press, 1956, 1959.

———. *Theory of International Politics.* New York: McGraw-Hill, 1979.

ticular state and nonstate actors in a particular time frame on particular issues. We might say that this "theory" is only useful for a single historical instance. Theories need to go beyond single instances; theories need to generalize across cases, events, incidents, and time frames. Theories need to apply to a group or class of cases that share similar characteristics. Consider this reformulated statement that incorporates generic concepts to get away from the single instance problem: *Whenever the economic inter-*

ests of parties within the government and society of a particular state have a
strong interest in obtaining greater access to the potential market and business
opportunities present in another state, and this protrade coalition possesses sig-
nificantly more power resources with which to influence national policy than do
other groups with contrary stances, we can expect that nontrade issues will be
deemphasized and/or delinked from trade issues in the ultimate policy decision.

Policy makers in both states can adjust their positions and behaviors in accordance with this generic knowledge in ways that will help them pursue their own best interests. Interested actors outside government circles can also use this understanding as the springboard for their own strategizing. Finally, academics can use this generic statement to explore cases where it holds true and cases where it does not in order to develop further refinements of the theory, or to discard it, or to construct new midrange theories.

How much do foreign policy makers consider the theories—grand or midrange—of scholars? Scholars around the world sit in foreign ministries (or state departments) and analyze the world and advise their governments. Sometimes these scholars are officeholders—such as U.S. President Woodrow Wilson, who was a professor of international relations and politics at Princeton University before he was president—or hold key ministerial/cabinet positions. Fernando Henrique Cardoso, the president of Brazil (1995–2003, serving two terms), was a leading scholar (in the Marxist–dependency theory tradition) in the study of asymmetrical power relations between rich and poor countries. In Canada, as another example, foreign policy and international relations scholars frequently spend part of their careers in universities, and part in the Department of Foreign Affairs and International Trade. Sometimes scholars write syndicated columns for newspapers or host talk shows that are broadcast around their countries. The work of scholars gets translated into the work of foreign policy makers, and that translation happens in many different ways. This is why there is an imperative that foreign policy studies have something to say about the world—something tangible and practical.

The three grand theories, their internal debates, and their derivative midrange theories have much to say about the world. Scholars in different traditions can and do examine the same set of events and arrive at different explanations about why those events occurred and how best to deal with similar events in the future. These theories give us different answers to the puzzles of the world because they begin with different starting assumptions, stress different "critical" variables, and have different ideal endpoints. It is also important to note that an analyst working within a particular tradition will ignore evidence that another analyst using a different worldview would find indispensable. When a scholar comes up with an answer to why an event occurred and whether it will occur again, we would be wise—especially as foreign policy makers—to ask ourselves: What tradition is this person in? What factors did this person ignore, disregard, or downplay? Will we imperil our policy if we ignore other potentially important variables?

As foreign policy makers as well as students of foreign policy, we should read every study with caution—with a critical mind—remembering that each scholar's orientation has led her or him to choose some variables over others. We might learn a great deal from this scholar's work, but the things we are not learning might be just as important. We would be wise, then, to critically mix and match our studies, looking for scholars of different orientations to offer us competing explanations that we can assess critically on the path to a more comprehensive understanding of events.

Let's review the dominant grand theories in brief.

Realism

Classical realists start with a pessimistic view of human nature and from this they make key assumptions about the "nature" of states and state behaviors. Humans are essentially self-interested (some would say necessarily selfish) and exist in a social condition characterized by the constant struggle to maintain autonomy from other self-interested humans. States also are self-interested actors existing in an **international system** characterized by the constant struggle to maintain autonomy (sovereignty) from other states.

Whereas in a national society some legal limitations are placed on the ability of individuals to infringe on the autonomy of other individuals, in the international system any "society" that exists is loosely formed with no ultimate guarantor of the sovereignty of states except the states themselves. Indeed, the dominant characteristic of the international system is **anarchy.** Neorealists or structural realists emphasize this, rather than human nature, as the starting point for their explanation of world politics.

Because of anarchy, states are compelled to be constantly vigilant, watching out for impositions on their autonomy. The best way to protect a state's autonomy—and thus ensure its survival—is to amass power resources that can be used to deter or defend against other states. All states are similarly motivated and thus can be expected to do what is necessary to survive—sometimes resorting to the use of armed violence against others to capture additional power resources that can be harnessed for the protection of the state. Power itself (or the things that together constitute power, such as military and economic might) is finite in the international system, so whenever a state lays claim to a certain amount of power resources, other states are deprived of those resources. For classical realists, international politics is a zero-sum game where the gains of one state equal the losses of another. International politics is also necessarily conflictual.

The realist perspective is state-centric. States and only states are international actors, or the only international actors of note, privilege, and agency. International organizations and nongovernmental actors are only important to study as instruments of states pursuing their own **national interests**. What goes on within a state also is unimportant because all states have the same operating motivation—protect the state (the national interest) by acquiring greater and greater amounts of power. The important topics to study from a realist perspective include power balances, relative versus absolute power, and the multiple uses of power by one state over another (or a group of states over another group). More recent realist scholarship focuses on whether to balance power or threats and states' pursuit of relative and contingent gains over others.

Globalization is a process that realists meet with some suspicion. Globalization both poses a serious threat to national autonomy and control and creates interdependencies that impede the pursuit of national interests.

Liberalism

Liberals start from a different assumption about human nature and end up with a different view about international politics. Humans, in the liberal view, cherish autonomy but do not assume that their autonomy is threatened by other humans. Instead, humans exist within many networks of relationships that help them achieve collectively what they cannot achieve on their own. Humans who have the opportunity to exercise self-determination will respect others' rights to the same and will value the social fabric that assists all individuals in self-realization. Just as national society should result from a system that respects the rights of individuals and serves the collective will of those individuals, international society should also be founded on principles that respect the rights of individual, self-determining states and serve the collective good. International politics, then, is characterized by—or can be characterized by—harmony among international actors. Because of this expectation that the future might find countries in harmony with one another, the liberal view is sometimes called idealism.

Liberals are pluralists. They conceptualize politics as the interaction of multiple actors pursuing multiple interests and using different types of resources and methods of interaction (such as bargaining, coalition building, arm twisting, and so on). States and nonstate actors of all sorts are important in different ways, depending on the issues at hand. Liberals focus on the formation of international law, organizations, and cooperative arrangements of many sorts, as well as on coercive statecraft directed at preserving some greater, collective good such as international peace or the promotion of human rights. Liberals value multiplicity and norms that protect and encourage multiplicity, all in the service of a greater, collective good.

Liberalism has a corollary in **liberal economic theory** in which it is proposed that free and open trade between countries can decrease the possibility of conflict between them. Essentially, the argument is that the more people trade, the greater the ties that bind them together. And the more

Introduction   21

people trade, the more they reap the benefits of trade together. In time, interdependencies and mutual gains will make war and violent conflict less likely, as all countries benefit from—and understand that they benefit from—their open relationships with one another. Globalization is a phenomenon that liberals welcome, even as they acknowledge that aspects of globalization need to be tempered in order to accommodate different peoples' concerns and interests.

Marxism

Before I explain the Marxist view on international politics, let's consider whether this worldview is still relevant with the collapse of the Soviet-led communist world. In brief, it is! The Marxist view was established before the founding of the Soviet Union as a critique and response to capitalism. Both of the grand political theories discussed above, realism and liberalism, are compatible with capitalism. Marxism constitutes both a response to the problems inherent to capitalism—an economic system—and a response to realism and liberalism—which describe political systems.

As with realism and liberalism, there is more to Marxism than I will describe here. The foundation of the Marxist view is that the economic organization of a society determines the political and social system. A society founded on capitalism, with its free market and private ownership of wealth and property, is a society divided into economic/social classes. Essentially, there are two classes—owners and workers. The societal norms and political system built on a capitalist-based economy are designed to maintain the continued profit taking of the owner class. Politics will be dominated by **elite** interests, and the institutions of government will be designed and directed to keeping the workers in an exploited, dependent position in order to preserve and increase the wealth of the owners. An international system based on capitalism is also a system divided into the owners, or the "haves," and the workers, or the "have-nots." The institutions of the rich states—such as their militaries—are used to maintain the world capitalist system, which serves elite interests. International institutions, similarly, are used to maintain the system in favor of the wealthy class/states.

Communist or Marxist states attempted to build a different political/social domestic order by instituting an economic system that rejected private ownership and rejected wealth-based social classes. Instead, centrally planned economies were constructed to serve the interests of all citizens—theoretically. Internationally, these states—primarily the Eastern bloc led by the Soviet Union—attempted to remove themselves from the capitalist world system in order to protect themselves from the inherent evils in that system. The Cold War conflict between the Soviet-led Eastern bloc and the American-led Western bloc was inevitable, according to the Marxist view, as capitalist states would use all means necessary to protect against the threat posed by communism.

Despite the collapse of the Soviet Union and the worldwide turn to liberal capitalism (a turn even manifested in the remaining communist states of China, Vietnam, North Korea, and Cuba), the Marxist critique of capitalism remains relevant. During and beyond the Cold War, Marxist discussions of international politics focus(ed) on how the world's rich states mobilize their resources and tools of statecraft to maintain and increase their wealth and predominance. International organizations, such as the United Nations, and international institutions, such as the World Bank and International Monetary Fund, serve as instruments of the rich (called the **core** or **centre**) states to maintain a world system that remains stratified into the rich few and the poor many. Because this view stresses the structure of the world system and the structural determinants of power within the world economic system, it is also referred to as **structuralism.**

A Marxist or structuralist observer might focus on how the policies of international lending agencies keep the developing countries submerged in debt and dependent on the core states for trade and investment. Similarly, such an analysis might discuss how the terms attached to international loans coerce developing countries to enact domestic economic policies that increase poverty and human suffering in order to be able to make the service payments on external debt. Marxists also examine the patterns in the use of force—unilaterally and multilaterally—by core states against dependent states as continuing evidence of inevitable class conflict.

In this era of globalization, the Marxist/structuralist perspective on international politics remains alive as an ongoing critique of the problems of a global free market system. In an interesting twist, globalization provokes strong opposition among realists and Marxists alike. The realists reject globalization because, as mentioned above, it erodes national sovereignty. That is, the opening of national borders and markets diminishes the ways in which central governments traditionally exert power. The Marxists reject globalization because there appears to be no safe harbor for poor people in the free market tsunami. The economic system being globalized is a wide-open liberal economic system; if states want to ride this wave to potential prosperity, they must disengage any "safety net" provisions designed to protect their poor and workers against the free market. Further, there is no countering force in globalization that will ensure a more equitable distribution of power in the system; thus globalization will only increase the structural power of the center at the expense of all others.

These worldviews don't focus on just different actors and issues but also on different levels of analysis. Realists are focused on the state—not on what's "in" the state but on relations between states based on differences in power. Thus realists study foreign policy at the system level—whether bilateral, regional, or global. The only exception to this is the study of rational

CONSTRUCTIVISM: ANOTHER WAY TO UNDERSTAND THE WORLD

Is it true that the world is a hostile place in which no other state can be trusted and every state must be constantly ready to prey or be preyed upon? Is anarchy a reality that states ignore at their own folly? If we start with realist assumptions about the world, we must go where the realists take us—to a self-help system in which violence is both natural and at times the preferred foreign policy instrument. If we change the starting assumptions, we can go to a differently constituted world. This idea has led scholars to use alternative grand theories to understand the world, such as liberalism.

There is an approach to understanding reality that, although not a grand theory per se, offers an alternative tool for analysis. This approach is constructivism. Constructivists argue that there is no more or less objective reality, but that reality is socially constructed from people's or, more precisely, society's perceptions of it. Society projects a certain understanding of reality onto the world—such as the "reality" of anarchy—and from this identities and appropriate behaviors result. States "make" the system (anarchic) and then the system they create "makes" the states (self-interested and predatory by necessity).

Constructivism does not offer us an alternative worldview, but a way to analyze the construction of institutions, identities, and behaviors within the worldviews. In chapter 4, constructivism is explained in more detail and used to understand "middle powers" and their foreign policies. Constructivism is "used" by many scholars to understand a wide range of issues and topics in the broad study of world politics; thus the reader should not conclude that constructivism is just a framework for studying middle powers!

---

actors. Realists often conflate leaders and countries; for instance, a realist may examine the calculations of Egyptian President Gamal Abdel Nasser leading up to the 1967 war between Egypt and Israel, with reference to Nasser and Egypt as if they were one entity. A realist would never examine the personal beliefs of leaders—all leaders, like all countries, are the same: they all pursue the national interests (the protection of the state and its power) in a rational, strategic, calculating manner. One of the most prominent post–World War II classical realists, Hans Morgenthau, said that this

A BRIEF DEMONSTRATION OF WORLDVIEWS

How can we explain the basic continuation of U.S. policy toward China from the George H. W. Bush to the Bill Clinton administrations?

The realist explanation. Considerations of domestic political campaigns notwithstanding, leaders of all political orientations will pursue the national interests of their state. What matters most in relations between the United States and China is that the multiple avenues of issues and policies combine to maintain and increase relative American power—political, strategic, and economic—over China. No single interest of "low politics"—such as human rights considerations—should ever override the single-minded pursuit of relative power, or "high politics." Leaders—whether they are named Bush or Clinton—understand and comply with this necessity of international politics. Bill Clinton the president came face-to-face with this reality and maintained the course.

The liberal explanation. "Intermestic" politics involve multiple issues and linkages. Policy strategies need to take into account the various ways in which issues can be pursued, both in the short term and in the future. Engaging China along multiple avenues will have the greatest long-term impact on China, in time compelling Chinese officials to modify their actions regarding the human rights of Tibetans. Concurrently, opening China's market to the outside world will, in time, increase the overall wealth and well-being of all states and all peoples. Bill Clinton the president was able to look beyond immediate, narrowly focused interests when he decided to maintain the course of "constructive engagement."

The Marxist explanation. Economic interests determine politics within and between states. The vested and powerful economic actors inside and outside the U.S. government can be expected to protect their own interests regardless of the cost to other policies and interests. Human rights and religious groups favoring a hard-line stance toward China could not hope to have meaningful impact on U.S. policy without sufficient economic leverage. Bill Clinton the president had more to gain by heeding the call of economic interests than by heeding the call of human rights groups. Given this calculation, he maintained the course toward greater economic ties with China.

expectation of rational uniformity was the beauty of studying politics among nations. Leaders deviated from this expectation only when they either were psychopaths or were trapped in the sway of democratic politics. We'll discuss the realist view of leaders in chapter 2. In chapter 4, we'll review some realist discussions of global politics, inquiring into the foreign policies of "great" or "major" powers and challengers.

Liberals, being pluralists, focus on all the levels of analysis, depending on the subject of the study. Liberals borrow from comparative politics and look at the persons, groups, structures, cultures, and so on within a state that may lead it to take certain foreign policy stands. They may examine the workings of international organizations—which is a system-level international relations interest. Liberals also explore the interaction of nonstate actors across state boundaries. Or they may look at the **belief sets** of individuals who form the foreign policy elite. The list goes on. Some of the studies reviewed in chapters 2, 3, and 4 derive from this pluralist viewpoint.

Marxists look at foreign policy from the system and state levels. At the system level, the asymmetrical relations between states are important. At the state level, Marxists study the common interests of economic elites in one state with the elites in another. Or they study how military industrial interests push a state into war. Group politics is important to Marxists, so we can find such explanations of foreign policy posed at the state and system levels, and some are explored in chapters 3–4.

Time to Back Up and Consider the Subject: Foreign Policy

Before we go any further we need to be clear about our subject: foreign policy. Charles Hermann calls foreign policy a "neglected concept."[30] He asserts, "This neglect has been one of the most serious obstacles to providing more adequate and comprehensive explanations of foreign policy." Hermann thinks that part of the reason for this neglect is that "most people dealing with the subject have felt confident that they knew what foreign policy was."[31] To put it colloquially, we know it when we see it. Ultimately, Hermann defines foreign policy as "the discrete purposeful action that results from the political level decision of an individual or group of individuals. . . . [it is] the observable artifact of a political level decision. It is not the decision, but a product of the decision."[32] Hermann defines foreign policy as the *behavior* of states.

Hermann rejects the idea that the study of foreign policy is the study of *policy*, but his is a minority view. Bruce Russett, Harvey Starr, and David Kinsella take an opposite and broader view: "We can think of a *policy* as a program that serves as a guide to behavior intended to realize the goals an organization has set for itself. . . . *Foreign policy* is thus a guide to actions

taken beyond the boundaries of the state to further the goals of the state."[33]
Although these scholars define foreign policy as a program or statement
of goals, they also stress that the *study* of foreign policy must involve
study of both the "formulation and implementation" of policy.[34]

Deborah Gerner takes foreign policy further when she defines it as "the
intentions, statements, and actions of an actor—often, but not always, a
state—directed toward the external world and the response of other
actors to these intentions, statements and actions."[35] Gerner combines
Hermann's interest in behavior with Russett, Starr, and Kinsella's emphasis on programs or guides. Note that in Gerner's definition the emphasis is on states but does not have to be on states. Other actors—such
as international cause groups, businesses, religions, and so forth—in the
international system formulate guidelines and goals that direct their actions toward other international actors. In this book, the emphasis is primarily on states, but other actors will appear from time to time as well.

We will use a broad definition of foreign policy that includes both statements and behaviors or actions. The study of foreign policy, however,
needs to consider more than what states declare to be their goals and how
they attempt to achieve them. The study of foreign policy needs to consider *how* certain goals arise and *why* certain behaviors result. Thus our focus is on how goals are decided upon. We will explore the factors that
cause a state to declare and embark on a certain foreign policy course. Our
emphasis will be on determining these factors and the processes by which
policy (statements and behaviors) is made. In summary, the "stuff" of our
foreign policy study includes processes, statements, and behaviors.

The Bridge between International and Comparative Politics

The study of foreign policy sits in the area of political science known as international politics, although you could say foreign policy sometimes
jumps over the fence into comparative politics. As a "field" of study, foreign policy analysis is relatively new, coalescing more or less in the mid-
1960s. There were, of course, scholars who studied foreign policy before
this time, but their pursuit was one of many within the broader study of
international politics.

The early study of foreign policy, like the study of international relations and comparative politics, reflected academic debates over the
proper "ways of knowing" that dominated social science research in the
1950s and 1960s. Foreign policy study arose in this era as a bridge between international relations and comparative politics. To understand
the construction of foreign policy study, we need to consider the development of international relations and comparative politics against real-
world politics.

Prior to the twentieth century, Deborah Gerner explains,

> neither foreign policy nor international relations constituted a distinct field. Diplomatic history probably came the closest to what we now label as "foreign policy," and much of what we call international relations came under the rubric of international law, institutional analysis, or history.[36]

Although the post–World War I years marked the strong emergence of the idealist (liberal) worldview and witnessed tangible efforts to incorporate idealist notions into the newly established League of Nations, the study of international relations and foreign policy was dominated by realism. According to Gerner,

> For the study of foreign policy, this essentially meant the study of the international actions of individual state leaders—frequently monarchs—who were believed to have few constraints on their actions other than those imposed by the external situation.[37]

Real-world events, such as states' nationalistic responses to the Great Depression and the mobilization for World War II, reinforced the appropriateness of the IR (international relations) emphasis on political realism. Growing fascism on the European continent, as well as the entrenchment of Soviet-style communism, caused significant out-migration of political scholars. Many of these scholars made their way to the United States, bringing with them "new and often broader perspectives about international relations and foreign policy."[38]

The study of comparative politics was established in the interwar period as a result of the same exodus of European scholars.[39] "Fascist Italy, Imperialist Japan, and Nazi Germany taught [these scholars] the dangers of mobilized masses from the extreme right end of the spectrum, while the politics of the Soviet Union taught them the dangers of mobilized masses from the left."[40] The new study of comparative politics was normative in its focus, exploring the development of "good" moderate participatory politics as found in the United States and some countries of Western Europe.[41]

In the post–World War II years, this new study of comparative politics coalesced around modernization theory (also called developmental economics), with its emphasis on state and economy building along the path of the Western model. In brief, this model proposed that all countries could develop into advanced industrialized countries with participatory democratic systems *if* they followed in the established footsteps of the United States and its Western friends. Moreover, as the Cold War emerged and deepened, the modernization/developmental model became the formula by which Western states, especially the United States, examined, judged, and intervened in developing states to protect them from the dangers of the mass politics of the left (communism) being exported by the Soviet Union.[42]

That is, the normative cause and theoretical model that characterized the study of comparative politics was adopted with alacrity by Western policy makers as one of many tools to be used to fight the Cold War.

The politics of the day also influenced the broader study of politics, as Laura Neack, Jeanne Hey, and Patrick Haney explain,

A principal strategy of the United States in the Cold War involved beating the Soviets through scientific advancements; academics were recruited to this cause. Federal funding for "scientific" research created a strong impetus among social scientists to become more "scientific" (and perhaps less "social" or "historical"). . . . This is also the era in which the majority of departments of politics or governments in the United States turned into departments of political science.[43]

International relations scholars joined this **positivist** movement in political science, although Gerner tells us that those who focused on foreign policy were temporarily left behind:

the fields of international relations and foreign policy, which had been intertwined, began to pull apart. International relations—or at least a significant subgroup of researchers represented after 1959 by the International Studies Association—became more scientific, with a goal of increasing knowledge through statistical tests and rational and dynamic modeling. Foreign policy theorists, however, were slower to adopt the behavioralist approach, and instead tended to continue in the classical tradition [derived from philosophy, history and law].[44]

As part of this positivist shift in international relations, a team of scholars produced two studies that proved critical to later foreign policy scholarship. In 1954 and 1963, Richard Snyder, H. W. Bruck, and Burton Sapin[45] presented a systematic decision-making framework in response to realism's privileging of national interest over human agency.[46] The emphasis for their framework was on decision makers:

It is one of our basic methodological choices to define the state as its official decision makers—those whose authoritative acts are, to all intents and purposes, the acts of the state. State action is the action taken by those acting in the name of the state.[47]

Snyder, Bruck, and Sapin rejected the realist notion that national leaders regardless of individual differences would make the same national interest-based foreign policy choices. Instead, they suggested that foreign policy choice derives from multiple sources, including the "biographies" of the individual decision makers as well as the organizational framework in which decisions are made. Snyder, Bruck, and Sapin pointed the way to studying foreign policy using multiple levels of analysis, a key theme of this book. Their work was taken up in James Rosenau's field-establishing work that appeared in the mid-1960s.

Charles Hermann and Gregory Peacock write, "If Snyder's framework invited scientific inquiry, Rosenau insisted upon it."[48] In his famous and foundational article, "Pre-Theories and Theories of Foreign Policy," James Rosenau sounded a "clarion call" to make the study of foreign policy into a science.[49] This is how Rosenau established the cause and scope of his call:

To probe the "internal influences on external behavior" is to be active on one of the frontiers where the fields of international and comparative politics meet. Initial thoughts about the subject, however, are bound to be ambivalent; it would seem to have been both exhausted and neglected as a focus of inquiry. Even as it seems clear that everything worth saying about the subject has already been said, so does it also seem obvious that the heart of the matter has yet to be explored and that American political science is on the verge of major breakthroughs which will make exploration possible.[50]

Rosenau was frustrated because foreign policy study had remained behind the times and, without significant recasting, would fail to benefit from the "major breakthroughs" on the horizon.

The nontheoretical state of foreign policy research is all the more perplexing when it is contrasted with developments elsewhere in American political science. In recent years the discipline has been transformed from an intuitive to a scientific enterprise, and consequently the inclination to develop models and test theories has become second nature to most political scientists.[51]

Foreign policy suffered, according to Rosenau, from the lack of a central theoretical framework (like realism in international relations) and the lack of a common **methodology**. He suggested that the common methodology be a commitment to comparative analysis, and that the central theory could be established through the subsequent efforts of scholars working within an agreed-upon framework. Rosenau offered his "pre-theory" framework—one in which he combined national attribute indicators to formulate "ideal nation-types." He hypothesized that factors at different levels of analysis might account for foreign policy differences that could be observed between these ideal nation-types. Using this "pre-theory," scholars could launch a systematic research program aimed at building a general body of theory that would, in time, define the scientific field of foreign policy.

In response to Rosenau's call, a "self-conscious" field of foreign policy was begun by a more or less cohesive group of scholars whose collective efforts come under the heading of "Comparative Foreign Policy,"[52] or what Neack, Hey, and Haney call the "first generation" of foreign policy study.[53]

In chapters 2–3 of *The New Foreign Policy*, I survey the scholarly progeny of Snyder, Bruck, and Sapin's work. In chapter 4, I survey the progeny of Rosenau's suggestions about ideal nation-types. Throughout this book, you will see the presence of these early contributors to the study of foreign policy in my emphasis on multilevel explanations.

Real-world events in the late 1960s and into the 1970s again influenced the direction of international relations, comparative politics, and foreign policy study. By the mid-1960s, most of the world's colonies had become independent states, entering the United Nations as a badge of their sovereign statehood. The countries of the "Third World" brought different issues to the United Nations and to discussions of world politics, as demonstrated by their domination of U.N. General Assembly debates, as well as by the oil crises of the 1970s. International relations scholars needed to develop frameworks for analyzing nonmilitary bases and definitions of power, as well as "find" a place for discussions of less than great power states. Further, the problems of Third World countries were not primarily strategic or military, but also involved issues of economic development and dependency, as well as issues of **state** and **nation building**. International relations scholars had to develop more diverse theoretical and conceptual tools to study this altered reality.

Western and non-Western international relations scholars began exploring alternative theoretical frameworks to realism. Some scholars in the West resuscitated the old idealist school under a newer, more reality-based rubric of "complex interdependence," or "transnationalism."[54] Today, the umbrella category of liberalism is applied to various works in this tradition. Other scholars—in the West and especially from developing countries—proposed that the world should be understood in terms of the historical development of political and economic relations among states that has resulted in a world of "haves" and "have-nots." These scholars drew on Marxist understandings of politics. As these contending paradigms emerged in international relations to challenge the dominance of realism, so, too, was realism's insistence on positivist-behavioralist methodology challenged. By the end of the 1970s, more complex qualitative as well as quantitative research efforts were underway.

Similarly, the emphasis in comparative politics on modernization theory/developmental economics came under significant challenge. There were some early critics of modernization theory such as Raul Prebisch, head of the U.N. Economic Commission on Latin America (ECLA). Prebisch and ECLA proposed in the 1950s that economic development in the developing world—or, the **periphery** of the world economic system—would always be impeded by ever declining terms of trade. Prebisch represented a Marxist variation called dependency theory, a theory with strong foundations in Latin America particularly and the broader developing world more generally. Although the dependency challenge to modernization theory was sounded in the 1950s, modernization theory remained dominant in comparative politics until the late 1960s and early 1970s. By this time, mainstream comparative politics had to make room for new voices and issues such as dependency theory.

Neack, Hey, and Haney describe the change in comparative politics in this time:

> Scholars from developing countries and Western "area specialists" who had rejected modernization theory were able to exploit the cracks in the crumbling modernization theory paradigm and assert the importance of studying complex domestic processes in comparative politics. . . . The study of domestic processes took a variety of forms in the 1970s, including the study of domestic class-based divisions caused by colonialism and perpetuated in post-independence dependent relations, political economy, state corporatism, and state-society relations. . . . The unifying feature of comparative politics from the 1970s onward was not a central theoretical core, but a central methodological agreement on the comparative method.[55]

Just as before, real-world political changes affecting international relations and comparative politics also affected the new field of comparative foreign policy. One result of the disequilibrium being felt in the fields of international relations and comparative politics was that divisions between the two were becoming less and less distinct. This was especially true in the case of political economy approaches to international and comparative politics. This blurring of divisions occurred precisely at the junction of these fields that foreign policy was supposed to bridge.

By the start of the 1980s, a variety of theoretical and methodological accountings from *both* international and comparative politics were adopted by foreign policy scholars. The impact of these accountings was evident in the growing number of contextualized, multilevel foreign policy analyses undertaken in the 1980s and into the early 1990s. This wave of scholarship has been called the "second generation" of foreign policy analysis by Neack, Hey, and Haney. A critical aspect of this second generation was the conscious choice by scholars to link their work to the major substantive concerns in foreign policy.

Second-generation foreign policy study reflected the complex issues of the times—the impact of the latest wave of **democratization,** the importance of the relative decline in U.S. economic power in the early to mid-1980s, the collapse of the Soviet empire and Soviet-style communism, the unprecedented international collaboration in the Persian Gulf War of 1991, and the December 1991 dissolution of the Soviet Union.

A New Millennium

The New Foreign Policy takes off from the second generation of foreign policy study, as the second generation was launched from the first. Just as the first and second generations reflected real-world politics, *The New Foreign Policy* reflects politics in this era of globalization. *The New Foreign Policy* is not necessarily a declaration of a third generation of foreign policy scholarship; instead, this book signals a refocusing of the rich research programs of the second generation on the politics of the new millennium.

The end of the old millennium and start of the new were marked by some monumental politics. From the mid-1990s until 2001, the American economy was in resurgence—a remarkable situation given American economic decline in the 1980s and a necessary situation given the global economic downturn of the mid and late 1990s (including the Asian economic "flu") and the "fact" of globalization. The early 1990s saw another resurgence—in the use of the United Nations to address humanitarian crises and to promote human rights. As the 1990s wore on into the new millennium, the United Nations fell out of favor and multilateral actions by groups such as the **North Atlantic Treaty Organization (NATO)** gained more favor. Some type of international response to conflict seemed in order since the world saw an outbreak of war and violence in the 1990s that only intensified into the 2000s. Refugee crises, HIV crises, sharp increases in illegal drug and small arms trafficking—all these seem to have become the norm in this new era. Two countries pushed their way into the elite nuclear weapons club when India and Pakistan tested their own weapons in 1998. At the same time, the new era has not been without some significant advances in the promotion of democracy and protection of basic human rights. But the benefits of the new era have yet to be felt by all and/or not met with the same welcome and enthusiasm, as suggested by the frequency of Islamic fundamentalist attacks against U.S. military and diplomatic personnel in the late 1990s. The September 11, 2001, terrorist attacks against New York City and Washington, D.C., brought the dangers and frustrations of the new millennium home to the United States.

Global politics in the new millennium include the following features that set the context for *The New Foreign Policy*. First, the United States is the world's single predominant—*super*—power, and the American post–World

War II **grand strategy** of building a liberal international trading order has succeeded. The economic and cultural currents that flow into and mold this order can collectively be called globalization. Second, globalization— briefly, the internationalization of economics and culture—erodes the distinctions between domestic and foreign politics at the same time that it creates strong countercurrents or backlashes among peoples attempting to assert their differences and their rights to these differences. Third, democratization seems to be accompanying globalization into the new millennium. But, where democratization requires the protection of individual human rights, globalization gives governments justification to vacate their responsibilities to their citizens. Further, democratization can release dangerous demands on governments, many of whom are inadequately prepared to manage the pace of globalization. Fourth, intrastate warfare is as much a presence in the new millennium as globalization and democratization. This intrastate warfare has an interstate connection that has turned into an international war on **terrorism**. *The New Foreign Policy* is intended as a guidebook for studying and considering state responses to these realities in the twenty-first century.

A Road Map of *The New Foreign Policy*

This book proceeds in four broad chapters. Chapter 2 focuses on the individual level of analysis. In this chapter, we examine how scholars have studied **leadership,** rational decision making, and **cognition.** As part of our discussion, we'll consider whether and how we might study leaders' moral positions and value stands.

Chapter 3 examines foreign policy from the state level of analysis. Here we examine how foreign policy is shaped by **national self-image** and culture, the link between democratic institutions and peaceful foreign policy behavior, and the ways in which domestic political opposition, partisan politics, **public opinion,** interest groups, and the media affect foreign policy.

In chapter 4, we move to the system level of analysis and consider the interaction of power and position on foreign policy behavior. We'll deliberate about the expected behavior of great powers, as well as the opportunities and constraints on non–great powers. We will take some time to discuss American foreign policy in the new millennium, especially in the aftermath of September 11. This chapter will also allow us to explore an alternative international relations theoretical account—constructivism—and to "test" this account by considering "middle power" foreign policy.

After breaking our study into levels of analysis, we arrive at chapter 5. Here, the need for multilevel or "nested game" foreign policy analysis is reasserted. In chapter 5, we explore how nonstate actors blur the lines between the levels, complicating the foreign policy game all the more for states. Although "foreign policy" remains the realm of national governments, we see in this chapter how critical individuals, nongovernmental organizations, and international organizations have become to the calculations of governments in the construction and execution of their foreign policies.

Review: Important Observations about Foreign Policy

- Foreign policy is made and conducted in complex domestic and international environments.
- Foreign policy results from coalitions of interested domestic and international actors and groups.
- Foreign policy issues are often linked and delinked, reflecting the strength of various parties and their particular concerns.
- The *stuff* of foreign policy derives from issues of domestic politics as well as foreign relations.
- Foreign policy analysis needs to be multilevel and multifaceted in order to confront the complicated sources and nature of foreign policy.

For Further Study

To read more about the China policies of the George H. W. Bush and Bill Clinton administrations, see Ramon Myers, Michal Oksenberg, and David Shambaugh, eds., *Making China Policy: Lessons from the Bush and Clinton Administrations* (Rowman & Littlefield, 2001). This volume contains chapters that span the levels of analysis, including chapters on individuals and interests in the executive branch of each administration, on the role of Congress, on the role of interest groups, and on external actors and politics that shaped China policy.

For reviewing international relations theory, consult these excellent compendiums: James E. Dougherty and Robert L. Pfaltzgraff Jr., *Contending Theories of International Relations: A Comprehensive Survey*, 5th ed. (Longman, 2001); and Paul R. Viotti and Mark V. Kauppi, *International Relations Theory: Realism, Pluralism, Globalism, and Beyond* (Prentice-Hall, 1998).

To study some of the classic statements on the levels of analysis, see Kenneth N. Waltz, *Man, the State, and War* (Columbia University Press, 1959); and J. David Singer, "The Level-of-Analysis Problem in International Relations," in *The International System: Theoretical Essays*, ed. Klaus Knorr and Sidney Verba (Princeton University Press, 1961).

For more on the development of the study of foreign policy, consult the following sources: Deborah J. Gerner, "The Evolution of the Study of Foreign Policy," in *Foreign Policy Analysis: Continuity and Change in Its Second*

Generation, ed. Laura Neack, Jeanne A. K. Hey, and Patrick J. Haney (Prentice-Hall, 1995), 17–32; Deborah J. Gerner, "Foreign Policy Analysis: Renaissance, Routine, or Rubbish?" in *Political Science: Looking to the Future,* vol. 2, *Comparative Politics, Policy, and International Relations,* ed. William Croty (Northwestern University Press, 1992), 123–86; Charles F. Hermann, Charles Kegley, and James N. Rosenau, eds., *New Directions in the Study of Foreign Policy* Allen & Unwin, 1987); Laura Neack, Jeanne A. K. Hey, and Patrick J. Haney, "Generational Change in Foreign Policy Analysis," in *Foreign Policy Analysis,* 1–16; James N. Rosenau, "Pre-theories and Theories and Foreign Policy," in *Approaches to Comparative and International Politics,* ed. R. Barry Farrell (Northwestern University Press, 1966), 115–69.

2

The Individual Level of Analysis:
Leaders, Rational Choices,
Cognition, and Morality

In This Chapter

- On the Definition of "Leaders"
- Rational Choice
- Rationality, Deterrence, Game Theory, and "Irrationality"
- Cognition: A Different View of Rationality
- Belief Sets, Images, and Cognitive Structure
- Moral Positions and Value Stands: A Departure
  Can We and How Might We Study Morals and Values?
  Leaders Who Put Broader Principles before National Interests
- Review
  Some Key Ideas from This Chapter
- For Further Study

On June 10, 2000, Hafez al-Assad, the president of Syria, died of a heart attack. Although most observers inside and outside Syria were certain who the next **leader** would be, this certainty did not arise via a constitutionally mandated chain of command. Assad had been "president" of Syria since 1971, seizing power through use of the military and brutality. (Assad had overthrown the military leader that he himself had supported in an earlier military coup.) Now, Assad's son Bashar would be the next president, designated and groomed for the post since the mid-1990s. Although this change in **leadership** was expected, it still caused much concern regarding Syria's foreign policy and internal stability. At the time of Hafez al-Assad's death, Syrian and Israeli negotiators had been involved in an on-again, off-again series of talks that in the best case scenario might finally bring some peace between the two countries. Assad firmly controlled Syria's position in these talks, as he controlled all aspects of Syrian politics. Bashar al-Assad, an eye doctor and Internet enthusiast educated in the West, could single-handedly change the course of the Syrian–Israeli talks—such was/is the power of the Syrian presidency.

On May 15, 2000, Keizo Obuchi, the prime minister of Japan, died from complications arising from a stroke suffered the month before. Obuchi had been prime minister since 1998, overseeing a rocky period for Japan during the Asian economic meltdown. His successor in the leadership post of the Liberal Democratic Party (LDP)—the party in control of Japan's parliament, the Diet—was Yoshiro Mori. This succession was only partially in doubt—the LDP would need to win the next election to remain the dominant party and various party leaders were, as always, politicking for the top spot. The LDP had governed Japan for nearly all of its post–World War II history and its top leaders already held key cabinet assignments. No major alteration in Japanese foreign policy was expected upon Obuchi's death, although low international confidence in Mori was expected to alter some of the details in Japan's foreign relations.

These two cases of leaders dying in office, their successors, and the possible impact of such leadership change on the affairs of each **state** demonstrate in a nutshell the importance of key individuals in the making and conduct of foreign policy. A change in leadership might lead to dramatic changes in a country's foreign policy, or it might make only minor changes. The extent of the change will depend on factors related to the individuals in question (and their key advisers) *and* to the type of government and political system. The latter takes us to the state level of analysis, the former to the individual level, but knowledge of both and the interplay between the two levels is, as always, essential to a fuller understanding of foreign policy making.

We do not need to look at examples of leadership change due to the death of an officeholder to wonder about the impact of such change on the country's foreign policy. Changes brought about by elections can also dramatically reorient a foreign policy—as when President Ronald Reagan abandoned the human rights focus of the Jimmy Carter presidency in favor of a hawkish, "cold warrior" policy orientation. Conversely, elections can result in basic continuity from one set of officeholders to the next—as in the case of the Democratic Clinton administration essentially continuing the Chinese policy of the Republican George H. W. Bush (Bush 1) administration despite early signs that abrupt policy change was in the offing.

Figure 2.1. A Tale of Two Bushes

The first cartoon depicts the artist's view that candidate George W. Bush was a "mini" version of his father, former President George H. W. Bush (Bush 1). "Mini Me" was a mini version of a character in a popular movie in 2000.

The second cartoon depicts a different Bush (2) presidency than that expected in the first cartoon. George W. Bush (Bush 2) started his presidency as a unilateralist who was determined to keep the United States out of world affairs as much as possible. The early Bush 2 administration turned out to be starkly different from the internationalist Bush 1 administration. After September 11, 2001, however, Bush 2 receives an "education" according to Pulitzer Prize–winning cartoonist Jim Borgman of the *Cincinnati Enquirer*.

Implicit in this discussion is an important assumption: leaders or individuals matter. Not all foreign policy observers would agree with this assumption. Realists in particular would reject it, as we will discuss later in this chapter. The presentation above is premised in part on the assumption that foreign policy will be altered—a little or a lot—by the change from Hafez al-Assad to Bashar al-Assad, from Keizo Obuchi to Yoshiro Mori, from Jimmy Carter to Ronald Reagan, and from George H. W. Bush (Bush 1) to Bill Clinton to George W. Bush (Bush 2). Leaders—or leadership—matters. An important question to explore from this assumption would be, How much do leaders matter? And why do leaders matter?

Mikhail S. Gorbachev is remembered as the last leader of the Soviet Union, not because he happened to be on watch over the collapse of the Soviet empire but because he made active, determined policy choices affecting the internal and external environments of the Soviet Union that led to its peaceful dissolution and contributed to the end of communist single-party states throughout Central and Eastern Europe. When the people of the countries of the former Soviet bloc took hold of their national destinies and undid communism, Gorbachev could have chosen to react with pleas, promises, threats, coercion, and even military force to hold the bloc together under Soviet control. The leader of the weakening superpower might not have been able to hold off the tide for long, *but he could have tried*, making the transition period fraught with tension and even bloodshed. Instead, Mikhail Gorbachev decided to let the Eastern bloc go—peacefully, gracefully. The decision credited to this single leader no doubt saved many lives and prevented much pain and destruction.

Gorbachev saw the Soviet Union and the world in which it operated as changing in fundamental ways. Had Gorbachev been an older man with different life-shaping experiences, he might have decided to hold on to Soviet power over the Eastern bloc and the former Soviet republics at all costs. Margaret Hermann and Joe Hagan explain Gorbachev's role and the importance of all leaders in this way:

> Leaders define states' international and domestic constraints. Based on their perceptions and interpretations, they build expectations, plan strategies, and urge actions on their governments that conform with their judgments about what is possible and likely to maintain them in their positions. Such perceptions help frame governments' orientations to international affairs. Leaders' interpretations arise out of their experiences, goals, beliefs about the world, and sensitivity to the political context.[1]

Leaders—even single, supreme leaders—do not work alone, cannot just consider their own judgments and concerns, and cannot afford to pay attention to one context (domestic or foreign) at the expense of the other. As noted in chapter 1, leaders are engaged in a **two-level game** between domestic and foreign interests. This two-level game often must be understood as it is interpreted by and filtered through the orientation of the leaders. In this way of thinking, leaders can be considered the nexus of the domestic and international political systems.

Hermann and Hagan take this a step further. After surveying the research on leadership, they conclude:

> The lesson learned so far is that international constraints only have policy implications when they are perceived as such by the leaders whose positions count in dealing with a particular problem. Whether and how such leaders judge themselves constrained depends on the nature of the domestic challenges to their leadership, how the leaders are organized, and what they are like as people.[2]

Gorbachev scanned the international environment and concluded that the old **security** threats which had made the Eastern bloc so critical to the Soviet Union had changed in fundamental ways. Further, he could see that Soviet restraint in the face of the self-opening of Eastern and Central Europe could earn the Soviet Union more international credibility and friendship, thereby allowing the Soviet leaders to turn inward to the serious crises proliferating in the domestic realm. Thus Gorbachev decided to view the tide of anticommunism rising in the Eastern bloc as a welcome and nonthreatening phenomenon.

Gorbachev was able to convince the rest of the Soviet leadership of the aptness of his interpretation of events in Eastern and Central Europe because they generally shared his view of political reality and because domestic problems required drastic action. With few significant threats to his leadership and a growing swell of support throughout Soviet society for change, Gorbachev could offer his positive assessment of change in the Eastern bloc and be assured that it would be accepted. We might say he was a man of the times, reading both the external and internal environments in a way that ensured an extraordinarily peaceful, radical change.

How leaders define situations that confront them has much to do with their personal characteristics, including social and educational background, previous experiences, ambitions, and worldview. In September 1970, air reconnaissance photos of southern Cuba convinced U.S. National Security Adviser Henry Kissinger that the Soviet Union was building a naval facility at Cienfuegos.[3] Kissinger's worldview and personal experience convinced him that the only way to protect **national interests** and stand up to totalitarianism was to confront the threat directly, promptly, and with force. Kissinger felt deceived by previous commitments made by the Soviet leadership to stay out of Cuba. Kissinger's boss, President Richard Nixon, had a much different interpretation of the nature of the situation. To Nixon, the situation was less a **crisis** than an example of "adventurism" that should be handled quietly through diplomatic circles.[4] Nixon believed that the Cuban missile crisis of 1962 had been mishandled by President John F. Kennedy (who had beaten Nixon in his first run for the White House in 1960), and he was determined to demonstrate better leadership.

Whose interpretation of the problem in Cienfuegos won? Kissinger was able to orchestrate a campaign of information "leaks" to the media in order to build the situation into a crisis in the minds of American political **elites** and public. By doing this, Kissinger forced Nixon into taking a strong and public stance against the Soviet action, rather than the quieter diplomatic approach Nixon preferred, in order to avoid appearing soft on U.S. national security. This example is interesting in the way it demonstrates both the importance of how leaders define and interpret the international (and domestic) environment, *and* the ways key individuals within a single administration (or **regime**) can and do differ in their interpretations. The ultimate decision maker—in this case, the U.S. president— is not always the person whose interpretation wins. For every policy decision, there may be different individuals with a stake in how a problem is defined and a policy response is built and executed.

It is important to step back from the proposition that leadership matters in order to explore how scholars approach the importance of individual differences in decision making. Although we might find some agreement on the point that how leaders define problems depends on their personal characteristics, we would not necessarily find agreement about whether this makes much difference in the foreign policy of a country. Basically, there are two very different schools of thought on this—the **rational choice** and the cognitive schools. Before we discuss these schools, I will define a few key terms.

On the Definition of "Leaders"

Before going further, it is important to define the word "leader." The easiest definition is the chief executive of the country: Iraqi President Saddam Hussein, Mexican President Vicente Fox, British Prime Minister Tony Blair, and so on. To denote a group of top decision makers, we use the word "leadership." Thus we might discuss the Blair cabinet or the Clinton administration as each country's leadership.

In this chapter, we will focus on national leaders *and not on individuals who do not represent states*. Thus it would be appropriate to examine George W. Bush (Bush 2) but not Osama bin Laden, although the two became irrevocably linked by the events of September 11, 2001. Bin Laden is not a national decision maker, and so he is placed in the category of "nonstate" actors. In chapter 5 we explore the impact of **nonstate actors**—such as bin Laden and the Al Qaeda terrorist network—on the foreign policies of states.

Another concept used interchangeably with "leadership" is "regime." "Regime" is defined as "the group that controls the central political structures of a national government."[5] The concept of a regime is flexible in that it is used to incorporate single leaders and different configurations of leadership groups. Sometimes the word "regime" is used to denote some kind of authoritarian leadership, but this use of the word is not definitional. Democratically elected leadership also can be referred to as a regime.

Foreign policy observers sometimes speak about leaders and their

---

"DECISION UNITS" AND PARTICULAR FOREIGN POLICY DECISIONS

The definition of leadership has been conceptualized as dependent on the number of actors involved in *particular* foreign policy decisions. Margaret Hermann and Charles Hermann offer three types of "decision units" or leadership configurations, each of which makes foreign policy decisions sometimes within a single state:

- A *predominant leader* is "(a) single individual [who] has the power to make the choice and to stifle opposition." Hermann and Hermann give the example of the U.S. president making a "spontaneous decision in response to an unexpected question at a press conference."
- Next, a *single group* is "(a) set of individuals, all of whom are members of a single body, [who] collectively select a course of action." They give as an example of a single group the Joint Chiefs of Staff.
- Finally, decision making can arise among *multiple autonomous actors* who "can act for the government" but cannot override the decisions of each other. Here they give as an example a foreign policy decision made between the White House, Joint Chiefs of Staff, and U.S. Senate.

References

Hermann, Margaret G., and Charles F. Hermann. "Who Makes Foreign Policy Decisions and How: An Empirical Inquiry." *International Studies Quarterly* 33 (1989): 361–87; quotes taken from 363–64.

countries, or capital cities and their countries, as if they were one entity. It isn't unusual to read in a news report that "today Moscow announced it will be postponing the sale of rocket technology to New Delhi." *Moscow* did not make any announcement; the word "Moscow" is exchanged for the name or names of key Russian decision makers. The sentence above could have just as easily stated: Today Russian President Vladimir Putin announced . . . It is also common to see the leaders and countries conflated: "Today Russia announced that it would be postponing the sale of rocket technology to India." Switching leaders for capitals or country names is most common among analysts who are identified with realism, as we will see in the next section. The practice is ubiquitous shorthand not limited to the realists.

Rational Choice

The rational choice approach to studying individuals in foreign policy making actually isn't about single individuals at all. This approach derives directly from the realist worldview that conceptualizes a state as a unitary actor. In international politics, by this view, states are only distinguishable by the relative power they hold, and not by their internal characteristics. Thus government type, history, economics, and the qualities of the individuals holding political leadership positions hold no importance in and of themselves to the analyst. The decisions taken by the leaders of the state are seen as the decisions of the state. This conflating of leader and state is possible because of a key assumption that realists make about leaders: any and all leaders act in ways consistent with the long-term and persistent national interest of the country. Since the national interest does not change, changes in leadership have no consequence.

The clearest statement regarding leaders and national interest and the study of foreign policy comes from the "father" of modern realism, Hans Morgenthau. In the statement below, note how the assumption binding leaders and national interests creates a simple model for the analyst to employ:

We assume that statesmen think and act in terms of interest defined as power, and the evidence of history bears that assumption out. That assumption allows us to retrace and anticipate, as it were, the steps a statesman—past, present or future—has taken or will take on the political scene. We look over his shoulder when he writes his dispatches; we listen in on his conversation with other statesmen; we read and anticipate his very thoughts. Thinking in terms of interest defined as power, we think as he does, and as disinterested observers, we understand his thoughts and actions perhaps better than he, the actor on the political scene, does himself.

The concept of national interest defined as power imposes intellectual discipline upon the observer, infuses rational order into the subject matter of politics, and thus makes the theoretical understanding of politics possible. On the side of the actor, it provides for rational discipline in action and creates that astounding continuity in foreign policy which makes American, British, or Russian foreign policy appear as an intelligible, rational continuum, by and large consistent with itself, regardless of the different motives, preferences, and intellectual and moral qualities of successive statesmen. A realist theory of international politics, then, will guard against two popular fallacies: the concern with motives and the concern with ideological preferences.[6]

The "concern for motives" or "ideological preferences" entails examining the characteristics of individuals or groups of individuals, or even examining the political dynamics within a country, pursuits that have no merit in the realist, rational choice view. Morgenthau does allow that, in rare cases, psychological disorders in an individual or the emotions of mass democratic politics may cause leaders to make decisions that are out of line with national interests. Morgenthau might warn that when studying most foreign policy decisions, follow the old advice given to fledgling doctors in medical school: When you hear hoof beats, think horses, not zebras. When you see a foreign policy decision, think rational decision making and not idiosyncrasy. The standard expectation is the one upon which to base your diagnosis or explanation.

How can rational choice theorists make the assumption that individual differences are insignificant when studying foreign policy decision making? Michael McGinnis, a rational choice adherent who eschews the use of the word "individual" in favor of "regime" precisely because "regime" takes our focus away from personalities, offers this explanation:

> Any individual who attains a position of major foreign policy responsibility will have been socialized through education and processes of political selection to pursue some set of common goals. Individuals differ in their perception of the national interest but role expectations reinforce a sense of common interests.[7]

For McGinnis, political culture and socialization *matter*, but not in a way that requires the study of such. Instead, culture and socialization produce regularities among the individuals who rise to national office, eliminating individual differences and any need to study those differences. Further, McGinnis's working assumption is that

> changes in foreign policy goals attributed to changes in individual leaders or ruling coalitions can be interpreted as random (but not nec-

essarily insignificant) fluctuations around a common "regime interest," which is based on domestic support structures and geopolitical
concerns which act as the primary sources of continuity in foreign
policy interests.[8]

The regime operates as a rational actor. McGinnis explains, "A rational
actor selects the action it perceives most likely to bring about the outcome
most preferred among the set of outcomes that are feasible given constraints on resources, time and information."[9] In McGinnis's explanation,
we see the basic decision-making model at the **core** of all rational
choice/realist discussions.

Decision making is defined as the "act of choosing among available alternatives about which uncertainty exists."[10] This definition is not limited
in its use to realists and rational choice analysts until we qualify it with the
critical assumptions of this school: states are unitary actors motivated by
matters of national interest defined as acquiring and securing power. The
first systematic discussion of the realist decision-making model was offered by Richard Snyder, H. W. Bruck, and Burton Sapin in 1954.[11] In their
"general decision-making model," they set out the following details: Since
states are unitary actors, the decisions and actions of the ultimate decision
makers can be considered the same as the decisions and actions of the
state. Since all states are said to pursue national interests, all states make
decisions in the same way. State decision making can be portrayed as a
process in which the ultimate decision makers examine the internal and
external environments, define the situation at hand, consider alternate
courses of action and then select the course of action which is best suited
to the pursuit of national interests. The actions are considered "planful,"
that is, the result of strategic problem solving and are embedded in an action-reaction interaction.

This decision-making model has often been imagined as a "black box."
We cannot see inside the box and have no need to, since all black boxes
(countries/regimes/leaders) work the same way. Information about the
problem at hand, possible courses of action, possible reactions, and esti-
mates of success for the different courses of action are fed into the box.
Inside the box, a basic utility calculation is made: which choice of action
best maximizes national goals and minimizes costs? A decision then results—or comes out of the box. The environment reacts to the decision/ac-
tion, and the reaction becomes part of a new set of factors that are fed into
the box again. One of the most famous and enduring applications of this
model appears in Graham Allison's *Essence of Decision*, in which he analyzes American and Soviet actions during the Cuban missile crisis.[12]

Of course, decision makers do not live in a perfect world, and so do not
have before them all the relevant information upon which to make the
best decision. In terms of daily affairs of state, this may not be a major

detriment to solid decision making since leaders have a chance to reconsider their choices in light of the steady flow of feedback. Even in crises, leaders make choices that are conditioned on the possible and real reactions to those choices, an issue we will take up shortly. Given the imperfect nature of available information, leaders make the best possible choice or even select the first option that satisfies the minimal requirements of a good choice (called *satisficing*).

Ben Mor presents an example of a rational choice study that turns on the issue of imperfect information.[13] Mor set out to understand why Egyptian President Gamal Abdel Nasser appeared to lead Egypt into war with Israel in 1967 when war with Israel was the very thing Nasser wanted to avoid.

Gamal Abdel Nasser was president of Egypt from 1954 to 1970. Egypt had been a primary enemy of Israel since Israel's creation as a modern state in 1948. Nasser had two primary goals: establish Egypt as the clear leader of the Arab states, and restore the displaced Palestinians to lands taken over by Zionists (i.e., Israel). In 1956, the Egyptian leader sought to nationalize the Suez Canal for purposes of prestige and economic power. The canal, opened in 1865, had been built by the British and operated by the British and French. It became the principal maritime route between the Mediterranean Sea and Indian Ocean, via the Red Sea. Nasser did succeed in nationalizing the Suez Canal, but only after a war with Israel in which Israel—with the collusion of the British and French—managed to quickly capture the Sinai peninsula. The end of the 1956 war saw the placement of the first official **peacekeeping** operation in U.N. history, the United Nations Emergency Force (UNEF). The purpose of UNEF was to keep peace in the Sinai by maintaining a cease-fire between Egypt and Israel, while maintaining the prewar borders of each state. Despite the recovery of the Suez Canal, the quick Egyptian losses and the agreement to allow foreign (U.N.) troops to be stationed on Egyptian soil were great humiliations to Nasser and Egypt.[14]

According to Mor, Nasser wanted to undo the humiliations of 1956 and regain Egyptian leadership in the Arab world especially vis-à-vis the Israeli problem *without* having to engage Israel in a war. Toward these goals, Nasser undertook a series of steps in May 1967—steps that could be interpreted as clearly provocative. First, Nasser ordered the Egyptian army into the Sinai Peninsula. Second, he ordered UNEF to withdraw from the Sinai.[15] Third, he ordered the blockading of the Straits of Tiran. The Straits of Tiran sit at the end of the Sinai Peninsula where the Gulf of Aqaba meets the Red Sea, roughly parallel to the Gulf of Suez. Blocking the Straits of Tiran effectively cut Israel off from direct access to the Red Sea via the Gulf of Aqaba. Israeli leaders—famous for their use of "red lines" establishing permissible ranges of action by their enemies—had already stated that any closing or attempted closing of Tiran would be considered an act of war. When Nasser ordered the blockade, Israel did nothing in *immediate* response. Nasser then signed a defense pact with Jordan on May 30. On June 5, Israel launched an attack, beginning the Six Day War.

Ben Mor's interest, as stated above, was to understand why Nasser appeared to take steps that provoked Israel into war with Egypt, when war was the one thing that Nasser wanted to avoid the most. Using a rational choice model, Mor details the calculations Nasser made along the way, some of which will be explored below. These calculations, though, need to be understood in the context of some key assumptions that Mor ascribes to Nasser. The first assumption was that Israel was a status quo country—that is, Israel benefited from the status quo and would not take steps to undo it. Second, and related to the first, Nasser assumed that Israel would not engage in a war in which it would be perceived as the initiator by the international community.

With these two starting assumptions, Nasser calculated that he had considerable room for movement vis-à-vis Israel. Nasser employed a clear **escalation-deescalation strategy** aimed at restoring Egyptian prestige in the Arab world and avoiding war with Israel. The strategy involved a series of moves; Nasser would make a move and then await the Israelis' reaction. As long as the Israelis made no countermove such as issuing a warning, initiating diplomatic discussions, or mobilizing troops, Nasser was free to continue with the next step. As soon as the Israelis signaled that Egypt had approached a "red line," Nasser would order a deescalation, register his *relative gains* over Israel in terms of enhanced prestige and strategic positioning, and avoid war. Thus utility maximization for Nasser meant registering some gains over the Israelis aimed at restoring some Egyptian prestige short of war.

Mor concludes that Nasser's decision making was rational, *given the limits of the information available* to Nasser. Unfortunately for Nasser, the external environment—Israel and other interested international actors—never provided him with the feedback necessary to sound decision making. Nasser approached and crossed a "red line," and did not know this until Egypt was under military attack. The failure, then, according to Mor, was not that Nasser's decision making itself was faulty, but that he lacked important information on which to calculate his next move. Ultimately, Mor places the blame for the Six Day War at the feet of Israel because Israeli leaders failed to provide adequate feedback to Nasser.[16]

Although this conclusion may seem to shift the focus of the analysis away from the primary research interest (which you could argue it does), Mor's study illustrates the importance of having or not having critical information on which to base any decision. The general decision-making model used by realists requires a constant stream of feedback for the process to maintain its integrity. Once a disruption in the feedback prevents relevant information from being learned, the process is skewed and the result might well be a policy failure. Disruption in information, or distorted information, is a key concern of analysts who study individual-level decision making from a cognitive framework. Rational choice analysts tend to accept the limitations of information as a variable that cannot be controlled and choose to focus instead on refining the decision-making model over several iterations or series of decisions.

Feedback, you'll recall, is vital to the basic rational decision-making model. Mor asserts that the Israelis' failure to provide proper feedback to Nasser led him to conclude that he was safe to continue to escalate when he had already crossed the Israeli "red line." But leaders do not need to wait on feedback before planning their next moves. They can anticipate any number of possible reactions from other actors to any particular move, plotting out different scenarios that might unfold. Choices are understood by the rational actor to be conditional and can be mapped out to follow different possible actions, reactions, and interactions.

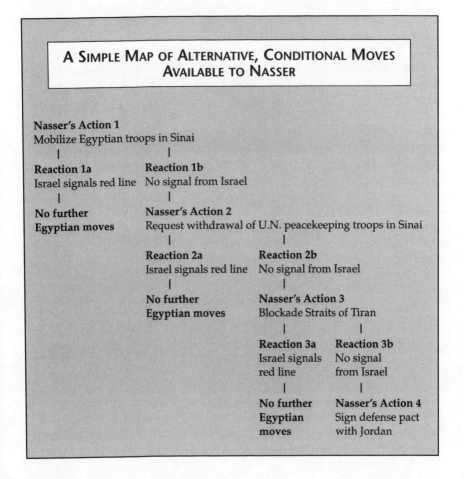

A SIMPLE MAP OF ALTERNATIVE, CONDITIONAL MOVES AVAILABLE TO NASSER

Nasser's Action 1
Mobilize Egyptian troops in Sinai

Reaction 1a
Israel signals red line

Reaction 1b
No signal from Israel

No further Egyptian moves

Nasser's Action 2
Request withdrawal of U.N. peacekeeping troops in Sinai

Reaction 2a
Israel signals red line

Reaction 2b
No signal from Israel

No further Egyptian moves

Nasser's Action 3
Blockade Straits of Tiran

Reaction 3a
Israel signals red line

Reaction 3b
No signal from Israel

No further Egyptian moves

Nasser's Action 4
Sign defense pact with Jordan

Nasser's decision making before the 1967 war shows that he was intent on escalating until given some clear signal or red line from the Israelis; then he would deescalate and count his relative gains. Nasser's first move—to mobilize Egyptian troops in the Sinai—was followed by no Israeli red line. Had a red line been signaled at that point, Nasser would have not made the second move—requesting the withdrawal of the U.N. peacekeepers. That is, the second move was conditioned on a certain reactive first move by the Israelis. Nasser was ready with his second move in either case. Each choice would be refined given the feedback from the Israelis and always with the primary goals in mind (winning relative gains against the Israelis while avoiding war).

Although Mor tells us that Nasser's provocations were calculated moves that were not intended to lead Egypt to war with Israel, war is not necessarily seen as a negative point along the calculated path of the rational actor. Media analyses of international events tend to privilege accounts in which conflict is seen as an acceptable short-term position on the road to larger relative gains. For example, in a *New York Times* report over failing peace talks between the Israelis and Palestinians in September 2000, Deborah Sontag considers why Palestinian leader Yasser Arafat would take an immovable negotiating stance on the disposition of Haram al Sharif (the Temple Mount to Israelis). Such an unrelenting stance gave Israeli Prime Minister Ehud Barak little room to maneuver, virtually guaranteeing continued conflict between the two sides. Arafat was willing to take this risk, suggests Sontag, because it served longer-term Palestinian interests. "Some Palestinian experts say Mr. Arafat thinks it less risky to protract the conflict than to seal a deal that would be perceived as selling out not just Palestinian, but also Arab and Muslim rights."[17] By this account, protracted conflict between Israelis and Palestinians may be an acceptable cost on the way to obtaining a goal more important to Arafat than peace with Israel.

Similarly, in a news report with the curious title, "Attack on Iraq May Be Outcome Hussein Wants," Robin Wright considers the calculations of Iraqi leader Saddam Hussein in January 1998. According to Wright,

After seven years of diplomatic battles with the United States, Iraqi President Saddam Hussein may actually welcome a major military assault, say analysts in the U.S. and diplomats from allied countries.

The Iraqi leader, they say, apparently sees a military showdown as a catalyst for settling a critical question: whether international sanctions, which have cost Baghdad $100 billion in lost oil revenues since 1990, will be lifted as long as he remains in power.[18]

Wright reports that the Iraqi leader might be willing to incur military strikes in the short term on the assumption that such strikes by the United

States would lead to international condemnation of America and international sympathy for Iraq. Ultimately, the United States would look like a bully and the sanctions on Iraq would be lifted, while Hussein stayed in power. Although the wisdom of such a calculation can be (and has been) debated, what is important for us is the clear presence of the rational choice model in these reports by political analysts. Whenever you read that conflict "serves" a purpose, try to discern the calculations that surround the steps in pursuit of that interest.

Returning briefly to the "tangled tale of Tibet," note that both the Bush 1 and Clinton administrations drew criticism for not linking issues of human rights to issues of trade in their China policies. Even the candidate Bill Clinton had been critical of delinkage. Ultimately, the defense each administration gave for its China policy was one that suggested many calculated moves on the way to a longer-term goal. Engagement with China would not only promote the short-term interests of American business and farm groups but also would integrate China into the world community. As this integration occurred, and as American business interests penetrated China, China would move toward greater opening both in terms of its relations with foreign partners and at home. Ultimately, down the road several years, the human rights situation in China would improve as China started to adhere to the behavioral expectations of the United States and the international community. That is, the United States could gain power over China in the long run in economic and political terms, as American interests penetrated the Chinese market and American political ideas penetrated the Chinese polity. China would be bound by its economic interdependence with the world economy, and it would have to curb its internal and external behavior or risk considerable loss. These calculations by two American presidents of different political parties demonstrate the realist proposition that leadership doesn't matter; what matters is the long-term, persistent, rational pursuit of national interests.

Rationality, Deterrence, Game Theory, and "Irrationality"

Realism, with its emphasis on rational choice, was the dominant grand theory of international relations throughout much of the twentieth century. Its dominance was at its peak at the close of World War II and the start of the Cold War. As the Cold War deepened and both the Americans and Soviets developed massive nuclear weapons capabilities, policy makers and realist scholars proposed that nuclear weapons were unlike other weapons in that their value was not in their potential use, but in the threat they posed. The possession of nuclear weapons (weapons of mass destruction) would *deter* any aggressor from striking out against the nuclear state because the threat of the retaliation with nuclear weapons outweighed any benefit that might be had through aggression. The *rational* choice of any leader confronting a nuclear foe was to avoid any action which might be punishable with nuclear retaliation.

In situations where both parties to a conflict held nuclear weapons, both were said to understand that aggression by either would likely result in unacceptable costs for both. Each side, then, was deterred and the situation was one of mutual or stable **nuclear deterrence.** Taken further, when both sides held sufficient nuclear weapons that a nuclear attack initiated by either side could be absorbed by the target and then matched with an equally punishing counterattack, the awareness of the likelihood of mutual assured destruction would deter both from provocative, directly confrontational acts toward the other.

Given the understood costs of a nuclear war (in terms of immediate destruction and longer-term aftermath), rational leaders would not entertain the idea of using nuclear weapons in a conflict. As already stated, realists proposed that nuclear weapons were not for fighting a war, but for deterring a war. One obvious difficulty with this is that recent history provides us with at least one example of a leader who was willing to think the unthinkable, all in the name of protecting the national interest (a realist pursuit). Former President Ronald Reagan was a committed realist in his approach to foreign affairs, yet, Reagan was also committed to the development of a strategy and capability for fighting and winning a nuclear war. He was not convinced that a nuclear "holocaust" was inevitable if either side in the Cold War initiated war with the other. Instead, Reagan urged his military strategists to think about what the United States needed in order engage the Soviet Union in nuclear war and win. The strategic defense initiative was seen as one way to win a nuclear war. There is no way to understand the Reagan desire for a winnable nuclear war fighting strategy outside a realist framework. Yet, nuclear deterrence—a concept that requires rational leaders to understand that the cost of using nuclear weapons is greater than any expected gains from such use—is a concept that comes straight from the realist framework as well.

For Reagan, "winning" the ultimate game between the United States and Soviet Union meant considering how to use nuclear weapons not as threats, but as weapons. This is but one contradiction in the realist/rational choice framework. There is yet another path by which we can encounter problems inherent to the rational actor model and **deterrence,** a path that also derives from realist scholarship.

The assumption that actors are rational decision makers is critical to a line of realist-based research called **game theory.** Game theory borrows from mathematical reasoning and the formal study of logic in order to develop mathematical models of the strategies adopted in the "games" of foreign policy, such as crisis and noncrisis **negotiations,** alliance formation, and arms racing. In the following explanation of game theory from

Dougherty and Pfaltzgraff, we can see the rational actor model inserted into an interactive relationship:

> Game theorists say . . . : If people in a certain situation wish to win—that is, to accomplish an objective that the other party seeks to deny them—we can sort out the intellectual processes by which they calculate or reach decisions concerning what kind of action is most likely to be advantageous to them, assuming they believe their opponents also to be rational calculators like themselves, equally interested in second-guessing and trying to outwit the opponent.[19]

All games contain common features: every player seeks to "win," certain rules govern the behavior of players in the game (with the primary rules privileging cost-benefit analyses and self-interest), players perceive that different moves are associated with different rewards or pay-offs, and all the choices made in the game are interactive. Some games are said to be zero-sum in that when one player wins, the other loses. Zero-sum games reflect the most distilled version of realism: when your country increases its power, it is only because my country has lost power. In other games, the results are non-zero sum, or mixed, in that players can register relative wins or gains over other players, reflecting the more sophisticated recent discussions of realism.

One of the most frequently discussed mixed motives games is that of the prisoners' dilemma. In this game, players attempt to "win," but the interactive choices they make leave each in a position of achieving only the best of the worst situation, rather than the best possible situation. Karen Mingst describes the standard setup of this game:

> The prisoners' dilemma is the story of two prisoners, each being interrogated separately for an alleged crime. The interrogator tells each prisoner that if one of them confesses and the other does not, the one who confessed will go free and the one who kept silent will get a long prison term. If both confess, both will get somewhat reduced prison terms. If neither confesses, both will receive short prison terms based on lack of evidence.[20]

Faced with this dilemma, and working on the assumption that each prisoner will choose what is in her/his own self-interest and that each has no reason to trust the other, both prisoners confess. Or, to put it another way, both confess because each assumes that the other—acting in self-interest only—will confess. Although neither "wins" by being set completely free, neither "loses" to the other by drawing the harsher penalty. The prisoners don't achieve the best solution—no jail time—but they achieve the best of the worst—a shorter sentence and *parity*. Parity—even in terms of mutual punishment—is preferred over sacrifice in a realist, self-help system.

The prisoners' dilemma illustrates the most fundamental realist problem: because no action is made in a vacuum but is, instead, part of a series of interactions with other actors, actors rarely can obtain ultimate security or freedom or superiority or whatever they seek to achieve over other actors. Instead, actors can only hope to obtain relative security or freedom or superiority, and so forth. Actors still make choices that would, under ideal circumstances, earn them the best possible result, but the interactive nature of choices means that the best is not possible in the realist world.

This dilemma can be taken further with far worse results. Borrowing from the notion of the prisoners' dilemma, realists admit to something they call the **security dilemma.** We can say that the security dilemma is the result of choices and behaviors a state makes to secure itself against unspecified, yet predictable outside threats. Although the initial step is only taken in self-defense, other states perceive it with suspicion and fear, and, due to the logic of **anarchy,** they must react to it. A cycle of action-reaction results. Ultimately, the states caught in this cycle find their environment to be more dangerous and more threatening than ever. To return to the first actor, the initial moves it made to increase its security have served only to lessen its overall security—and the security of others as well, thus the state is trapped in a dilemma. Realists acknowledge that this dilemma is real and unfortunate, but also as inevitable as conflict in the **international system.** As if the situation in which the rational pursuit of security ultimately creates more insecurity isn't problem enough with the rational choice model, we can use the setup of the prisoners' dilemma to demonstrate the rationality of *engaging* in nuclear war.

According to deterrence theory, it is more rational not to use nuclear weapons because both sides to a conflict understand that the ultimate costs of using such could never be worth the potential benefits. But, in a competitive, prisoners' dilemma-type relationship (as always exists in the realist world), "winning" is the best possible result and "losing" is the worst. In between is "breaking even" with one's competitor. The rational choice is to attack first. If your opponent does nothing, you win. Since your opponent is also a rational actor, it also has decided to pursue a "win" and attack. Both sides attack and both sides suffer war, but break even with the other. The best possible solution is not possible; the best of the worst—mutual war, even mutual nuclear war—is both possible and rational.

Robert Jervis, one of the leading early scholars in the cognitive school to which we turn shortly, proposes that deterrence theory is dangerous because decision makers and scholars misperceive the "rationality" of others. Jervis authored a number of articles and books in which he presents a number of important misperceptions made by decision makers. For example, Jervis hypothesizes that "actors tend to overlook the fact that evidence consistent with their theories may also be consistent with other views."[21] One "partner" in a relationship premised on stable nuclear deterrence might accept the "fact" of **mutual assured destruction (MAD)**, and assume that the other "partner" also accepts this "fact." But what if the second partner is not operating on the assumption of MAD? What if the second actor believes, as President Ronald Reagan did, that MAD was not inevitable and that a nuclear war could possibly be won? The actor who believes that MAD is incontrovertible and who bases decisions on this could be confused and alarmed by the "inconsistent" behaviors of the other partner—or, at the very worst, this actor could be destroyed by the opponent who was looking at the "facts" and drawing very different conclusions all along.

As another example, Jervis hypothesizes that it may be very difficult for an actor to understand that the other actor is "playing an entirely different game."[22] During the Cold War, the Soviet Union and the United States seemed at times to be "playing" the nuclear "game" with very different rules. The Soviets had a policy of "no first use" of nuclear weapons. Soviet leaders pronounced that they would not be the first to introduce nuclear weapons into any conflict, *but* once such weapons were introduced by others, the Soviets would use them to the fullest and maximum extent. American leaders refused to make a pledge of no first use. Instead, American leaders retained the right to use nuclear weapons as needed, but they pledged to use those weapons in a limited, rational manner, deescalating to conventional weapons as the situation allowed. Both sides assumed that the other would appreciate and conform to the other's expectations and rules—but what guarantees were there that this would happen? Who would yield to the other's rules? When? There was *within* the view of each side a certain rationality, yet on a battlefield the failure to understand that two different rationalities were at play could have resulted in nuclear holocaust. Let's turn now to a competing perspective that offers us a way to examine different "rationalities."

Cognition: A Different View of Rationality

As the preceding discussion makes clear, not every analyst has been satisfied thinking about people as decision-making "boxes," utility maximizers, or rational actors (based on a single notion of rationality). Scholars have long studied great leaders as well as notorious ones in order to understand their motivations, thoughts, and actions. But, in the post–World War II era, political biographies of leaders were regarded by mainstream political scientists as too unscientific for the nascent field of foreign policy analysis. The study of individuals needed to take on the same rigor as the competing study of rational decision making.

The move toward incorporating a more thorough, scientific investigation of individuals into the study of foreign policy takes off in the 1950s. In the aftermath of World War II, behavioral scientists and psychologists had begun to examine issues such as whether aggression was inherent to humans or a learned (socialized) behavior that could be unlearned. Kenneth Waltz and Jerel Rosati—writing in different time periods and with very different orientations—credit the peace researchers of the 1950s with bringing the insights of psychology into the study of foreign policy.[23] The motivation of peace researchers was simple: if humans learn to make war, then they can learn to make peace. If, instead, aggression is part of human nature, perhaps aggression could be channeled into nonviolent pursuits. Behavioral scientists and psychologists were studying **cognition**—which the *American Heritage Dictionary* defines as "the mental process or faculty of knowing, including aspects such as awareness, perception, reasoning, and judgment." The insights from the study of cognition could be used to shape peaceful leaders and peaceful countries.

A key starting assumption for the study of cognition is that humans do not necessary think "rationally," or, more to the point, that "rationality" itself is context-driven. Individual differences can and do have a huge impact on foreign policy decision making, but it is possible to systematize our understanding of basic human thinking, developing constructs that have utility in a variety of settings.

In his important early work on misperception, Jervis offers this starting point for understanding the focus of cognitive foreign policy study:

In determining how he will behave, an actor must try to predict how others will act and how their actions will affect his values. The actor must therefore develop an image of others and of their intentions. This image, may, however, turn out to be an inaccurate one; the actor may for a number of reasons misperceive both others' actions and their intentions.[24]

Why might actors misperceive? What are the processes that cause this to happen?

The evidence from both psychology and history overwhelmingly supports the view . . . that decision makers tend to fit incoming information into their existing theories and images. Indeed, their theories and images play a large part in determining what they notice. In other words, actors tend to perceive what they expect. Furthermore, . . . a theory will have greater impact on an actor's interpretation of data (a) the greater the ambiguity of the data and (b) the higher the degree of confidence with which the actor holds the theory.[25]

Is the process that Jervis proposes an example of *irrational* thinking? Jervis says that it is not, or, rather, that we need to rethink "rationality" in terms of the logic of the actor's existing beliefs and images. Borrowing from others, Jervis asserts there is a "psycho-logic" that structures each individual's cognitive processes. To combine this notion with one of Jervis' hypotheses on misperception stated above, we might say that I have a logical structure to my beliefs that makes it difficult for me to understand why you look at the same world I do and draw very different conclusions. Indeed, I may not even be able to comprehend *that* you draw different conclusions. Miscommunications and antagonistic foreign policy behaviors can easily result from the clash of different, often unknowable, yet internally rational beliefs.

Another important early contributor to the study of cognition is Irving Janis. Janis proposes that that in every situation there is a "decisional conflict" that distorts decision making.[26] A decisional conflict refers to the situation in which opposing tendencies within an individual interfere with what realists would call "rational" decision making.

A quick example is in order. Imagine a meeting of top foreign policy decision makers meeting in a cabinet session. Present at the meeting is a new appointee, a young "rising star." This new member might have several personal and professional goals wrapped up in the meeting. She might want to be well-liked and well-respected by all the others in the cabinet, and to have an impact on the group's process and final decision. During that meeting, another cabinet member—older and very influential—begins to make an argument in favor of one particular course of action. As the youngest member listens to the older member explain his reasoning, the youngest member begins to feel rising alarm. She believes the speaker is fundamentally wrong and potentially could take the group and the country down the wrong path. But, as she looks around the room and notices other key cabinet members nodding in agreement, she begins to doubt her own view about what is right. Wanting to be part of the group, wanting to be respected and accepted, the younger member feels *conflicted* about speaking out—it would be correct to speak out, but it would jeopardize her standing in the group if so many others agree with the older speaker.

During the Lyndon Johnson administration, a similar sort of self-censorship was exercised by some conflicted members of President Johnson's Vietnam War decision-making circle. This self-censorship was encouraged by the fairly ruthless exclusionary practice exercised by President Johnson in his so-called Tuesday lunch group. People who spoke out against the direction favored by the group were told pointedly not to return for the next group meeting.

Adopting a realist-like view, we might conceptualize the opposing tendencies that most people feel in any given social interaction as "distortions" in "rational" decision making. These distortions might be imagined as screens or filters that keep altering the direction in which thoughts are processed. The presence of these filters limits the range, creativity, and responsiveness of the decision maker, as Jerel Rosati suggests:

> Where the rational actor perspective assumes individual open-mindedness and adaptability to changes in the environment, a cognitive approach posits that individuals tend to be much more closed-minded due to their beliefs and the way they process information—thus, they tend to resist adapting to changes in the environment.[27]

Alternatively, what one scholar might interpret as a distorted cost-benefit analysis, another scholar might interpret as a value stand. The rising star in the scenario above might go with her beliefs, staking a value position against the older speaker's view that overrules a cost-benefit calculation.

Belief Sets, Images, and Cognitive Structure

Scholars have tried to elucidate the various kinds of screens or filters that produce "nonrational" decisions. A number of concepts are foundational to this work, starting with the rather simple notion of **belief sets.** A belief set is a more or less integrated set of images held by an individual about a particular universe. This set of images acts as a screen, letting in information that fits the belief set and keeping out information that does not.

One illustration of a belief set is the enemy image. Images of other international actors can be categorized according to stereotyped views of the motivations of the subject and the behaviors that result from such.[28] The "enemy" is imagined as evil by nature, with unlimited potential for committing evil acts. The enemy is also imagined as a strategic thinker and consummate chess-master—establishing and carrying out a plan bent on destroying its enemies and their way of life. When a foreign policy maker holds a fairly strong enemy image of an opponent, only those images that confirm the inherently evil and cunning nature of the opponent are stored and remembered. Images that suggest a more complicated nature in the opponent, or that suggest less capability by the opponent are screened out. Arguably, the inability of the U.S. leadership and intelligence community to predict the sudden and terminal collapse of the Eastern bloc and the Soviet Union can be attributed to a firmly entrenched enemy image that failed to take note of signs of a rapidly deteriorating Soviet empire and a differently oriented Soviet leadership under Gorbachev. Enemy images may do more than cause an actor to miss signs of change in the enemy, the presence of strong enemy images may sustain international conflict over time, a prophetic conclusion drawn by Ole Holsti in the 1960s regarding American decision makers' images of Soviet leaders.[29]

A belief set is a fairly simple idea the elements of which can often be depicted in simple metaphors. When a leader is described as a "dove," the image of a dove of peace is evoked, suggesting the leader is inclined to interpreting international events in an optimistic way and to acting cooperatively with others. When a leader is described as a "hawk," the image of a bird of prey is evoked. Predator birds must be constantly alert to threats and opportunities in the environment, and they never turn away from the use of force when such use can further self-interest.

A related concept is **cognitive consistency**—the idea that the images contained in a belief set must be logically connected and consistent. Cognitive theorists claim that when an individual holds conflicting beliefs, the individual experiences an anxiety known as cognitive dissonance. Individuals strive to avoid this dissonance and the anxiety it produces by actively managing the information they encounter and store in their belief sets.

It is important to note here that the idea of the individual as a cognitive manager actively attempting to avoid dissonant information does not necessarily mean that individuals cannot learn something new. Scholars who study learning among foreign policy makers study the "development of new beliefs, skills, or procedures as a result of the observation and interpretation of experience."[30] Learning is possible and belief sets can change.

Janice Gross Stein's study of Mikhail Gorbachev provides a good explanation of the conditions under which beliefs can change. Stein argues that learning—a change in held beliefs—occurs easiest on problems that are "ill-structured" in the mind of the individual. An ill-structured problem is akin to an incomplete belief set. Gorbachev's primary interests within the Central Committee and, after 1980, within the Politburo, centered on the domestic economy of the Soviet Union. On topics of external security, Stein asserts, including the United States, Gorbachev held few preexisting beliefs. According to Stein, "learning is the construction of new representations of the problem"; new representations of a problem occur most easily when there is an underdeveloped existing representation of the problem in the mind of the individual.[31] Gorbachev was unconstrained by well-structured existing beliefs about Soviet external security, and so he was "free" to learn. Stein argues that Gorbachev was prompted to learn new ideas about Soviet security and about the United States by the failure of Soviet policy in Afghanistan. Learning, then, requires two elements: the lack of strongly established beliefs and some "unanticipated failures that challenge old ways of representing problems."[32] Learning requires some prompt and some need.

Beliefs that are firmly held and supported by one's society and culture are more rigid and unlikely to change. Moreover, individuals are assumed to be limited information managers—or **cognitive misers** who rely on cognitive shortcuts to understand new information. The shortcuts are images in their belief sets that look like some idea they already hold. Individuals not only use preexisting beliefs to screen out dissonant information, but they also use existing beliefs to *interpret* new information. The new information is "recognized" as similar to an existing belief and so is stored as the same. Great distortion can occur in this act of interpreting and storing, but the distortion is necessary because it is quicker and easier, and it helps individuals avoid dealing with new and potentially dissonant information.

Matthew Hirshberg provides a demonstration of the rigidity of preexisting beliefs and the reconstruction of information to make it resemble preexisting beliefs. Hirshberg presented fictional news stories to three groups of college students to test two hypotheses. His first hypothesis was that "the stereotype of a prodemocratic America serves to maintain its own cultural dominance by filtering out information that does not fit it, making it difficult for Americans to test the validity of their preconceptions."[33] The fictional news accounts portrayed the United States intervening in three different ways: (1) on the side of a democratic government besieged by rebels, (2) on the side of an unspecified type of government besieged by communist rebels, and (3) on the side of an unspecified type of government besieged by democratic rebels. When asked to recall the events depicted in the particular story read, most students recalled that the United States had intervened in support of **democracy.**[34] The students' strongly held belief that the United States always supported democracy and freedom caused them to re-create the information in the news account to fit what they believed.

Hirshberg tested a second hypothesis on what is called attribution bias. An attribution bias or error is triggered by information that is inconsistent with preexisting beliefs and cannot be re-created to fit those beliefs. The attribution bias involves both the enemy image discussed above and another perceptual move called the mirror image. The starting belief is that we are a people who are inherently good and well-intentioned. Our opponent, on the other hand, is evil and has malevolent intentions—the opposite or mirror image of us. In an attribution error, the individual goes a step further in order to explain behavior, especially behavior that does not fit one's beliefs about one's own country as good and well-intentioned. When our evil opponent does bad things—like using military force or coercing another country into a one-sided trade arrangement—it is because such bad behavior is in our opponent's nature. Conversely, we are by nature good and so only do good things. When *we* do bad things, it is because we have been forced to do so by external events. When an individual must explain a behavior that is inconsistent with preexisting foundational beliefs, cognitive scholars say the individuals attribute the inconsistent behavior to outside circumstances.

Hirshberg's second hypothesis was tested with fictional news accounts

---

ATTRIBUTION BIAS: YOU MADE ME BOMB YOU, I DIDN'T WANT TO DO IT

Attribution bias can be found in media reports and in statements issued by governments to explain their behavior. During the Bosnian war of 1992–1995, U.N. peacekeeping troops were scattered around parts of Bosnia and Croatia to try to limit the violence and thereby stem the outflow of refugees. As history has demonstrated, however, the peacekeepers were not an effective deterrent or buffer, and they often found themselves under fire.

In one episode, the Croatian government sought to retake a sector that was under the watch of U.N. peacekeepers. A demand was issued for the peacekeepers to give up their position. The peacekeepers refused, prompting a warning from the Croatian government about what might happen if it received no compliance with its demand. When the peacekeepers refused to move again, the Croatian army proceeded to bomb the U.N. position. The official explanation—a clear manifestation of the attribution bias—was that the peacekeepers had given the Croatian government no other choice but to bomb them. The Croatian government further announced, "Croatia deeply regrets and is very sorry for what happened. We were doing our very best to avoid such incidents before commencing military activities."

References
"Croatian Jets Strafe UN Observation Posts." *Reuters World Service*, August 4, 1995, Lexis-Nexis.

---

that either depicted the United States dropping "tons of incendiary bombs," causing "panic" and "horror" among villagers, or depicted it dropping "tons of relief supplies," causing "joy" and "glee" among villagers.[35] After having his subjects read one version of the fictional accounts, he had them answer questionnaires on the "nature of the United States" and why it acted as reported. Hirshberg found that 70 percent of those reading about the dropping of relief supplies agreed that it was American nature to do so (an internal attribution bias). However, he did not find significant statistical support for the external attribution bias—that the United States dropped bombs because it was forced by external events.

When preexisting beliefs are used to interpret, re-create, or explain away behavior, cognitive scholars say that the individual is acting as a cognitive miser, using shortcuts to deal with the new information. The name given by some scholars to these cognitive shortcuts is a schema. A schema is a shortcut like a menu that is more or less particular to place and event. The schema a leader "uses" when facing a trade dispute is different from the schema that same leader uses when dealing with a diplomatic or military dispute. When scholars study schemas, they are interested in identifying the nature or internal structure of schemas and the policy decision that might result from different schemas.

For example, it is well-known that individuals use analogies to understand a new situation and to determine a course of action. An analogy is a comparison made to similar events or phenomena. For instance, if a leader uses the "Munich analogy" to determine a course of action, he or she has decided that events at hand resemble the events of 1938 when the British Prime Minister Neville Chamberlain "appeased" Adolph Hitler. In the Munich treaty—which essentially amounted to a green light for Germany to move east into Czechoslovakia, thereby sparing countries to the west—Chamberlain proclaimed that he had bought "peace in our time." But the Munich treaty did not satisfy Hitler's aggression; he ultimately brought war to countries in all directions. When a leader says that a new situation brings to mind the "Munich analogy," he or she is saying that it does no good to try to appease an aggressive leader; instead, the aggressor must be met with immediate and decisive force. Keith Shimko writes that when individuals use a schema to understand a new problem, they "fill in the blanks of current events with knowledge accumulated from past experiences."[36] Once a leader decides a new situation resembles the effort to appease Hitler, the leader need not seek out detailed information about the new situation in order to know what policy is necessary.

Policy makers can cause problems for themselves in their use of analogies. We can see this in a diplomatic tussle that resulted from remarks made by the Israeli prime minister in the immediate aftermath of the September 11, 2001, terrorist attacks on the United States. In pursuit of Arab support for its campaign against international **terrorism,** the George W. Bush (Bush 2) administration announced in early October that it was in favor of a long-standing demand of the Arab world—Palestinian statehood. This announcement prompted a speech by Israeli Prime Minister Ariel Sharon in which he made use of the famous analogy discussed above:

I call on the Western democracies and primarily the leader of the free world, the United States: Do not repeat the dreadful mistake of 1938 when enlightened European democracies decided to sacrifice Czechoslovakia for a convenient temporary solution. Do not try to appease the Arabs at our expense. This is unacceptable to us. Israel will not be Czechoslovakia. Israel will fight terrorism.[37]

The Israeli prime minister's use of the Munich analogy provoked a public rebuke from the White House press secretary: "The president believes that these remarks are unacceptable. Israel can have no better or stronger friend than the United States."[38] Opposition Party members from within Israel also condemned Sharon's remark, pointing out that Israel and the United States shared the same interests in eliminating international terrorism. Sharon subsequently retracted the remark—in part—agreeing that the United States was a good friend of Israel's.

Before prompting an angry U.S. retort, Sharon's use of the Munich analogy set the course for abandonment of the most recent cease-fire between Israel and the Palestinian National Authority (this conflict is explained in much greater detail in chapter 3). Within a few hours of his use of the Munich analogy, Sharon ordered Israeli tanks, infantry, helicopter gunships, and armored bulldozers into parts of Palestinian-controlled Hebron. Analogies can signal leaders' intentions to embark on certain courses of action. Rather than allow Israel to be sacrificed by the United States in order to curry Arab favor, Sharon demonstrated that he was prepared to take Israeli security into his own hands, setting his own policy direction. Abandoning the cease-fire was a clear statement to this effect, especially in the face of U.S. pressure on Israel to be more accommodating with the Palestinians in order to help along the Bush 2 administration's new war on terrorism.

When a leader makes use of an analogy, it is possible to make a safe guess about the kind of behaviors that follow. Once a leader identifies an opponent as another Hitler and therefore the lessons of Munich must apply, we can safely predict that the leader thinks that some kind of forceful reply to the new Hitler is in order. Once a leader declares that his or her country will not be abandoned in the same way that Czechoslovakia was abandoned, we can safely predict that the leader will demonstrate his or her willingness and capability to go it alone. If we as analysts can map out the operating beliefs of a leader we are studying, looking for the analogies and other pronouncements that demonstrate the leader's worldview, we can use this "map" to explain why certain policies were made and certain actions taken. A cognitive map that details both the normative beliefs held by an individual and his or her behavioral beliefs is called an operational code.

Alexander George is the scholar who brought the discussion of operational codes to the forefront in foreign policy study in the late 1960s. George defines the operational code as a "political leader's beliefs about the nature of politics and political conflict, his views regarding the extent to which historical developments can be shaped, and his notions of correct strategy and tactics."[39] Delineating a leader's operational code involves a two-step process, as described by Stephen Walker and colleagues:

First, what are the leader's philosophical beliefs about the dynamics of world politics? Is the leader's image of the political universe a diagnosis marked by cooperation or conflict? What are the prospects for the realization of fundamental political values? What is the predictability of others, the degree of control over historical development and the role of chance? Second, what are the leader's instrumental beliefs that indicate choice and shift propensities in the management of conflict? What is the leader's general approach to strategy and tactics and the utility of different means? How does the leader calculate, control, and manage the risks and timing of political action?[40]

Operational code studies typically depend on an examination of the writings and statements of a leader from which philosophical beliefs can be extracted. With a clear articulation of a leader's beliefs about the world, these beliefs can be matched against the leader's real foreign policy decisions and behaviors in order to elaborate his or her instrumental beliefs. Ibrahim Karawan examines the writings and statements of Egyptian President Anwar Sadat in order to elaborate his operational code. Karawan sought to understand Sadat's ultimate decision to make peace with Israel in the 1979 Camp David Accords.[41]

Anwar Sadat assumed the presidency of Egypt in 1970 upon the death of Gamal Abdel Nasser. Recall that earlier in this chapter we explored the rational choices made by Nasser in the events leading up to the 1967 war between Egypt and Israel. The losses incurred by Egypt and the Arab states collectively in the 1967 war—the Old City of Jerusalem, the Sinai peninsula, the Gaza Strip, the West Bank, and Golan Heights—caused Nasser to lose his leadership position in the Arab world. Although Nasser attempted to resign from the presidency after the 1967 defeat, his popularity among Egyptians remained high and he remained as president until he had a heart attack and died.

According to Karawan, Sadat took over the Egyptian presidency committed to setting Egypt on a different foreign policy course. Rather than follow the pan-Arab policy of Nasser, Sadat embarked on an "Egypt first" policy course. Karawan claims that Sadat's writings and speeches indicate that "Egypt first" was the driving philosophical belief of Sadat's operational code.[42] The instrumental belief that follows from this is that Sadat would negotiate Egypt's future without regard for the opinions and interests of the other Arab states. To illustrate Sadat's "Egypt first" operational code, Karawan points to Sadat's speeches and actions at several key junctures in the 1970s.

For instance, in 1973, Egypt and Syria launched a concerted two-prong attack on Israel. Egyptian forces managed to reclaim a small part of the Sinai peninsula in this attack, a victory Sadat attributed to the power of Egyptian **nationalism**.[43] This was the first time an Arab leader made battlefield gains against Israel. Following his "Egypt first" philosophy and despite the fact that he had engaged in the war alongside ally Syria, Sadat declared a unilateral cease-fire and negotiated a subsequent disengagement without consulting or *even informing* ally Syria. Similarly, Sadat pursued peace with Israel in the 1978 Camp David Talks, which led to the 1979 peace treaty between Egypt and Israel, in order to pursue Egypt's national interests. Sadat's decision to engage in peace talks with Israel and his agreement to the terms of the Camp David Accords occurred in the absence of any consultation with or consideration of the other Arab states. Sadat's pursuit of Egyptian national interests vis-à-vis Israel constituted the behavioral manifestation of his driving philosophical belief.

Sadat's pursuit of his "Egypt first" philosophy caused the other Arab states to turn their backs on Egypt. His decision to negotiate peace and normal relations with Israel ultimately gave incentive to some Egyptian Islamic fundamentalists to assassinate Sadat in 1981. But his actions in the 1970s flowed directly from his primary beliefs. The elaboration of Sadat's operational code explains the foreign policy he followed, that is, the elaboration of Sadat's cognitive map points out the direction of the course he set for Egypt.

Some scholars have been interested in mapping out the cognitive complexity or simplicity of decision makers. Allison Astorino-Courtois explains, "The cognitive complexity-simplicity construct reflects the degree to which individuals both *differentiate* and *integrate* various sources of information in considering a decision problem."[44] Peter Suedfeld and colleagues elaborate: "Integrative complexity is an attribute of information processing that generally indicates the extent to which decision makers search for and monitor information, try to predict outcomes and reactions, flexibly weigh their own and other parties' options, and consider multiple potential strategies."[45]

The study of integrative complexity involves an examination of the public utterances of leaders. The utterances, or statements, are scored as to whether they demonstrate simple information processing, more complicated contingency-based reasoning, or highly complex, multicausal information processing. Scholars have found that leaders demonstrating higher levels of complexity tend to be more cooperative in their international initiatives than those demonstrating lower levels.[46] However, in situations of prolonged stress, such as the 1962 Cuban missile crisis or the months leading up to the 1991 Persian Gulf War, the measured integrative complexity decreases for all decision makers as they begin to feel that their time and options are running out.

In many respects, these scholars equate cognitive complexity with rational decision making, and cognitive simplicity with decision making through the use of preexisting beliefs:

At the lower end of the complexity scale, the amount of information used in cognitive processing is limited . . . decision makers often rely on analogs or stereotyped images, and discrepant information is either ignored or discounted. . . . Complex thinking, on the other hand, involves a broader search and use of varied information sources concerning the decision problem. Discrepant information is integrated most thoroughly at higher levels of cognitive complexity, and more flexible consideration is given to the complete set of options and outcomes relevant to a decision situation.[47]

By equating high levels of complexity with the tasks typically associated with rational decision making, this line of research begins to bridge the differences between rational choice and cognitive studies.[48]

Moral Positions and Value Stands: A Departure

A standard foreign policy book would include a discussion of rational choice, decision making, cognition, or some combination or survey of these three topics, but rarely a discussion of moral positions and value stands. *The New Foreign Policy* departs significantly from the past in this respect. Yet note the following disclaimer: *This section is a call to study rather than a presentation of what has been studied.* Its brevity should not suggest that the study of morals and values is unimportant, but that they have been understudied or largely neglected in the broader study of foreign policy decision making. Here, we'll consider a few reasons why morals and values should be considered, offering encouragement for those who would undertake a more systematic, broad-reaching study of ethical foreign policy decision making.

The *Penguin Dictionary of International Relations*—an otherwise excellent resource for students, teachers, and practitioners—does not include entries for "moral" or "value." The *American Heritage Dictionary* includes this definition of moral: "Of or concerned with the judgment of the goodness or badness of human action and character . . . Conforming to standards of what is right or just in behavior; virtuous." This same source provides this among the definitions of value: "A principle, standard, or quality considered worthwhile or desirable." These definitions fit our purposes here quite well.

We can consider several broad questions when studying the morals and values of leaders. Is it possible to undertake a study of the morals and values of leaders and leadership? *Should* we undertake the study of morals and values? Are there lessons to be learned from such studies that might lead to morally based foreign policy decisions and actions? Like every subject taken up in this book, we could spend many, many volumes examining these questions. Here we'll just touch on them, even as I insist that the study of moral positions and value stands should be a part of the study of foreign policy.

Can We and How Might We Study Morals and Values?

The answer to the first question posed above—is it possible to undertake a study of the morals and values of leaders and leadership—is a simple yes. In the first instance, worldviews—or grand theories—are premised on moral judgments about what is and is not important, as well as on ideas about the fundamental nature of human existence. Despite this, there is strong disagreement between the grand theories of international relations regarding *whether* morals should be considered at all in the study of politics. Hans Morgenthau warned against injecting "interpersonal" issues such as morality into politics. Morals are important between individuals, but leaders who concerned themselves with moral issues would lose track of national interests defined as power. Conversely, idealists or liberals long have considered the moral bases for personal and interstate relations, even to the point of constructing "codes" that regulate what is just and proper behavior between them.[49] Feminist scholars, now a large "wing" of the liberal/idealist school, suggest that a major source of conflict in the world derives from the very fact that typical national leaders have been socialized since infancy to reject their natural, moral connections to other humans in favor of the primary masculine value of autonomy.[50]

When mainstream scholars include morals and values in their analyses, they generally are included in lists of background characteristics that shape a leader's perception of reality, ambitions, desire for power, desire for cooperation, and so forth. For example, consider Tom Princen's study of President Jimmy Carter's mediation efforts in the talks that culminated in the 1978 Camp David Accords between Israel and Egypt. Princen's primary research interest was to study how a mediator perceives mediation and his or her role as mediator, and whether the end-product of such mediation reflects the mediator's perceptions about mediation (that's a mouthful!). Carter had clearly articulated value stands that he applied to every situation he faced as president. Princen writes that Carter "believed in the basic goodness of humankind, [and] that conflict could be overcome if the protagonists understood each other and appreciated each other's basically good intentions."[51] Princen asserts that Carter's mediation style was influenced first and foremost by his belief in the goodness and basic rationality of humans, and second by his engineering background. If Carter could bring together Israeli leader Menachem Begin and Egyptian leader Anwar Sadat and if they could see that the other truly desired peace, then he could "engineer" a bridge between the two in the shape of an enduring peace agreement.[52]

Princen examines the statements made by the primary participants of the Camp David talks, and especially Carter's written recollection of the talks, to demonstrate whether and how Carter's mediation efforts were

shaped by his principles. Ultimately, Princen concludes that Carter's initial morality-based approach to mediation failed, leaving him to resort to
hard bargaining and power politics. Begin and Sadat did not respond well
to Carter as helpful engineer, but they were quite ready to deal with Carter
as U.S. president. Princen's study serves as a useful model for how to or-
ganize and conduct research into the impact of morals and values on foreign policy behaviors, even though he concludes that power politics
overrode a moral position in this case. Before we concede this point entirely to Princen, though, we might remember that Carter's values *did*
have a crucial *shaping* impact on his initial decision to bring the Egyptian
and Israeli leaders together. As Princen himself explains,

As for a U.S. role, Carter saw both a moral and a political dimension.
First and foremost, Carter saw a moral obligation to seek peace. He
and his country owed it to all concerned—the Israelis, the Arab countries, and the Palestinians—to bring peace to the region. With the ever-
present threat that another Middle East war would engage the two
superpowers in direct conflict, world peace demanded a solution.[53]

Princen's study, as already noted, serves as a useful model, especially to
scholars who worry that investigating the impact of moral and value
stands on foreign policy decision making will "muddy up" our inquiry.
Such research can be done systematically.

Leaders Who Put Broader Principles before National Interests

Princen notes Carter's belief that the United States had an obligation
and responsibility to "world peace," which required action on the Arab-
Israeli conflict *regardless* of American national interests. There were U.S.
interests to be served by an Arab-Israeli accord, to be sure, but world
peace "demanded" action and then U.S. national interests could/would
be served. Carter stands among the ranks of some noteworthy world leaders who put the greater good before their national interests *and* saw their
own national interests as integrated into the greater good.

Consider the case of former Costa Rican President Oscar Arias Sánchez.
Arias taught political science at the University of Costa Rica before he entered politics. In 1986, after a decade and a half of government service,
Arias was elected president. One of his greatest priorities on becoming
president was to achieve peace in Central America.

The countries of Central America witnessed one armed conflict after another since the late 1940s, with the violence intensifying from the late 1960s
on. In 1983, the leaders of Mexico, Venezuela, Colombia, and Panama
drafted a peace plan for Central America known as the Contadora plan, but

"fundamental differences in interpreting the plan kept it from succeeding."[54] American interests in the region and with individual countries there contributed to these fundamental differences.

Arias, acting on his own, signaled a strong and tangible break from "business as usual" in Central America by closing down Costa Rican–U.S. military ties. Then he contacted the leaders of the five Central American countries about reviving the Contadora plan or whether a new peace plan was possible. Arias and the five Central American leaders succeeded in designing a new plan, one signed by all in August 1987. Peace was the goal for Arias, a goal *not* balanced against economic and political interests, although, to be sure, the economic and political interests of all Central American countries would be served by peace. Later that year, Arias received the Nobel Peace Prize for his contribution to bringing peace to Central America. Arias used the money that accompanied the Nobel Prize to fund the nonprofit Arias Foundation for Peace and Human Progress.

In order to fully understand why Oscar Arias Sánchez worked for peace in all of Central America more than he worked for the immediate national interests of Costa Rica, we would have to "think outside the box" to see the man for who he was/is. But we don't have to invent a new "box." As mentioned earlier, long before the study of politics and government became the study of political science, great leaders were studied for the lessons and models they and their lives might offer. The study of individual leaders privileges issues of right and wrong, of moral standing and compassion. We can reclaim political biography as an important source for understanding leaders and moral foreign policy decision making.

Moreover, **globalization**'s mass culture makes single leaders and their moral stands more immediate and relevant to the entire world. When Nelson Mandela called on his countrypeople to find ways to reconcile with and make amends to one another in order to begin a just, moral, and democratic South Africa, this great man's words and moral acts were noted around the world. When Vaclav Havel became prime minister and later president of the Czech Republic, he was asked why his government had not imprisoned those from the communist era who had in previous times imprisoned him and his colleagues. His answer in paraphrase was, Because we are not them. Goodness, justice, and decency guided these great national leaders to make **governance** decisions that valued human life and dignity, and the dawning era of globalization helped disseminate the news.

It is widely said that Neil Armstrong's famous words upon stepping onto the surface of the moon in 1969 were heard by everyone everywhere in the world who was within range of a radio. This was a momentous uniting of people on a day of human triumph, inspiring them to want to do more and better or hope for better. In this day of global media, personalities take on a much more potent force when they speak out on behalf of something better. Globalization helps spread their message (although it is sometimes the evil side of globalization that they speak against!).

Foreign policy scholars can contribute to the construction of a morally just international order by studying the single cases of national leaders whose basic commitment to humanity and morality helped them make positive changes in this world. As some leaders rise up to the level of "global leaders," foreign policy scholars can aspire to the role of "public intellectuals," contributing to a greater collective good.

The New Foreign Policy might serve figuratively as "good offices" to facilitate the reinclusion of morality into the study and conduct of foreign policy. Some might argue what *standard* should we use? Wouldn't the choice of any particular standard deny voice to others? Some might argue about the impracticality of ever agreeing on a single ethical or moral standard. But there are many standards to which states already have agreed. From 1919 through 1989, states signed on to seventy-nine different treaties and accords, which together Dorothy Jones calls the States' Ethical Code.[55] These international instruments covered a range of state-state behaviors, as well as expected behaviors of states toward the people within their own borders. In the model of Dr. Martin Luther King Jr., who called on the United States to live up to its moral principles, there are international leaders like Oscar Arias Sánchez, Nelson Mandela, and Jimmy Carter whose moral leadership calls on the peoples of the world to live up to commonly accepted standards. By incorporating more examinations of moral leadership into foreign policy studies, scholars can be voices on the side of the 1938 Declaration in Favor of Women's Rights, the 1938 Declaration against Persecution for Racial or Religious Motives, the 1948 Universal Declaration of Human Rights, and the 1959 Declaration on the Rights of the Child, to name but a few international standard setters. Such a focus within foreign policy analysis would bridge the gap between the scholarly and "real" worlds and serve some fundamental, moral, good.

Review

Realist rational choice/decision-making models and cognitive approaches to the study of individual decision making attempt to isolate important components of the decision process at the smallest unit of analysis—the individual. It is important to remember that the individual per se is not the subject of realist scholars. Instead, realists focus on the abstraction of the national leader to describe the rational cost-benefit analysis at the heart of all foreign policy decision making. Cognitive scholars question the notion of abstract, universal rationality, preferring instead to examine how individual differences and beliefs impact decisions made.

When we explore the factors influencing foreign policy making and behavior at any particular level, we try to isolate a subset of important factors to understand one part of the foreign policy puzzle. Such a move does not imply that other factors deriving from other levels of analysis are not important. Rational choice scholars depend absolutely on system-level politics, which influence the range of choices available to the decision maker. Some even make passing reference to domestic or state-level factors when they suggest that the socialization of leaders makes them all tuned into critical national interests, or that institutional processes even out individual irrationalities, ensuring rational decision making by institutions. Cognitive scholars also point toward system- and state-level factors that influence the shaping of belief sets. As we'll see in the next chapter, some concepts developed by cognitive scholars are applied at the aggregate level to societies or national cultures. By isolating individual-level factors, we seek to understand foreign policy making from one angle (or through using a zoom lens on a camera), but we do not rule out the influence of factors from other levels of analysis.

Some Key Ideas from This Chapter

- When we say that "leadership matters," we suggest that leaders play crucial roles at the nexus of international and domestic politics.
- "Leadership," like "regime," refers to the highest decision making unit of a country. These concepts can be used to refer to single leader as well as to different configurations of leadership groups.
- Realists propose that the study of individual leaders is inappropriate and irrelevant since all leaders, regardless of who they are and their own individual differences, act to safeguard and forward the national interests. National interests are enduring interests that exist above and beyond differences in officeholders.
- Decision making, according to the realists, involves strategic calculations of policy based on simple cost-benefit analyses.
- Cognitive scholars question whether there is a universal rationality, electing instead to examine bounded rationality within particular belief sets.
- According to cognitive scholars, individual belief sets are structured, integrated, internally logical sets of images that help individuals efficiently manage new information.
- Also according to cognitive scholars, preexisting belief sets make it difficult for individuals to recognize new information as new information and make it difficult for individuals to recognize and understand that others think differently than they do.

For Further Study

For an introduction to the work on leaders and leadership, see Margaret G. Hermann and Charles F. Hermann, "Who Makes Foreign Policy Decisions and How: An Empirical Inquiry," *International Studies Quarterly* 33 (1989): 361–87; and Timothy McKeown and Daniel Caldwell, eds., *Diplomacy, Force and Leadership: Essays in Honor of Alexander George* (Westview Press, 1993).

To explore some of the earliest, foundational work on rational decision-making models, see Richard Snyder, H. W. Bruck, and Burton Sapin, "Decision Making as an Approach to the Study of International Politics," in *Foreign Policy Decision Making: An Approach to the Study of International Politics* (Macmillan, 1962); David Braybrooke and Charles E. Lindblom, *A Strategy of Decision* (Free Press, 1963); and Sidney Verba, "Assumptions of Rationality and Nonrationality in Models of the International System," in *International Politics and Foreign Policy,* ed. James N. Rosenau, rev. ed. (Free Press, 1969).

To learn more about early works on game theory, see Robert Axelrod, *The Evolution of Cooperation* (Basic Books, 1984); and a special issue of the journal *World Politics,* October 1985.

For more on the early works on perception, cognition, and foreign policy study, see Ole R. Holsti, "Cognitive Dynamics and Images of the Enemy: Dulles and Russia," in *Image and Reality in World Politics,* ed. John C. Farrell and Asa P. Smith (Columbia University Press, 1967); Alexander George, "The 'Operational Code': A Neglected Approach to the Study of Political Leaders and Decision making," *International Studies* 13, no. 2 (1969); and Robert Jervis, *Perception and Misperception in International Politics* (Princeton University Press, 1976).

Updated, comprehensive discussions of cognition can be found in Jerel Rosati, "A Cognitive Approach to the Study of Foreign Policy," in *Foreign Policy Analysis: Continuity and Change in Its Second Generation,* ed. Laura Neack, Jeanne A. K. Hey, and Patrick J. Haney (Prentice-Hall, 1995); Nehemia Geva and Alex Mintz, eds., *Decision Making on War and Peace: The Cognitive-Rational Debate* (Lynne Rienner, 1997); and Richard Herrmann and Michael Fischerkeller, "Beyond the Enemy Image and Spiral Model: Cognitive-Strategic Research after the Cold War," *International Organization* 49, no. 3 (1995): 415–50.

For more on the use of analogies and metaphors, see Yuen Fong, *Analogies at War* (Princeton University Press, 1992); George Lakoff and Mark Johnson, *Metaphors We Live By* (University of Chicago Press, 1980); Dwain Mefford, "Analogical Reasoning and the Definition of the Situation: Back to Snyder for Concepts and Forward to Artificial Intelligence for Method," in *New Directions in the Study of Foreign Policy,* ed. Charles F. Hermann, Charles W. Kegley Jr., and James N. Rosenau (Unwin Hyman, 1987).

To read some first-person accounts (by former foreign policy decision makers, humanitarian aid workers, peacekeepers, and members of **international organizations,** among others) that advocate for explicit moral and ethical choices in our foreign policy decisions, consult two excellent volumes: Jonathan Moore, ed., *Hard Choices: Moral Dilemmas in Humanitarian Intervention* (Rowman & Littlefield, 1998); and Jeffrey Hopkins, ed., *The Art of Peace: Nobel Peace Laureates Discuss Human Rights, Conflict, and Reconciliation* (Snow Lion Publications, 2000).[56]

3

The State Level of Analysis: National Culture, Institutions, Domestic Politics, and Society

In This Chapter

Denmark and the Netherlands are two small European countries situated on the northwestern coast of the continent. Both have approximately the same amount of territory—43,094 square kilometers for Denmark and 41,526 square kilometers for Netherlands—although the Netherlands has three times the population of Denmark—almost 16 million people for the Netherlands, and just over 5 million people for Denmark. Both are founding members of the **United Nations** and **NATO**, and members of the **European Union**. Finally, both have parliamentary political systems.

Despite their similarities, there is a difference between the two countries that some scholars have attributed to a difference in **national self-image**. For example, in a cross-national study that includes Denmark, Ulf Hedetoft depicts the Danes as being "peaceful nationalists" who are somewhat disdainful of countries whose **nationalism** has led them to war—especially war against Denmark:[1]

> Political defeats in war(like) situations have regularly been used to boost the country's cultural nationalism and the reputed "homogeneity" between state and people. This anomaly is based on three distinctive criteria: Denmark is small; Denmark is not the aggressor; Denmark has survived.[2]

Hedetoft writes that in sport as in war, the Danes hold a different view of themselves when compared to others:

> The UK has its violent, racist "hooligans"; [Germany] has its often intimidating "Schlachtenbummler" (soccer rowdies); but Denmark takes pride in its "roligans," i.e., "peaceful supporters," and laps up the international praise it can collect on that account.[3]

Internationally, the Danes contribute substantially to U.N. peacekeeping, in line with the notion of "peaceful supporters," but as a people they tend to be reluctant to cooperate too quickly with others. In particular, the Danes are famous for the "no" vote they cast on the Maastricht Treaty on European Union in June 1992. The Maastricht Treaty is the plan for the broadening of the European Community into the European Union—a monetary and economic union that gives citizens of each member state European citizenship and ushered in the single European currency, the euro, among other things. In order for union to go forward, voters in each of the signatory states needed to approve it. When the Danes took a vote on union, they voted no, demonstrating their reluctance to jump onto any bandwagon, no matter how carefully planned. In May 1993, the Danes took another vote and this time agreed to union on the promise that Denmark would be exempted from certain expectations in the EU.

The Dutch could also be considered "peaceful supporters" of the international system, but there is no reluctance on their part to participate. The Netherlands is a country that takes the lead in the writing and promotion of international law. The Hague has been the long-standing home of the International Court of Justice and, since 1993, has been the site of the International Criminal Tribunal for the former Yugoslavia (ICTY). The Hague is also home to the International Criminal Court (ICC), established formally in July 2002. What is especially remarkable is that the Dutch people have paid most of the costs of the ICTY since its inception.

Peter Baehr asserts that the Netherlands is a country unusually committed to the rule of law internationally and to human rights law particularly, because of the combination of system-level factors and national self-image. On the system level, the Netherlands always has been dependent on international trade, and the development of international law was crucial to protecting the interests of such a small state. In terms of national self-image, the Dutch as a people believe they must "do some good" in the world, a belief that derives from their religious heritage.[4] This combination of **national interest** and national self-image creates an interesting domestic political arena where all four major political parties—and therefore parliament—stand committed to an activist human rights policy. Because of this widespread agreement, the details of such policy are left to the Foreign Ministry. By law and practice, Foreign Ministry officials work side by side with human rights **nongovernmental organizations (NGOs)** to plan and execute Dutch human rights foreign policy.

To understand how the Netherlands came to be called the "international legal capital of the world" by former U.N. Secretary-General Boutros Boutros-Ghali, or to understand why Denmark voted no on Maastricht, we need to go "inside" each country to explore the dynamics at play within each. A more complete understanding of these phenomena would require us also to examine where each country "sits" in the world (in terms of the power hierarchy of states) and its relations with other countries (i.e., system-level factors), but an examination of the inner workings of each country can yield interesting insights into how and why these countries follow the distinct foreign policies that they do.

Foreign policy study that proceeds from the state level of analysis involves examining different features of a country to see which of those factors shape its foreign policy. At this level of analysis, we include leaders and leadership as important factors, but we add into the mix the country-specific context. This level of analysis is the one that most directly borrows from the insights of comparative politics and regional area specialists. The focus here is *what goes on within states* that ultimately has an impact on what goes on between states.

There are two broad categories of factors that we examine at the state level: governmental and societal. Governmental factors include the type of political system, the type of **regime** that sits atop the government, the division of powers and authority between government institutions, bureaucratic in-fighting among government agencies, and the size and institutionalization of bureaucracies. Societal factors include the type of economic system, the history of the people(s) in the country, the ethnic, racial, and religious mix of the people, the number and activities of interest groups and political parties, and the role of the media in setting the public agenda. These two categories are not exclusive; for instance, it would prove informative in some cases to study state–society relations, the lobbying of government officeholders by interest groups, and the mobilization of **public opinion** by national leaders.

There have been some serious efforts to develop midrange theories of foreign policy at the state level of analysis, and some of these go back to the "founding" of the field. In his foundational work (discussed in chapter 1), James Rosenau hypothesized that three state level factors influenced foreign policy choice and behavior: size (large or small by population), economic system (developed or underdeveloped as determined by gross national product), and political system (open or closed as determined by whether the country is democratic or not). Rosenau proposed that these factors could be grouped into eight configurations or "ideal nation-types."[5]

As has been stated elsewhere,[6] Rosenau did not go on to propose what types of foreign policies might be associated with each country type, but he did encourage other scholars to take up this exploration. He also proposed that for each ideal type, scholars might benefit from utilizing one particular level of analysis over others. Rosenau called his proposals combined a "pre-theory" designed to stimulate research that might lead to the development of theories of foreign policy, including theories proceeding from the state level of analysis.

Despite Rosenau's call, study at the state level has not progressed to the point where robust general midrange theories have been produced. Scholars have important things to say about the role of culture or formal institutions of government or the media or other state level factors in the making of foreign policy, but with one exception: none of these insights have been studied across enough countries and time frames and by enough scholars to have yielded some propositions that are widely accepted and widely applicable. (The exception is the proposition of the **democratic peace** or pacific democracies, a proposition we will consider later in this chapter.) Foreign policy inquiry at the individual and system levels is marked by greater theoretical development around various propositions or midrange theories. We can account for this difference in some measure by recalling the dominance of the realist school of international politics, a school which greatly influenced study at the individual level (as in **rational choice** decision-making models) and system level of analysis. We can also attribute this difference to the rather rigid (and needless) boundary that has existed between the study of international and comparative politics.

ROSENAU'S IDEAL NATION-TYPES IN HIS "PRE-THEORY"

In James Rosenau's "pre-theory" of foreign policy, he proposed that countries could be typed by size, level of economic development, and political system. After deriving eight ideal nation-types from these variables, he then hypothesized that foreign policy making originated at different levels of analysis for each nation type. Foreign policy scholars were to develop more elaborate hypotheses and tests from Rosenau's pre-theory, thereby contributing to the scientific field of comparative foreign policy study.

Rosenau's Pre-theory by Nation Type, Example, Key Levels of Analysis

1. Large, developed, open; example: United States; key levels of analysis: role, societal, governmental, systemic, individual
2. Large, developed, closed; example: Soviet Union; key levels of analysis: role, individual, governmental, systemic, societal
3. Large, underdeveloped, open; example: India; key levels of analysis: individual, role, societal, systemic, governmental
4. Large, underdeveloped, closed; example: China; key levels of analysis: individual, role, governmental, systemic, societal
5. Small, developed, open; example: Netherlands; key levels of analysis: role, systemic, societal, governmental, individual
6. Small, developed, closed; example: (former) Czechoslovakia; key levels of analysis: role, systemic, individual, governmental, societal
7. Small, underdeveloped, open; example: Kenya; key levels of analysis: individual, systemic, role, societal, governmental
8. Small, underdeveloped, closed; example: Ghana; key levels of analysis: individual, systemic, role, governmental, societal

References
Rosenau, James N. "Pre-theories and Theories of Foreign Policy." In *Approaches to Comparative and International Politics*, edited by R. Barry Farrell, table 6.1, 133. Evanston, Ill.: Northwestern University Press, 1966.

Despite this relative theoretical "underdevelopment," the study of governmental and societal factors in the making of foreign policy has yielded some interesting insights, some of which we explore in this chapter.

National Self-Image

"National self-images . . . consist, at least in part, of idealized stereotypes of the 'in-nation' which are culturally shared and perpetuated."[7] The Dutch view that their country should "do some good" in the world is a manifestation of aspects of the Dutch self-image that comes out of a common sense of history, religious imperative, and social obligation. As suggested earlier, Baehr attributes the substantial strength and depth of Dutch commitment to an international legal system, particularly on human rights issues, in part to this Dutch national self-image.

National self-image, likes its close sibling nationalism, can have a good face and a bad face. Historically, the good face of nationalism is linked to the demand for self-government, or **democracy.** Similarly, a positive national self-image can contribute to stable **governance.** As Matthew Hirshberg writes, "The maintenance of a positive national self-image is crucial to continued public acquiescence and support for government, and thus to the smooth, on-going functioning of the state. . . . This allows government to go about its business, safe from significant internal dissension, and to expect a healthy level of public support in times of crisis."[8]

Like the Netherlands with its national self-image constructed on the notion of doing some good in the world, Canada has a similar national self-image—that of the "helpful fixer" and "peacekeeper *par excellence.*"[9] Canadian self-image, like Dutch self-image, is attributed in part to religious heritage. J. L. Granatstein writes,

> Probably the idea [of the helpful fixer and peacekeeper *par excellence*] emerged out of the missionary strain in Canadian Protestantism and Roman Catholicism that saw Canadian men and women go abroad in substantial numbers in the nineteenth and twentieth centuries to bring the word of God to India, Africa, and China . . . the "do-good" impulse that they represented was a powerful one, and it had its strong resonances in the Department of External Affairs.[10]

Granatstein goes on to explain that many members of the early Canadian diplomatic corps (in the interwar period) were the children of missionaries or clergy and had been born abroad.

The self-image of Canada as the peacekeeper par excellence is backed with substantial evidence: Canadian U.N. Ambassador Lester Pearson won the Nobel Peace Prize in 1957, along with U.N. Secretary-General Dag

Hammarskjöld, for developing the idea of neutral peacekeeping. Canada has been a leading participant in nearly all of the U.N. peacekeeping operations. Extending the notion of "keeping the peace" into other political dimensions, Canada has been one of the leading countries in accepting refugees from war-torn areas. Further, Canada's foreign policy since the end of the Cold War has been reoriented to addressing a wider notion of "human security," a concept that requires attention to the problems of civilians in war zones, the use of children as combatants, and rebuilding war-torn societies.[11] In 1997, Canada was a leading state in the International Campaign to Ban Land Mines, a campaign involving for the first time concerted efforts by states and nongovernmental organizations (in fact, the nongovernmental organizations led the way). On March 1, 1999, the Convention on the Prohibition of the Use, Stockpiling, Production, and Transfer of Antipersonnel Mines and on Their Destruction—also known as the Ottawa Treaty—came into force with ninety-four states as signatories, a product of Canada's strong commitment to peace and security in the world.

History also demonstrates that nationalism can have a negative face—represented most starkly in nationalist wars and genocide committed against members of select "out-groups." Similarly, national self-image can have a negative effect on a country's foreign policy. For example, Matthew Hirshberg tested the hypothesis that a positive, patriotic self-image interferes with Americans' ability to keep watch over the government's foreign policy behaviors. In his experiment, Hirshberg's subjects were only able to recall details of fictional news stories that featured the United States doing stereotypically good things, and his subjects re-created the details of news stories that featured the United States doing bad things (such as supporting nondemocratic governments against prodemocracy dissenters) in order to select out the negative information about the United States. His findings show that "Americans rarely interpret or remember things in . . . ways that threaten their patriotic self-image." As a result, he concludes:

even if American news consisted equally of information consistent and inconsistent with this [patriotic American] stereotype, Americans would, at least in the short term, tend to find its confirmation in the news. The stereotype interferes with information otherwise capable of cuing alternative perspectives. This increases popular support for military interventions that are or can be viewed as instances of a benevolent America protecting freedom and democracy from a perceived threat, such as communism. It also allows politicians and officials to elicit such support by promoting the application of the stereotype to specific conflicts.[12]

The danger in this is that "in the end, citizens' abilities to critically monitor and evaluate American foreign policy is [sic] impaired, and the

---

CANADIAN NATIONAL IMAGE BECOMES A MEDIA HIT

In 2000, a television commercial for a Canadian beer called "The Rant" whipped up a nationalist frenzy across the country by invoking key aspects of what it means to be Canadian, including peacekeeping. In the ad, a young Canadian man walks up on a large, empty stage (carrying a can of the beer, of course) and stands before a huge Canadian flag to declare:

> I'm not a lumberjack. Or a fur trader. I don't live in an igloo, eat blubber or own a dogsled . . . I have a prime minister, not a president. I speak English and French, not American . . . I can proudly sew my country's flag on my backpack. I believe in peacekeeping, not policing; diversity, not assimilation. And that the beaver is a truly proud and noble animal. A tuque is a hat, a chesterfield is a couch. And it's pronounced zed. Not zee. Zed . . . Canada is the second largest land mass, the first nation of hockey—and the best part of North America. . . . My name is Joe. And I am Canadian.

Although the ad was done partly in jest, it became so popular that it was performed live at sporting events to crowds who "ranted" along, and the actor in the ad even participated in a cross-country "rant" marathon in honor of Canada Day.

References

Kettle, Martin. "Mocked Canada Finds Hope and Glory in a Beer Ad." *Guardian* (London), May 25, 2000, 19. The ad's sponsor, Molson Beer, maintains a Web site where Canadians (presumably) can add their own pro-Canadian "rant." The site has an appropriate Web address: <www.iam.ca> (last accessed November 27, 2000).

Macintosh, Donald, and Donna Greenhorn. "Hockey Diplomacy and Canadian Foreign Policy." *Journal of Canadian Studies* 28, no. 2 (1993): 96–112. This is an academic article that discusses the importance of hockey to the Canadian national image and foreign policy.

---

ability of government to pursue unsavory policies with impunity is enhanced."[13]

Alastair Johnston sees a dynamic at play between positive self-image and a negative stance toward out-groups: "The creation of and intensification of group identities . . . positively correlates with the degree of competitiveness with the out-group."[14] Johnston contends that government efforts to promote active nationalism and group identity have a direct impact on relations between states:

Identity construction, and its intensity, determine anarchy and how much fear and competition results. Applied to international relations, then, the literature would suggest that changing intensities of in-group identity affect the degree of outwardly directed realpolitik behavior, regardless of changes in structural environment.[15]

At issue for Johnston is recent Chinese government policy aimed at constructing a Chinese ethno-identity and nationalism. By Johnston's argument, we can expect such a policy—if successful—to correlate with an increasingly self-interested, aggressive, and competitive foreign policy, even in the absence of external threats to China.

National self-image contains a message (implicit or explicit) about those *outside* the nation—our **nation** is good, therefore other nations are not (as) good. This mirror image may even suggest that vigilance must be the constant order of the day or the good nation will be at risk. Studies of siege mentality, such as Daniel Bar-Tal and Dikla Antebi's study of Israeli **siege mentality,** suggest that governments are given permission to conduct aggressive, preemptive foreign policies in order to protect the good nation from the actions of evil nations. Bar-Tal and Antebi define siege mentality as "a mental state in which members of a group hold a central belief that the rest of the world has highly negative *behavioral* intentions toward them." This culturally shared and perpetuated belief is complemented by the belief that the group is alone in the world, that it cannot expect help in times of crisis from anyone and therefore "all means are justified for group defense."[16] Siege mentality is more than a group-shared paranoia; paranoia is an unfounded fear of others, whereas an historical, evidentiary basis exists for siege mentality.

Yugoslavia in the postcommunist era is an excellent example of a country manifesting strong elements of siege mentality. The former Yugoslavian President Slobodan Milosevic manipulated historical examples of Croatian and "Turkish" or Muslim attacks on the Serbian nation to foster a strong and particularly aggressive modern Serbian nationalism. Milosevic used this nationalism to wage war on Croatia and then Bosnia in the early 1990s toward the goal of creating a greater Serbia. When Milosevic turned Serbian nationalism on the ethnic Albanian people of the Yugoslavian province of Kosovo in early 1998, his Serbian forces managed to displace or kill a third of the total population in a matter of weeks. This prompted nearly two months of NATO air strikes against Serbia, which only reinforced Serbian siege mentality and nationalism. These air strikes came on the heels of nearly a decade of international economic sanctions against Yugoslavia for its involvement in the Bosnian war. Ultimately Milosevic was forced from power through elections and a "people's revolution," but the new Serbian leaders demonstrated the same suspicion of the intentions of the outside world. Countries exhibiting high degrees of siege mentality require careful handling by the outside in order not to cue automatic distrust and noncooperation. Bringing Yugoslavia back into the community of states will take time and patience given the intensity of Serbian nationalism and siege mentality during the 1990s.

The leaders of the former Soviet Union displayed siege mentality when they viewed their country as a "besieged fortress" in the 1950s. There was clear cause for suspicion about the intentions of other countries. By 1955, the United States had managed to form military **alliances** with a series of countries that, taken altogether, nearly encircled the Soviet Union and Communist China. Present-day, post-Soviet Russia appears to have retained this suspicion about the outside world, even as it struggles with an age-old identity conflict over whether it is essentially a Western country or a unique Slavic country. "The first tendency pushes Russia toward the West, while the second one results in Russia pursuing a policy of self-isolation," notes Sergei Chugrov.[17] A conflicted national self-image results in a conflicted, sometimes contradictory foreign policy as competing tendencies vie for control over who and what defines the nation.

Culture and Institutions of Governance

Culturally maintained national self-image does more than just influence the broad notions and directions of a country's foreign policy. National self-image and the culture that supports it also influence the types of institutions constructed within a state and the foreign policy decision-making authority allotted to those institutions.

It should go without saying that a people's culture will influence the shape and type of its political structures when that people is self-governing. For example, once we have found that a country exhibits high degrees of siege mentality, it should come as no surprise to find mandatory, universal military conscription. The urgent need to protect the in-group results in the practical need for a strong military. The need for a strong military necessitates conscription. In Israel, all Jews and Druse must serve in the military—men for thirty-six months and women for twenty-one months. Switzerland's well-known image as a neutral country contains the same elements of distrust of out-groups. Swiss men between nineteen and twenty years of age must perform fifteen weeks of active military duty, followed by ten three-week reservist training periods over the subsequent twenty-two years.

Moving in almost the completely opposite direction is Japan. After its defeat in World War II, Japan reconstructed itself into a antimilitaristic country, as signified by the adoption of its Peace Constitution. Chapter II, Article 9 of the Japanese Peace Constitution reads:

Aspiring sincerely to an international peace based on justice and order, the Japanese people forever renounce war as a sovereign right of the nation and the threat or use of force as means of settling international disputes.

In order to accomplish the aim of the preceding paragraph, land, sea, and air forces, as well as other war potential, will never be maintained. The right of belligerency of the state will not be recognized.

Japanese nationalism since 1945 has been channeled into its pursuit of economic security, especially the goal of reducing reliance on imported raw materials through the development of "technological autonomy."[18] These two dominant cultural norms—antimilitarism and economic nationalism—inform and reinforce the institutions of governance as well as define appropriate foreign policy behavior. For instance, on the issue of human rights, the Japanese believe that they are in no position to preach to others given their militaristic past, opting instead to pursue straightforward, nonpolitical economic goals in bilateral relations, especially in Asia.[19]

As might be expected, the Japanese government agencies in charge of pursuing economic security are privileged over those tasked with military defense. What is surprising is the degree to which this is true, as elaborated by Peter Katzenstein and Nobuo Okawara. The three most powerful state institutions—and the ones with essential control of national security policy—are the Ministries of Foreign Affairs, Finance , and International Trade and Industry.[20] Conversely, the Japanese Defense Agency (JDA) does not have cabinet-level status, and "inherent in the civilian-military arrangements inside the JDA is a strong bias against any military interpretation of Japan's national security requirements."[21] The civilian staff of the JDA is "colonized" by members of various ministries. The JDA has no mobilization plan, no emergency civil defense system, nor rules for engaging the enemy. It even lacks a military court system.

Japanese military defense rests on three pillars: the Peace Constitution, the Japanese-American Security Treaty, and the Charter of the United Nations. Two of the three pillars are only partially defined by the Japanese, contributing to increasing "dual-game" conflicts between Japanese culture and international expectations. American pressure on Japan to commit greater resources toward its defense, along with international pressure on Japan to play a more significant role in U.N. peacekeeping, run headlong into Japanese cultural and institutional rigidity. Various scholars have suggested that this conflict will never be won by the international forces, as domestic factors are more determinative of policy choices than are international factors.[22]

This same conclusion—that domestic factors are more determinative of policy choices than are international factors—is expressed in Elizabeth Kier's historical study of the relationship between French culture and military doctrine in the interwar years:

> Even during times of increased international threat . . . the international system is indeterminate of choices between offensive and defensive military doctrines. . . . Civilian concerns about the military's power *within* the state often have the greatest effect on doctrinal developments.[23]

Kier's assertion is that between the world wars there were competing subcultures in France, rather than a single, inclusive (sub)culture regarding political-military relations. These competing subcultures offered different "policy prescriptions about the organizational form of the army; the left wanted short-term conscripts, the right a professional army."[24] In the mid-1920s, a coalition of moderate and left-wing parties imposed short-term conscripts on the military, *despite* the clear and growing menace of Germany. The internal threat posed by a professional army was perceived to be greater than the clear and present external threat. The French army, in turn, decided that the only viable military doctrine using short-term conscripts was to strike a defensive posture,[25] a poor choice as shown a few years later when Germany invaded and occupied France.

Culture, Institutions, and the Democratic Peace

The greatest concentration of scholarly activity on the impact of culture and institutions on foreign policy has been on the idea of the democratic peace. This research finds its intellectual roots in philosopher Immanuel Kant's proposition that democracies are peace-loving countries.[26] In the first modern variation on this idea, it was asserted that democracies are less likely to go to war than nondemocratic states. In a later version, the idea was refined to the proposition that democracies do not fight wars with other democracies. If true, a world of democracies would be a world freed from war. When national leaders, such as former President Bill Clinton, speak about "enlarging the circle of market democracies," they speak (and sometimes act) on the assumption that the idea of the democratic peace is more than an idea, it is an operating reality.

There are two explanations of why democracies are or should be more peaceful than nondemocracies—the first explanation emphasizes the culture of democracies and the second emphasizes domestic institutional structures. The cultural explanation proposes that "liberal democracies are more peace loving than other states because of the norms regarding appropriate methods of conflict resolution that develop within society."[27] Further, "leaders choose to employ the standards and rules of conduct which have been successful and acceptable at home in their international interaction."[28] Leaders of democracies are not constrained by peaceful standards when dealing with nondemocracies, since nondemocracies cannot be expected to be similarly constrained. The second explanation stresses the constraining role of democratic institutions on foreign policy decision makers. The division of and checks on power within democratic governments and the ultimate restraint of officeholders having to face voters in regular elections prohibit violent (and costly) foreign policy behaviors.[29]

The idea of the democratic peace has generated much excitement and much criticism. Critics point out a number of weaknesses in the proposition: that interstate war is rare; that the number of democracies at any given point in history has been small; that, for the bulk of the second half of the twentieth century, most democracies were primarily Western states bound together in military alliances against the Soviet bloc; and that these same democracies were also the world's richest states bound together by class-based interests. The democratic peace idea also has been accused of being another justification for Western imperialism.[30] This criticism is that Western states claim moral cause to impose their political and economic structures on other peoples in the name of creating a more peaceful world. During the Cold War, these same states claimed the need to defend democracy against communism as their justification for **neoimperial** policies in the developing world. Other criticisms of the democratic peace literature focus on the **methodology** or the manner in which democratic peace research is conducted.

Despite the criticism, proponents declare that the proposition of the democratic peace is so robust that it amounts to the only "law" in the study of international relations.[31] The criticisms have not deterred research programs intent on fleshing out the nuances of the proposition. For example, in a recent variation and extension, Brett Leeds and David Davis expand the dependent variable—war—to include a wide range of cooperative and conflictual behaviors in which states engage. Looking at data from the period of 1953 to 1978, they conclude that democracies exhibit far less conflictual behavior than do nondemocracies and, importantly, display a greater range of *cooperative* foreign policy behaviors, regardless of whether their partners or targets are democratic or not.[32] This finding, if replicated in other studies and for longer time periods, could resurrect the first proposition about the democratic peace that democracies are more peaceful than other types of states.

Domestic Political Opposition

Adding more fuel to the pacific democracies debate is both argument and evidence from Edward Mansfield and Jack Snyder that in the transitional period, *countries undergoing democratization* are more likely and not less likely to become aggressive and war prone.[33] Using data for the years 1811–1980, Mansfield and Snyder examine the war proneness of democracies, autocracies, and mixed regimes (displaying both democratic and nondemocratic elements). Their findings suggest how volatile a transition to democracy, measured over one, five, and ten years, can be:

- "an increase in the openness of the selection process for the chief executive doubled the likelihood of war";
- "increasing the competitiveness of political participation" increased chances of war 90 percent;
- "increasing the constraints on a country's chief executive" increased chances of war 35 percent;
- when "high levels of mass participation in politics" occurred in regimes moving from mixed to democracy, the chance of war was 50 percent;
- states going from full autocracy to full democracy "were on average about two-thirds more likely to become involved in any type of war."[34]

What accounts for these findings? Mansfield and Snyder suggest that the dynamics of democratization combine to form an unstable mix of "social change, institutional weakness, and threatened interests."[35] As citizens are freed to participate in politics through political party and interest group activities, they begin to make demands on the central government. These demands must be met or quelled, all the while that the power of the central government to make an effective response is being reduced as a new constitutional order is instated. The government, then, must build and maintain a **policy coalition** among diverse and vocal interests while hanging on to its crumbling power and **legitimacy.** Mansfield and Snyder conclude that "one of the simplest but riskiest strategies for a hard-pressed regime in a democratizing country is to shore up its prestige at home by seeking victories abroad."[36]

Russia as Illustration

Historical examples are used to demonstrate their findings, but Mansfield and Snyder also point to the recent past and post-Soviet Russia and its war in Chechnya as an illustration of these dangerous, unwieldy dynamics at play. Fifteen countries were formed at the collapse of the Soviet Union, but there might have been at least one more. One month before the collapse of the Soviet Union, the independent state of Chechnya was declared by a former Soviet general, Chechen nationalist, and newly elected president. Chechnya, one of twenty-one Russian republics (administrative units), sits in southwestern Russia, along the northern border of the former Soviet Republic of Georgia (now an independent country). The Chechen people are Sunni Muslims and their land contains considerable oil reserves.

Russia did not recognize the Chechen unilateral declaration of independence, but it also made no move to do anything about the "breakaway" republic until late 1994. In December of that year, the Russians launched a massive military invasion of Chechnya. Most of the Russian fire power was concentrated on the capital city of Grozny, the home of almost half of the republic's population. Grozny was nearly flattened by the Russians, yet it did not fall to them for almost two months. Fighting throughout Chechnya raged on until 1996, despite the overwhelming force employed by the Russians against the Chechen guerrillas.

Why did Russian leaders delay responding to the declaration of independence in 1991? Why was there no response even when Russian troops were expelled from Chechnya a short time later? Russia indicated that it would not honor the declaration but made no moves to resist the expulsion of Russian troops. It is safe to argue that the Russian leadership was too preoccupied with managing all the other changes in Russia—as well as those in some of the former Soviet Republics—to give Chechnya much notice. When the Russian leaders did move to reestablish control of Chechnya, it was probably to reestablish control in all of Russia, not just in Chechnya.

For example, fourteen months before the Russian troops launched the invasion of Chechnya, Russian troops were ordered to fire upon the Russian Duma (parliament). Then Russian President Boris Yeltsin had been feuding with the Duma over constitutional changes he wanted. The Duma was full of various and sundry parties and factions, many of whom were left over from the Soviet days and opposed to Yeltsin's overall political agenda, especially his economic reforms. Fed up with the Duma, Yeltsin called in the troops and launched a two-day shelling of the White House where the Duma sits. The action killed as many as 150 people but was fairly popular among the Russian public and went without much official notice by foreign governments. Yeltsin did get the constitutional changes he wanted, but the reconstituted Duma remained fairly defiant and argumentative.

A Model of the Forces at Play

Let's hold the Russia and Chechnya case there for a moment and add another scholar's work to the discussion. Joe Hagan offers a useful model for considering the likelihood that leaders might resort to risky foreign policy actions. The decision to use force or to engage in all sorts of risky international behaviors is the result of the dual game that top decision makers play between the international and domestic environments.

According to Hagan, leaders have two fundamental priorities in the domestic environment: build and maintain policy coalitions and retain political power. Building and maintaining policy coalitions is necessary for leaders to propose and execute policies and programs. Retaining political power means just what it says, whether the leaders are **autocratic** or democratic, or somewhere in between. All leaders require the support of some key domestic actors in order to stay in power, even the most authoritarian. Hagan's model is useful because it applies equally well to different types of political systems, and to different types of top leadership.

Building and maintaining policy coalitions and retaining political power are particularly difficult in highly politicized contexts in which a large and vocal opposition exists. When the issue at hand is a foreign policy matter and it becomes linked to questions about the legitimacy of the leadership, Hagan proposes that leaders resort to three different political strategies to manage the challenge posed by a vocal domestic opposition: (1) accommodation, (2) insulation, and (3) mobilization.[37] Each of these strategies carries with it a certain propensity to engage in risky foreign policy behaviors.

The **accommodation strategy** involves bargaining with the opposition and controversy avoidance. Here "leaders seek to contain opposition, and thus retain political power, by avoiding publicly disputed policies and actions that make the country appear weak in international affairs or are closely associated with a widely acknowledged adversary."[38] Restraint in foreign policy is the expected result of an accommodation strategy. In the **insulation strategy**, the leadership attempts to deflect attention from foreign policy through suppressing and overriding the opposition, or even through coopting the opposition by favors and promises. If successful, we would expect no change to occur in the chosen foreign policy course. Finally, a **mobilization strategy** involves the manipulation of foreign policy and amplified risk taking. Leaders assert their legitimacy by confronting the opposition through appeals to nationalism, imperialism or the "scapegoating" of foreigners and/or through claims that they have a "special capacity" to maintain the country's security and status abroad. When successful, this strategy works by "diverting attention from divisive domestic problems."[39]

When they describe the unruly forces at play in a democratizing country, Mansfield and Snyder essentially describe Hagan's mobilization strategy: "One of the simplest but riskiest strategies for a hard-pressed regime in a democratizing country is to shore up its prestige at home by seeking victories abroad."[40] Returning now to the Russia and Chechnya case, when Yeltsin decided to send troops into Chechnya in December 1995, it was in the context of a volatile Russia on the verge of economic and political meltdown. Mansfield and Snyder write,

One interpretation of Yeltsin's decision to use force in Chechnya is that he felt it necessary to show that he could act decisively to prevent the unraveling of central authority, with respect not only to ethnic separatists but also to other ungovernable groups in a democratizing society. Chechnya, it was hoped, would allow Yeltsin to demonstrate his ability to coerce Russian society while at the same time exploiting a potentially popular issue.[41]

Of course, Chechnya was an internal security problem for Russia, not a foreign policy issue. But the same forces that propelled Russian leaders to use force in Chechnya were apparent in Russian relations with the other former Soviet Republics in this same time period. Neil MacFarlane points out the degree to which Russia was engaging in aggressive foreign policy behavior:

> Elements of the Russian military assiduously manipulated the civil conflicts in the [Transcaucasus] region (notably the Nagorno-Karabakh conflict between Azerbaijan and Armenia and the conflicts between Ossets and Abkhaz on the one hand and Georgians on the other in the Republic of Georgia) in order to return the governments of the region to a position of subservience. . . . Azerbaijan is the only country in the Transcaucasian region with no Russian forces within its border, but it has been under significant Russian pressure to allow a return of the Russian military, coordination of air defense systems, and joint border control. Many have interpreted Russian support of the Armenian side in the Nagorno-Karabakh dispute as a means of bringing Azerbaijan to heel.[42]

Rajan Menon, in an article that appeared in print the summer before the Russians launched their invasion of Chechnya, gives this same basic domestic politics calculation for determining whether Russia would assert its neoimperial face in the former Soviet Central Asian Republics.[43] The likelihood of neoimperialism—a "risky" foreign policy behavior using Hagan's term—depended upon the strength of proimperial coalitions versus the "democratic reformers" led by Yeltsin. The proimperial coalition was composed of groups nostalgic for different reasons for the old Soviet empire. This same coalition was part of the problematic Duma that Yeltsin decided to shell in October 1993. Shelling the Duma might be considered an insulation strategy as described by Hagan. But it might be difficult to maintain the guise of democratic reformer if one uses military force against one's own parliament too often!

Instead, Menon proposes that Yeltsin engaged in an accommodation strategy to deal with the proimperial groups:

More important than the existence of such coalitions is the extent to which Russia's governing democratic elites feel compelled by their weakness to engage in appeasement and accommodation toward these coalitions. They have done so to avoid being outflanked by ul-tra-nationalists, who have successfully manipulated the symbolic ap-peal of a virile defense of Russian interests and ethnic Russians in the former Soviet republics.[44]

Unable or unwilling to coopt the opposition, Yeltsin switched strategies and co-opted the powerful symbols of the opposition in order to assert his own regime's special capacity to preserve the security and prestige of Russia. Yeltsin's strategic policy spoke of the former Soviet Republics as the "near abroad" in which Russia had special rights, "obligations" and "responsibilities." And democratic reformers noted that Russia had a se-curity interest in "our own foreign countries," that sometimes would re-quire the use of Russian "peacekeepers" therein.[45]

Menon warns that, in adopting an accommodation strategy, "forces within the state capable of countering neoimperial elites and offering al-ternative paradigms of statecraft have been weakened."[46] The reformers become trapped by the coopting of neoimperial rhetoric, increasing the possibility of neoimperial behavior. Menon worried about the Central Asian Republics, but he might have looked within Russia to see where Yeltsin would turn next to legitimize his power.

Yeltsin's military campaign in Chechnya in 1994–1996 did not play out the way he had hoped. Domestic and international opposition to the cam-paign arose quickly. Indeed, Yeltsin could blame the new climate of **politi-cal opening** for the failure of his Chechnya policy, at least in part. Russian journalists quickly exposed the campaign for its barbarity, stupidity, and costliness. Other actors in the newly created Russian **civil society** actively opposed the war. One group, the Committee of Soldiers' Mothers of Russia (CSMR), was a particularly vocal opponent, organizing demonstrations and the March of Mothers Compassion march from Moscow to Grozny in spring 1996. As reported by the *Inter Press Service*, "Hundreds of mothers went to Chechnya to take their sons away from the battlefront. Some car-ried out **negotiations** themselves with the Chechen army to secure the re-lease of sons held as prisoners of war."[47] Once the protests began, they did not end until a cease-fire was arranged in August 1996.

However, in 1999, Yeltsin restarted the military campaign in Chechnya, after a number of unsolved "terrorist" bombings of civilian apartment buildings and public spaces in Russia. Perhaps because the economic and social fabric of Russia was still so unstable and perhaps because the gov-ernment successfully scapegoated the Chechen rebels for the bombings, the public rallied behind the military campaign. At the start of 2000, Yeltsin's hand-picked acting president and soon to be elected successor

Vladimir Putin also enjoyed considerable public support for his own military campaign in Chechnya. In one campaign stunt designed to take advantage of popular support for the new war in Chechnya, Putin visited troops in Grozny aboard a two-seat Sukhoi-27 fighter bomber.[48]

The Palestinian-Israeli Conflict as Illustration

Hagan's model of how leaders attempt to manage domestic opposition, retain power, and maintain a policy coalition through insulation, mobilization, or accommodation is useful for framing cases beyond instances of countries undergoing democratization. Hagan suggests that the model can be used regardless of regime or political system type. Let's look at another brief case for illustration.

In 1996, Yasser Arafat was elected president of the Palestinian National Authority (shortened to the Palestinian Authority, or PA), the governing body of the Palestinian people living in the West Bank and Gaza. Arafat was also the leader of Fatah, one of several Palestinian organizations that joined together under the umbrella framework known as the Palestine Liberation Organization (PLO). Arafat served as chairman of the PLO in its long struggle to reclaim territory subsumed by the state of Israel in its 1948 unilateral declaration of independence and its subsequent wars with Arab states. The West Bank and Gaza were captured by Israel in the 1967 war from Jordan and Egypt, respectively.

The government of Israel and the PLO signed a peace treaty in 1993. This treaty set in place mechanisms for future negotiations regarding the transfer of authority and land in the West Bank and Gaza to the PA. The amount of territory to be transferred to the PA, the enumeration of details regarding whether the PA was to be partially or fully independent of Israel, and the resolution of competing claims on Jerusalem were left to subsequent negotiations.

Also in 1996, Benjamin Netanyahu was elected prime minister of Israel in a landslide election, defeating sitting Labor Prime Minister Shimon Peres. Although a hard-liner by reputation, and the leader of the conservative Likud Party, Netanyahu began the transfer of some territory to the PA as part of the continuing peace process. After a series of deadly suicide attacks against Israelis, Netanyahu stopped some troop withdrawals from, and lifted a freeze on Jewish settlements in, the disputed territory. Yet in October 1998, negotiations between the Israelis and Palestinians resulted in a three-stage agreement for the transfer of more lands. Netanyahu completed the first stage of this transfer and then was defeated in Israeli elections by Ehud Barak in 1999.

Barak led a coalition called One Israel to a landslide victory over Netanyahu. One Israel was a fragile coalition of divergent parties, including Barak's own Labor Party. Soon after Barak's election, the Knesset—in a demonstration of the fragility of Barak's coalition—elected to the power-ful role of speaker one of the leaders of opposition Likud. Barak and Yasser Arafat signed the Wye River Agreement under the mediation of President Bill Clinton in September 1999. Barak transferred land and re-leased two hundred political prisoners in the second part of the three-stage peace process. In July 2000, President Clinton sponsored another series of talks at Camp David in order to initiate the third stage of the peace process. These talks failed to produce an agreement and both Barak and Arafat indicated that the position of their respective sides had hard-ened. Arafat announced that the PA would make a unilateral declaration of independence in September absent further agreement with the Israeli government.

Although Arafat postponed the unilateral declaration, events in late September 2000 brought the peace process to a deadly halt. Ariel Sharon, one of the leaders of the opposition Likud Party, and a group of followers and Israeli troops went to a disputed site in the Old City of Jerusalem, a place the Jews call the Temple Mount and the Muslims call Haram al-Sharif (Noble Sanctuary).[49] Sharon's goal was to demonstrate Israeli commitment to maintaining full access to the Old City. His very public display on a Friday, which is a day of special religious observation for Muslims, prompted a Palestinian crowd to form in protest. Rocks and bullets were thrown—the rocks from the Palestinian side, the bullets from the Israel side—and months of active low-intensity conflict erupted. In this conflict, the death toll was taken disproportionately on the Palestinian side.

The Hagan framework can be used to explore responses to this conflict on both the Palestinian and Israeli sides. On the Palestinian side, Arafat governed with the assistance of the PA, a small council of Arafat ap-pointees. For our purposes, we can consider the PA to be a nondemocratic regime in this time period, not in transition to democracy. Arafat had a major domestic opponent in the person of Sheikh Ahmed Yassin, the spir-itual leader of Hamas. Hamas was formed in 1987 at the start of the *in-tifada*, or Palestinian uprising, in Gaza and the West Bank. Its purpose was twofold—to provide humanitarian assistance to Palestinians in Israeli-occupied territory and to coordinate military/terrorist activities aimed at the Israelis. Sheikh Ahmed Yassin spent eight years in Israeli prison until released in 1997 in a deal made between Israel and Jordan. Yassin had pro-claimed that Israel was attempting to destroy Islam and so loyal Muslims had a religious obligation to fight against Israel. Arafat and the PLO also had been committed to the violent elimination of the state of Israel, but this position was reversed in 1989 (the same year that Yassin was impris-oned by Israel). It should go without saying that Yassin and Hamas op-posed the agreements made between Arafat and the Israeli government.

In the first week of fighting after the Sharon visit to Haram al-Sharif, seventy Palestinians were killed in the streets while confronting Israeli security forces. During that week, the Israeli government demanded that Arafat reestablish order in the West Bank. Arafat's reply was to express outrage, but he made no move to deploy an effective Palestinian police presence to quell the uprising. As Israeli leaders continued to demand that Arafat assert control and the Israeli defense forces were deployed, Arafat's leadership began to be called into question. Either Arafat could not control the uprising or he did not want to control it; the former suggested that the political balance had shifted in favor of a dangerous element in the Palestinian community, the latter suggested that Arafat condoned the use of violence to force Israeli concessions in negotiations. Neither explanation implied good things for the peace process.

One explanation of Arafat's lack of effective police response is that the political power *had* shifted in the Palestinian community, putting into doubt Arafat's ability to retain political control, much less retain a strong coalition in support of further agreements with the Israelis. During the first week of fighting, the Hamas politburo leader Khaled Meshal announced at a seminar in Tehran, Iran, that the Palestinians had no option but to engage in armed struggle with the Israelis.[50] On Friday, October 6, Hamas called for a "day of rage" against Israeli rule—the first of many. The "day of rage" call was answered by a mass outpouring in the West Bank and Gaza with the end product being ten Palestinians killed and dozens injured. Significantly, Arafat's Fatah issued support for the "day of rage" *after* it was clearly under way.[51]

Once begun, the street uprising and violence continued. International efforts to broker a cease-fire were met at times with obstinacy from both Arafat and Barak and, at other times, with agreements that subsequently were broken. Arafat kept insisting that the Palestinian people were only defending themselves against the Israeli military and that a multinational investigation be conducted into the causes of the violence.

Arguably, Arafat's hard line toward Israel had started months before at the Camp David talks. Arafat's approach to Camp David and later his threat to unilaterally declare the independence of Palestine might have been manifestations of his decision to employ a mobilization strategy (as per Hagan's model). Perhaps Arafat calculated that he needed to assert a hard face toward the Israelis to demonstrate his commitment to his people and his special capacity to lead the Palestinians to statehood. Taking a tough negotiating stance with the Israelis might slow down the peace process in the short term, but reinvigorating his regime against domestic opposition— Hamas—was the first, pressing priority. Arafat's initial refusal to order an effective Palestinian police presence to stem the riots might be seen as the continuation of this risky behavior. There was a symbolic Palestinian police presence in the streets, but Arafat insisted that the uprising was a spontaneous response of the people which would stop when the Israelis stopped using violence and conceded to a multinational investigation.

Unfortunately, Arafat's mobilization strategy worked to the advantage of Hamas. Until Fatah announced its support for the first "day of rage," Arafat's regime had said nothing publicly to encourage violence against Israelis. Hamas forced Arafat's hand in calling for the "day of rage," forcing him to adopt a violent pose or risk being seen as unsupportive of the people's right to defend themselves against Israeli aggression.

On the other side of this particular dual game, Arafat's support for the first and subsequent days of rage provided evidence for Israeli right-wing hard-liners of Arafat's "true" intentions and untrustworthiness. This, in turn, would only create strong domestic opposition to Barak's government. It is possible to use the same analytical framework to consider Barak's negotiating stance at Camp David in July and his decision to use the Israeli army against the Palestinian street violence. In brief, Barak's fragile One Israel coalition was all but gone by the time of the Camp David talks. By late November, after two months of violence in the West Bank and Gaza, Barak was forced to call for early elections in the face of mounting domestic political attacks on his government. Before Barak made the call for new elections, he had issued ultimatums to Arafat, approved significant escalations in the use of military force, and desperately courted Ariel Sharon to join a new emergency government. Barak's bid to woo Sharon failed, while peace with the Palestinians—still Barak's long-term foreign policy goal—seemed more remote with each passing day.

Applying the Hagan concepts, we can say that Barak's use of military forces against the Palestinians manifested his adoption of a mobilization strategy. This was adopted to demonstrate that Barak and his government were willing and able to defend the state of Israel against all threats, implying that his political opponents possessed no special capacity for safeguarding the nation. Barak's subsequent efforts to bring Ariel Sharon into an emergency government can be seen as a coopting, accommodating move, signaling Barak's desire to preserve some maneuvering room for his long-term foreign policy agenda. Significantly, Barak maintained throughout the crisis that the peace process was not dead and could be recommenced.

As an interesting and relevant footnote on what scholars have revealed about the purported relationship between democratic states and peaceful international behavior, consider the research of Brandon Prins and Christopher Sprecher. Prins and Sprecher ask whether variations in the *type* of democratic government have any impact on the democratic peace idea. They examine a dataset with information on militarized international disputes and on the cabinet structures of fifteen Western parliaments from 1946 to 1989.[52] One of their hypotheses was that "Single-party governments will have the fewest decisional constraints and therefore the greatest freedom to reciprocate militarized disputes." Along these lines, they also proposed that "coalition and minority governments will possess

Figure 3.1.   The "Danger" of Negotiating with Democracies

Cartoonist Tom Toles illustrates one of the "dangers" of negotiating with democracies. Yasser Arafat is the only person left at the negotiating table after elections in the United States in 2000 and Israel in 2001 caused leadership changes. In the United States, Bill Clinton was prevented from running for reelection because of constitutional limits on the number of terms a president can serve. In Israel, the inability of Prime Minister Ehud Barak to contain the violence that erupted in the fall 2000, in Israel, the West Bank, and Gaza, led to his defeat in February 2001 elections. Despite Arafat's tough talk in the cartoon above, many observers felt that he had a better chance negotiating with Clinton and Barak than with their successors, George W. Bush and Ariel Sharon.

greater constraints on decision making and as a result the likelihood of reciprocation [of militarized acts] should decrease while these types of government hold the reins of power."[53]

Applying these hypotheses to Barak's situation in the summer and fall of 2000, we might predict that his fragile **coalition government**'s response to Palestinian street violence would be less likely to involve the use of reciprocated violence than would the essentially unified, Likud-dominated government of his predecessor, Benjamin Netanyahu. But, as stated previously, Netanyahu's response to a series of Palestinian suicide bombings in 1996 resulted in a postponement of Israeli troop withdrawal and a lifting of the freeze on Jewish settlement in the affected areas. Netanyahu did *not* reciprocate violence in the occupied territories, and he later completed a first-stage transfer of territory to the PA in the West Bank.

Indeed, Prins and Sprecher's own research disconfirms their hypothesis. Contrary to expectations, they found

> coalition governments are more likely to reciprocate disputes in general, and particularly more likely to reciprocate with the actual use of military force. This may be more a result of single-party governments avoiding the electoral risks involved in escalation, rather than a clearcut active attempt by coalition governments to militarily engage dispute opponents.[54]

Democracies as a general category may be less likely to use force than nondemocracies, but different types of democracies exhibit different domestic political configurations that might affect their foreign policy decision making about the use of force or the pursuit of peace, trade agreements, diplomatic recognition, and the whole range of foreign policy activities.

Partisan Politics and Intragovernmental Divisions

Despite the claims of realists, as well as the often heard American claim that "**partisanship** ends at the country's shores," partisan differences sometimes are reflected in countries' foreign policies. For example, in the United States when a Democrat occupies the White House, the standard expectation is a pro-Israeli foreign policy orientation, while a Republican president is expected to be more pro-Arab. Democrats are supposed to be doves on issues of international peace and more inclined to **multilateralism,** while Republicans are supposed to be hawks and more **isolationist** or **unilateralist**. On the other hand, the Democratic Party is more suspicious of free trade, while the Republican Party is in favor of lifting government-imposed impediments to world market forces. Thus we might conclude that Republicans are more isolationist (on some issues) and more globalist (on other issues) than are Democrats—a conclusion that contains some contradiction.

Beyond the obvious notion that different parties might have different foreign policies, a more intriguing topic is how differences *within* a single government or within a single party can impact policy. The study of intragovernmental or intraparty impact on foreign policy making is underdeveloped beyond the single case of the United States. What follows, then, is a discussion of some studies that are suggestive of the types of questions that might be asked in future comparative foreign policy research.

Juliet Kaarbo proposes that parliamentary decision making should take a different form than decision making in presidential democracies, for three reasons: "the concentration of authority in the executive, the collective responsibility of the cabinet, and the imperative of negotiating differences for the cabinet's survival."[55] Within coalition governments particularly, Kaarbo hypothesizes that disproportionate decision-making influence may be exerted by junior partners. "A party is 'junior' in terms of the structural distribution of power and resources in the political context of the parliamentary system—it controls fewer parliamentary seats than its senior coalition partner."[56]

Kaarbo analyzes eight case studies involving German and Israeli coalition governments to test the plausibility of eight hypotheses that might explain when junior partners have disproportionate influence on policy. Her eight cases reveal the most support for the hypothesis that the "locus of authority" is critical in determining when junior partners may and may not have inordinate influence. When foreign policy decision making is centered in the cabinet, junior partners exert disproportionate voice because the junior partner is "equalized" or elevated in presence relative to its actual representation in parliament. When decision making is delegated to the Foreign Ministry and that portfolio is held by a member of the senior party, the junior party will have a relatively weak voice. Similarly, when decision-making authority is moved to the entire parliament, the junior party's voice is equal only to the actual number of seats it holds.

Kaarbo gives as an example the unusual power held by the junior partner in Israeli cabinets during the 1970s. The National Religious Party was able to throw its support behind different governments, succeeding in bringing governments down or setting them up. When the National Religious Party switched sides in 1976, it brought down the Labor government and helped bring to power the Likud government led by Menachem Begin. However, the National Religious Party was opposed to territorial concessions to any Arab state, so Prime Minister Begin's participation in the 1977 Camp David Accords between Israel and Egypt did not sit well with this junior partner. Aware that he would not convince the National Religious Party to support the accords, Begin took the final decision making to the Knesset, where Likud held a narrow margin over all parties, thereby diluting the junior party's ability to stop the ratification.[57]

Kaarbo also finds support for the hypothesis that unified junior parties exert greater influence when the senior party is internally divided, and lesser influence when the senior party is unified and the junior party divided. The junior partner can exert much greater influence on the final decision when it is able to exploit divisions among senior members, forming temporary single-issue coalitions.[58] Kaarbo finds support for the proposition that junior partners who undertake a "strategy of influence" involving threats to withdraw from the coalition also have inordinate influence on policy decisions. The threat is effective because of the fragile nature of coalition governments, and because of the desire of all top decision units to maintain political power and policy coalitions. Junior partners who threaten to leave can win a key voice in making policy, key portfolios, or even side payments on other issues.[59]

Recall the domestic political problems faced by Ehud Barak during the Israeli-Palestinian crisis in fall 2000. When Barak was unable to convince Ariel Sharon to form a new emergency (coalition) government, he turned to the coalition in place to shore up support for his crumbling political power. In particular, Barak turned to the ultraright religious party Shas, a junior coalition member, and offered a side payment for its continued support of the government. The side payment was that Barak would review the national policy requiring all Jews to serve in the military to find an exemption for Orthodox Jews, something Shas had long desired.

Similar bargaining and politicking can be found among different members of single-party executive branches. In the first case explored in this book, the Clinton administration's China policy was dramatically altered when economic-based agencies' heads gained the upper hand over political- and defense-based agencies' heads. Such intra-agency competition (and also cooperation) has been studied under the model of bureaucratic politics.[60] This model proposes that the heads of agencies will promote the agency's perspective and interests in higher-level decision-making circles. Thus, for instance, the secretary of commerce will promote the interests of Commerce regarding trade with China, the secretary of defense will promote Defense's interests, and the secretary of state will promote State's interests. When decisions are made, each agency head promotes the stand that best serves her or his agency. In the most fundamental sense, this is a description of how political officials represent their constituents—an elected officeholder represents the voters in her district or town, an agency head represents the collective interests of his agency. Policy decisions are the result of bargaining, **coalition building**, even bullying among these agency heads. The bureaucratic politics model is used frequently to study instances of U.S. foreign policy making, but it remains underutilized in the study of other countries' policy making.

Despite the lack of systematic study of bureaucratic politicking beyond the U.S. case, scholars and observers may have something like this model in mind when they discuss intraparty and/or intragovernmental political differences. For example, in a *Foreign Affairs* essay, Andrew Pierre addresses the political divisions within the Vietnamese Communist Party (VCP) and how these might impede Vietnam's ability to compete in a globalizing world. Since North Vietnam militarily overcame South Vietnam in

1975, Vietnam has been a one-party, communist state. Pierre offers this description of political life in Vietnam:

The Vietnamese Communist Party (VCP) still pervades all dimensions of life in the country, even if it faces an uncertain future. This dominance is key to understanding contemporary Vietnam. The VCP's exclusive role in government is constitutionally mandated, and advocacy of a multiparty system is forbidden. Party members control the top echelons in the ministries, the military, the internal security services, the media, and the many state-owned enterprises. Accordingly, drawing a distinction between government and party is close to meaningless.[61]

Since there is little power divested in the government, and most power in the party, the way to understand Vietnam's foreign policy is to explore intraparty, intraleadership differences.

Pierre describes the VCP in 2000 as divided behind three men and their supporters:

Vietnam is run by a "troika" of the president, the prime minister, and the general secretary of the VCP. The current top leadership, selected in late 1997 by the 18-member Politburo, was a cautious compromise. Prime Minister Phan Van Khai, an economic reformer, was intended to balance General Secretary Le Kha Phieu, a conservative and dedicated party worker who had climbed the ranks as a political commissar within the army. President Tran Duc Luong stands in the middle. . . . Le Kha Phieu has emerged as the most aggressive and powerful within the troika. . . . Meanwhile, Phan Van Khai, having tried and failed to obtain greater political support for economic reform, has offered to resign and is clearly on his way out.[62]

This fragmentation between leaders is replicated in the party ranks, that is, among the "constituents" of the three leaders. Pierre proposes that this fragmentation—while still unresolved—has led to policy paralysis, "as evidenced in the year-long delay in agreeing to the recently signed trade deal with the United States."[63] The ascendance of communist hard-liner Le Kha Phieu signals difficulties ahead for Vietnam; as the world quickly changes around Vietnam, Le Kha Phieu and his constituents may "bunker in" rather than adapt to the changes.

Looking at the same country, Zachary Abuza proposes that even the hard-liners may be changing, allowing Vietnam to adapt. Abuza writes that, since 1986, Vietnam's foreign policy making has been decentralizing—albeit slowly—under the policy of *doi moi* or renovation.[64] Various factors contribute to this decentralization, particularly changes in party leadership from political generalists to functional experts on the state level, and the disappearance of significant security threats and globalization on the system level.

We might envision Vietnam's institutions of governance as two pillars—party and government. Government institutions have been a facade, with real power residing in the corresponding party organs. Abuza suggests that since the late 1980s decision-making authority has moved down to different functional entities in the party structure, and sometimes it has slipped over the barriers to government agencies. This decentralization and empowerment of government agencies is encouraged by other countries and **international organizations** that insist on working with government rather than party officials. Mark Sidel agrees with this assessment in his discussion of the significant generational change under way in the VCP *below* the top leadership level.[65]

If Pierre is correct that hard-line forces are on the resurgence in the VCP, this might be in response to the slow decentralization proposed by Abuza and the generational change noted by Sidel. Observers of different countries and political movements around the world have noted a "fundamentalist" or "nationalist" backlash to globalization. As globalization reinforces the decentralization started by the VCP, elements within the VCP react by attempting to put on the brakes. Who "wins" this struggle will depend on the strength of the different factions—both domestically and internationally. In the short run, the hard-liners in the VCP may be able to slow the pace of economic and political reform, but the pressures from within for tangible economic progress and from without may hasten decentralization and the end of VCP control in the long run.

A similar situation faces Turkey—although Turkey is a multiparty state and the situation involves an intragovernmental rather than intraparty political difference. But the impetus for the brewing trouble in Turkey is linked to pressure emanating from both the domestic and international realms, or the state and system levels of analysis.

In Turkey, the intragovernmental tension is between the civilian, elected government, and the military. The Turkish military plays the role of the guardian of the country, protecting it from domestic forces that threaten its foundation—Kemalism. Kemal Atatürk was the father of modern Turkey, or "Father of the Turks." Eric Rouleau, the former French ambassador to Turkey from 1988 to 1992, explains, "Modern Kemalism is a faith simple in formulation and broadly positive in content. It has two major elements: the indivisibility of the nation and its territory and the secularism of the republic."[66] The military has broad and peremptory power in Turkey, using Kemalism as a justification for coups and threatened, "virtual" coups:

> The latest, in February 1997, has come to be known in Turkey as the "virtual" or "postmodern" coup, because the troops never actually left their barracks: a thinly veiled ultimatum from the army high command

sufficed to bring down the coalition government headed by the so-called Islamist Necmettin Erbakan.[67]

The issue at the core of the differences between elected governments and the armed forces is **EU (European Union)** membership. All the important political actors in Turkey, including the military, want EU membership, but the military has not been willing to allow politicians who are so inclined to meet the conditions for EU membership. After a stop-and-go relationship, the EU decided in 1999 to allow Turkey to proceed toward membership, requiring only that Turkey meet the conditions of the so-called Copenhagen rules. These rules require all candidates for admission to establish democratic institutions, the rule of law, and the protection of individual and minority rights. For Turkey, however, adherence to the Copenhagen principles would require the reformulation of the very constitution that the military put in place and that gives the military its special guardian powers.

One of Brussels' [the EU's] main targets has been Article 118 [of the Constitution], which establishes the National Security Council (NSC), a kind of shadow government through which the pashas [top generals] can impose their will on parliament and the government. The NSC is made up of six high-ranking military officers and five civilians. Once a month, decked out in full dress uniform, the chief of staff and the heads of the army, navy, air force, and national police, along with a sixth general acting as the council's general secretary, meet with Turkey's president, prime minister, and the ministers of defense, foreign affairs, and the interior. The council is empowered to examine all the affairs of state, whether relating to domestic or to foreign policy. Its deliberations are never made public, and even when decisions are announced, they are presented as "recommendations" to the government.

Civilians ignore these recommendations at their peril.[68]
· Rouleau submits that civilians in liberal circles welcome EU insistence on constitutional changes—including relegating the NSC to an informal, consultative body—but the military rejects such out of hand. Thus the broad consensus that exists on a primary foreign policy objective—EU membership—is held hostage to the military's desire to maintain its special license in Turkish politics. Political reformers who are encouraged by external forces may be thwarted in their efforts to comply with EU standards by a military unwilling to forgo its power. Similarly, in Vietnam, would-be economic and political reformers, encouraged by globalization and the promises of liberalization, are thwarted in their efforts by the Vietnamese Communist Party, which also is unwilling to abjure its special power.

For Vietnam and Turkey, as well as the Barak government in Israel and the Clinton administration regarding China policy, divisions among key political actors—whether within a single cabinet, within a single party, or among different governmental actors—can cause a foreign policy about-face or stalemate, or even contribute to an incoherent foreign policy. Conversely, agreements among key political actors on the broad outline of foreign (and domestic) policy can lead to coherent, consistent foreign policy, and to considerable freedom for foreign policy decision makers. As a brief example, the Netherlands is firmly committed to the promotion of international human rights as a primary foreign policy goal. The four major political parties all emphasize this in their party platforms. "As no political party has ever achieved an absolute majority in the parliamentary elections, cabinets are always formed on the basis of party coalitions that reflect the composition of parliament."[69] Cabinet ministers, then, tend to have high security in their positions, and the foreign minister, particularly, has "considerable political freedom." The strong party and societal agreement on the importance of international human rights, along with the Dutch constitutional system, combine to create a largely invariant foreign policy.

Public Opinion

As already noted, an interesting feature of Dutch human rights foreign policy is the degree to which governmental and societal actors unite behind international human rights. Peter Baehr asserts that Dutch public opinion—as expressed by the major political parties that control parliament (government) and the high membership rate in Dutch human rights nongovernmental organizations (society)—supports and commands a strong human rights foreign policy. Since the late 1970s, the interaction between the Dutch Foreign Ministry and human rights NGOs has gone beyond the typical; beyond education and advocacy roles, human rights NGOs have served as official, formal members of Dutch government delegations to international conferences.[70] This interplay of public opinion, interest groups, political parties, and domestic political institutions is another interesting avenue to explore.

First, it is valuable to discuss how scholars envision the impact of public opinion on foreign policy making. There are two basic views on this: the first suggests a strong impact and the second denies any real impact. The first view derives from the **pluralist model** of policy making. This view is "a 'bottom-up' approach [which] assumes that the general public has a measurable and distinct impact on the foreign policy making process. In sum, leaders follow masses."[71] The second view "representing the conventional wisdom in the literature suggests a 'top-down' process, according to which popular consensus is a function of the elite consensus and elite cleavages trickle down to mass public opinion."[72] This view is consistent with realism, as it envisions a persistent national interest pursued by elites and a passive, acquiescent, or inconsequential mass public.

Ole Holsti's study of the impact of public opinion on American foreign policy cautions that the relationship between policy and public opinion is more complex than that suggested by the two views above. Holsti dispels the notion that the American public is unknowledgeable about or indifferent to foreign affairs, but he asserts that the public acts as a cognitive miser, making use of mental shortcuts when confronted with international issues. Recall from chapter 2 that when scholars conceptualize individuals as cognitive misers, they suggest that people do not exert great cognitive energy when confronted with new information. Instead, the new information cues preexisting shortcuts such that the new information is made to match information already "stored." In this, the new information is remembered in a way that is consistent with the individual's preexisting **belief set.** Holsti concludes that the American public makes use of cognitive shortcuts that follow a pragmatic internationalist orientation.[73]

The **linkage,** however, between public opinion and policy formation is more difficult to demonstrate. Holsti says that although American policy makers tend to be more inclined to **internationalism** than the American public, the policy makers are restrained by their *perception* of what the public will tolerate. Policy makers *believe* the public is harder to convince about internationalist policies—especially policies that involve international cooperation and/or the possible deployment of U.S. troops abroad—and the lack of public support could jeopardize any undertaking.[74] Thus there is no direct linkage between public opinion and policy formation, but policy makers' perceptions of public opinion—in the immediate and future sense—set the parameters for foreign policy behavior.

Although scholars have provided evidence to the contrary, it seems intuitive that pluralistic countries—democracies—should exhibit more of the bottom-up impact of public opinion on foreign policy, while nondemocratic countries would be more likely to exhibit the top-down relationship. Public opinion should matter more in democratic states because these states are democratic. Public opinion in nondemocracies, on the other hand, should be a nonfactor in foreign policy making, or should play at best an instrumental role for elites. The research, however, does not support these simple generalizations. Instead, public opinion is seen to have an indirect impact on policy making in democratic states, while public opinion in nondemocracies matters more than an elite-driven model would allow. This gray area is more understandable when we recall that policy makers' perceptions of public opinion are crucial. We'll take up the case of public opinion in nondemocracies first.

WHAT DO AMERICAN FOREIGN POLICY ELITES THINK THE AMERICAN PUBLIC THINKS ABOUT FOREIGN AFFAIRS AND WHAT DOES THE PUBLIC THINK?

There is a shared understanding between foreign policy makers and analysts—or the foreign policy elite—about what the American public will tolerate regarding U.S. international involvement, especially regarding the deployment of American troops. Steven Kull and Clay Ramsay of the survey research Program on International Policy Attitudes (PIPA, www.pipa.org) describe this understanding:

> In the post–Cold War period, US troops have been used in a variety of operations for which the link [to national interests] is less direct or even arguably marginal. In such cases, it is widely believed among the US policy elite, public support for operations is, at best, tenuous and likely to collapse in the face of US troop fatalities. The public response to the deaths of eighteen US Rangers in Somalia in October 1993 is viewed as a key example. Most significant, this belief about the public appears to have had a significant impact on US foreign policy, leading policy-makers to hesitate from using force when they might otherwise have done so, and when using force to do so in a more cautious fashion than would be ideal from a military perspective.[1]

This shared belief is easily found in influential foreign policy outlets. For instance, in a short essay in *Foreign Affairs* instructively titled "Where Are the Great Powers? At Home with the Kids,"[2] Edward Luttwak argues that demographic change in the United States and Europe—especially low birth rates and family size—has led these publics to vigorously oppose the use of troops abroad for nearly any reason. According to Luttwak, policy makers are all too aware that

> Parents who commonly approved of their sons' and daughters' decisions to join the armed forces, thereby choosing a career dedicated to combat and its preparation . . . now often react with astonishment and anger when their children are actually sent into potential combat situations. And they are apt to view their wounding or death as an outrageous scandal, rather than as an occupational hazard.[3]

The importance of this change to Luttwak is that the most powerful countries no longer act to maintain international order, since order must often be kept through the deployment of troops and the use of military force. The United States, Russia, Great Britain, France, Germany, and Japan have the ability to act like great powers and maintain world order, "but their societies are so allergic to casualties that they are effectively debellicized, or nearly so."[4]

However, this shared understanding among the foreign policy elite does not stand up well against public opinion polls, as Kull and Ramsay demonstrate. In their review of polls taken during the 1990s on a number of real and hypothetical events involving the deployment of and possibility of fatalities among U.S. troops, Kull and Ramsay conclude that the

> polls show little evidence that the majority of Americans are prone to respond to fatalities by wanting to withdraw US troops. If anything, the public is more likely to want to respond assertively. The critical determinant of the public's response is not whether US vital interests are involved but whether the operation is perceived as likely to succeed.[5]

Further,

> support for continuing an operation is likely to be sustained provided that the public has support for the operation in the first place and believes that it is likely to succeed. If these conditions are not met, then it is possible that fatalities will contribute to a decline in support for the operation and even a desire to withdraw. However, even when confidence in a mission is low, this will not necessarily lead to a desire to withdraw. A majority has expressed a lack of confidence that the Bosnia mission will succeed; nonetheless, a majority supports US participation.[6]

An additional finding by Kull and Ramsay that really stands this particular myth on its head is that support for U.S. troop participation remains strong even when the public mistakenly believes that fatalities have occurred, and the public *vastly overreports* the extent of these fatalities. In a 1998 poll by PIPA, 63 percent of the respondents reported that Americans had been killed by hostile fire while on peacekeeping duty in Bosnia, when none had actually been killed. Despite this perception, 65 percent of the respondents supported U.S. participation in the operation. Similarly, in a 1999 PIPA poll, 56 percent believed U.S. troops had been killed (none had), while 63 percent still supported U.S. participation.[7]

Similarly, *Foreign Policy* featured an "interview" in the fall of 2001 with "virtual John/Jane Q. Public" that demonstrated clear internationalist sentiment among the American public. The interview responses of J.Q. Public were constructed by Steven Kull using the results of extensive polling data. According to Kull's reading of many polls, J.Q. Public believes:

- "[The United States has] to stay involved [in world affairs]. We are so interconnected with the rest of the world nowadays. I also think we have a moral obligation to try to do something when people are starving or when innocent people are being killed."[8]
- "Countries need to work together [in the United Nations]. Everybody should pitch in. And the United States should be willing to do its fair share."[9]
- If other countries contribute more troops to an international peacekeeping operation than the United States does, it is appropriate for the U.S. troops to be under foreign command.
- "Sometimes I think the United States can become too powerful. It kind of throws things out of balance. And people end up resenting us—you know, the ugly American and all that."[10]

In the same interview, though, some sobering evidence is offered on how poorly informed Americans really are. For example, J.Q. Public thinks the United States spends some 20 percent of the federal budget on foreign aid; it actually spends less than 1 percent. And J.Q. believes that U.S. troops constituted 50 percent of the Bosnian peacekeeping mission as of 2001; the U.S. troops amounted to 18 percent of the total deployment.

Imagine what the American public might support if it had better command of the facts of U.S. international involvement! Despite poll findings to the contrary, though, policy makers and analysts remain stubbornly convinced that the American public is isolationist and will not tolerate troop casualties, and from this belief policies are made.

Notes

1. Steven Kull and Clay Ramsay, "The Myth of the Reactive Public," in *Public Opinion and the International Use of Force*, ed. Philip Everts and Pierangelo Isernia (Routledge, 2001), 205.

2. Edward N. Luttwak, "Where Are the Great Powers? At Home with the Kids," *Foreign Affairs* 73, no. 4 (1994): 23–28.

3. Luttwak, "Where Are the Great Powers?" 25.

4. Luttwak, "Where Are the Great Powers?" 27.

5. Kull and Ramsay, " Myth of the Reactive Public," 205.

6. Kull and Ramsay, "Myth of the Reactive Public," 224.
7. Kull and Ramsay, "Myth of the Reactive Public," 219.
8. "Vox Americani," *Foreign Policy* interview, *Foreign Policy*, September–October 2001, 29–38; quote from 29.
9. "Vox Americani," 29–38.
10. "Vox Americani," 30.

In Nondemocratic Systems

Shibley Telhami conducted interviews of policy makers and average citizens and examined media reports in Egypt, Syria, Iraq, Jordan, Tunisia, Israel, and the West Bank in 1990 and 1991. His goal was to determine whether public opinion had any impact on the foreign policies of Arab states. None of the Arab states is democratic; Egypt is arguably the Arab country that leans closest to democracy, but it does not feature a fully elected and representative government with constitutional protection of individual and minority rights.

In Arab countries, Telhami proposes, government legitimacy derives not from elections but from the mass public's perception of the given regime's adherence and faithfulness to powerful transnational symbols. There are two symbols that transcend borders and ideological differences among Arab states: support for the Palestinian people's right to **self-determination** and statehood, and **anticolonialism** (which translates into anti-Israeli and anti-American sentiments).[75] Arab regimes compete with one another for regional leadership, because (among other reasons) obtaining regional leadership is proof of one's service to the two pan-Arab symbols.[76] Should a public perceive its government to be weak in supporting these two symbols, street protests and rioting result, and social movements opposed to the governing regime may take root. Arab governments challenge each other's leadership by attempting to manipulate public opinion in the target state through media campaigns aimed at questioning the loyalty of the target regime. "Successful" regimes are able to control the media messages to which their publics are exposed, and thereby keep people off the streets at less expense than using coercion.

Telhami gives examples of what he proposes. During the 1950s and 1960s, Egypt attained regional leadership by using military power and **leverage** against Israel and Western interests. But the Camp David Peace Accords with Israel in 1977–1978 removed Egypt's prestige on both transnational symbols. Egyptian President Anwar Sadat was assassinated not long afterward by fundamentalist Islamists *from within* Egypt. Since that time, the Egyptian government has needed to expend considerable resources to fight the internal threat posed by the organized and potent Islamic Brotherhood.

With the changes that occurred internationally at the end of the Cold War and collapse of the Soviet Union, Arab leaders worried about unimpeded U.S. dominance in the region. Telhami explains that these regimes took different views on the best way to respond to this altered order. Egyptian and Syrian leaders were convinced that the time was not right to get on the wrong side of the United States. They urged caution until a new global order emerged. The Iraqi regime proposed that the Arabs might unite to balance against U.S. domination, while the Jordanian and Palestinian leadership worried that disaster was pending because the United States and Israel would unite against Arab interests.[77] The key for each Arab regime was to portray its views—to its own and to the others' publics—in ways that demonstrated continued support for pro-Palestinian and anticolonial goals.

At a regional summit in Baghdad in May 1990, the Iraqi regime attempted to claim leadership of the Arab world, broadcasting a call to the pan-Arab public to rally behind its plan for direct and specific Arab counterweight to the U.S.-Israeli threat. Telhami asserts that the Egyptian and Syrian governments were able to maintain their cautious policy by blocking the media dissemination of Saddam Hussein's message to their own publics.[78]

Within a few months, Iraq had invaded Kuwait with more calls from Saddam Hussein to the pan-Arab public to rally behind Iraq's first strike at Western domination. Egyptian and Syrian leaders chose to join the U.S.-led coalition against Iraq, a move that these regimes were able to portray to their own publics as in line with the pan-Arab themes. Thus "the information campaign deprived Iraqi leaders of extensive access to the masses they sought to mobilize."[79] There were no significant public demonstrations in Egypt and Syria against the decision to join the U.S.-led fight. Conversely, Jordanian leaders did not attempt to block or counter the broadcasted Iraqi views. Most public demonstrations against the U.S.-led coalition and in favor of Iraq took place in Jordan, a country in which the leadership took no official stand in favor of either side of the war.

In the fall and winter 2000, it was possible to see again the impact of public opinion on Arab leaders. By this time, many Arab states had reached some accommodation and somewhat normalized relations with Israel and the United States. The eruption of violence between the Palestinians and Israelis (already discussed earlier in this chapter) put the Arab regimes in a precarious position. People throughout the Arab states were mobilized and on the streets in the tens of thousands in support of the Palestinians, calling on their governments to declare war against Israel. The Arab regimes needed to walk a dual-game tightrope—speaking in outrage about Israeli violence against Palestinians to placate their own people, while being careful not to go too far and jeopardize relations with Israel or the United States. In Yemen, the government decided to take the side of the street protestors and called for an Arab war against Israel,[80] despite the fact that U.S.

military ships were using Yemen's ports for refueling at the time. Within days of this call, a terrorist attack on the USS *Cole* in a Yemeni port caused massive damage to the ship and killed sixteen U.S. service personnel.

The goal of these Arab regimes was to preempt any public protest that might take on the shape of organized political movements threatening their power at home and limiting policy options abroad. The terrorist attacks on New York City and Washington, D.C., on September 11, 2001, posed numerous public opinion management challenges to these regimes.

Consider the situation of the **Palestinian National Authority (PA)** and its leader, Yasser Arafat. Within hours of the attacks on the World Trade Center and the Pentagon, video from East Jerusalem showed Palestinians of all ages *and* PA police celebrating news of the attacks. Arafat and PA senior officials quickly moved to suppress media coverage of any public celebrations.[81] Their campaign initially took two forms: (1) they accused the media of misrepresenting Palestinian reaction and (2) they "told local representatives of foreign news agencies and television stations on several occasions that their employees' safety could be jeopardized if videotapes showing Palestinians celebrating the attacks were aired."[82] PA officials then staged several media events to demonstrate Palestinian support for the United States. These actions were taken to deal with one part of the **nested game**—the need to control the message to the outside world and thereby preserve some foreign policy options.

On the other side of the nested game, senior Palestinian officials moved swiftly to confront street demonstrations aimed at the PA itself. Recall from earlier in this chapter that Hamas and its leaders posed a serious challenge to Arafat's control. During the *intifada* that started in September 2000, Hamas was able to rally people into the streets and against Israeli forces at will, causing many to question Arafat's ability or willingness to govern. After the United States began air strikes against Osama bin Laden's terrorist camps and Taliban positions in Afghanistan in response to the September 11 attacks, Palestinians demonstrated their lack of confidence in the PA and Arafat by turning on PA police. In one incident, PA police opened fire on the crowd, killing two, one of whom was a young teenager. *Washington Post* reporter Lee Hockstader filed this report about the fracas: "Journalists at the scene and other witnesses ranked the violence with some of the worst clashes between Palestinians and Israeli forces during the past year of fighting."[83] Hockstader explained Arafat's dilemma this way,

The question is whether he can face down a resurgent, home-grown Islamic opposition, enforce the latest cease-fire with the Israelis and cast his political lot with the U.S.-led war against terrorism—as he appears to want to do—without igniting a wave of street violence that could crush his increasingly fragile rule.[84]

Arafat's may be one of the weaker Arab regimes—indeed, his regime suffers from the ultimate weakness in that it does not have full **sovereignty** and independence—but his predicament is emblematic of the situation facing the others. The silence from the Egyptian and Saudi Arabian regimes after September 11 and especially after the start of the U.S. military campaign that came in response to September 11, suggests that these regimes wanted to keep a low profile in order not to inflame their own publics. Osama bin Laden was, after all, a hugely popular figure among the Egyptian and Saudi populations.

In Democratic Systems

As we return to democratic systems, recall that in the case of the Netherlands public opinion in support of a strong human rights foreign policy was channeled through human rights NGOs and the four major political parties. Democratic systems by their nature allow for more public involvement in the policy-making process. But, as already pointed out, scholars have wondered about the processes by which public opinion gets translated into influence on the foreign policy–making process in democracies. The articulation of public opinion by formal or informal interest groups appears to be critical to the process in which public opinion shapes policy in any type of political system.

Thomas Risse-Kappen examines the relationship between public opinion and foreign policy making in the United States, France, the former West Germany, and Japan. He concludes that "mass public opinion mattered" in each case, in that it "set broad and unspecified limits to the foreign policy choices."[85] Public opinion had an important *indirect* effect as it appears that "the main role of the public in liberal democracies is to influence the coalition-building processes among elite groups."[86] Further, Risse-Kappen maintains, "For both the political elites and societal actors, mass public opinion proves to be a resource for strengthening one's position in the coalition-building process."[87] Public opinion, then, is the leverage used by elites and interest groups in establishing their claims to dominate a policy coalition.

Additionally, the degree of both societal fragmentation and centralization of political authority are critical parameters in understanding the impact of public opinion on foreign policy. In countries with great societal political fragmentation, such as France, no mass public opinion exists on foreign policy issues. French social fragmentation is "complemented" by the highly centralized nature of political authority; both conditions combine to limit severely the impact of public opinion on foreign policy making. The United States presents a different picture on these two variables. American society is politically heterogeneous, but far less so than French society. Thus it is possible to identify certain policy orientations among segments of the mass public. Whereas centralized political authorities tend to control the formation of policy networks in France, in the United States political authority is decentralized, allowing societal groups to dominate the formation of policy networks.[88] Risse-Kappen concludes that public opinion has more impact on U.S. foreign policy making than it does in the other three cases for these very reasons.

Interest Groups

How might interest groups in a heterogeneous society attain the opportunity to put their stamp on foreign policy? In his study of the impact of interest groups on the Clinton administration's China policy (a case explored in detail in chapter 1), John Dietrich suggests that interest groups which possess broad leverage over many different policy areas are able to exert greater influence on the making of a particular policy than are single-issue groups. Business and farm groups were critical to the success of the Clinton administration's policies on numerous domestic and foreign policy issues. Once these groups joined forces with the economic executive branch agencies and protrade members of Congress, this policy coalition in support of delinking China trade from human rights was unbeatable. Human rights groups, conversely, tended to be single issue and they had less ability to link their interests to broader policy coalitions. Knowledge of their own limited leverage in the Clinton administration convinced human rights groups to back away from their prior insistence that trade be linked with human rights conditions, all toward the goal of, at minimum, staying relevant to the political game.

Similarly, Yossi Shain's study of African American and Arab American lobbies in the United States reveals that some ethnic interest groups have greater impact than others on foreign policy making when those groups are more integrated into the broader American political game. Less successful interest groups remain peripheral to the American mainstream.[89] Shain writes to counter the fear voiced by some that the rise of influential ethnic lobbies with strong ties to real or symbolic homelands will lead to a "Balkanization" of U.S. foreign policy. He suggests that the opposite is occurring: as ethnic lobbies join the American political mainstream, embracing the values and political clout associated with it, they become strong voices in support of a U.S. foreign policy that is premised on core American values.

By way of example, Shain contrasts the isolationist black power movement with the integrationist civil rights movement.

Black Power separatists of the late 1960s advocated national liberation and rejected the civil rights movement's vision of a color-blind, integrated America. Their crusade was bolstered by the successful struggle for independence of African states and by the rise of Third World ideology. Conversion to Islam was a reaction to the perception of Christianity as "a slave religion." Yet, by the early 1970s, black separatism was already waning, as more and more black leaders . . . preached the gospel of power-sharing and pluralism and denounced Black Power as reverse racism. Moderate black leaders realized that only by playing an insider's game and embracing the American electoral system and its democratic values could they hope to become equal participants in American society.[90]

Integration into the American mainstream deepens the potential impact of ethnic lobbies on policy making because these groups' interests broaden to encompass a variety of issue areas, thereby increasing their ability to join policy coalitions. Concurrently, once ethnic interest groups demonstrate their commitment to pluralism, they no longer pose a threat to groups already in the mainstream, also increasing the likelihood of cross-group coalitions on foreign *and* domestic policy issues. To return to Shain's example:

In the African American community, the integrationists' mode of foreign affairs is best represented by TransAfrica. From its inception, TransAfrica considered African American involvement in African and Caribbean affairs to be an additional mechanism for domestic empowerment. In the crusade to reverse America's posture toward South Africa, TransAfrica endeavored to apply Martin Luther King's domestic strategy of challenging Americans to live up to their democratic creed.[91]

To bring together some elements discussed above, we can conclude that public opinion matters, but its impact on policy making is indirect. Public opinion seems to matter most when it has been filtered through either the perceptions of elite policy makers or interest group and political party activity. There is another filter that needs to be considered here—the mass media.

Media

Our final section in this review of state-level sources of foreign policy making and behavior concerns the impact of the media. The above discussion of public opinion in Arab countries considered Telhami's argument that state control of media is critical to maintaining the legitimacy of nondemocratic regimes, introducing the idea that the media play an instrumental role for national leadership. But, as with many issues, the full story is more complicated.

There exists in the minds of some observers and policy makers a phenomenon called the **CNN effect.** Political scientist and former U.S. Assistant Secretary of Defense for international security affairs Joseph Nye explains the CNN effect in this way:

> The free flow of broadcast information in open societies has always had an impact on public opinion and the formation of foreign policy, but now the flows have increased and shortened news cycles have reduced the time for deliberation. By focusing on certain conflicts and human rights problems, broadcasts pressure politicians to respond to some foreign problems and not others. The so-called CNN effect makes it harder to keep some items off the top of the public agenda that might otherwise warrant a lower priority.[92]

Nye sees the CNN effect as real and potentially harmful to reasoned policy making. Because the news broadcasts "24/7," the media sometimes force issues into the open on which policy makers would be happier to keep a low profile. This, in turn, lessens deliberation time and the search for the most reasonable policy response.

Those who believe that the CNN effect is real propose that it turns on public opinion. Once the media broadcast images of mass starvation, ethnic conflict, or some other sort of mass suffering, the images arouse strong emotions in the public. The public then turn to their elected officials and demand some strong and morally correct response. That is, the public, aroused by images of suffering in the media, demand that officials "do something." Elected officials, wanting to stay in the public's favor for all sorts of obvious reasons, respond with some sort of **humanitarian intervention,** military intervention, or whatever action is needed in the immediate term.

This suggests that the media play a powerful role in setting the public agenda. How powerful is this role? Jonathan Mermin poses this question about the American media: "Journalists necessarily engage in agenda setting, in deciding out of the vast universe of events what to report and what to ignore. *But in setting the news agenda, what rules do journalists follow?*"[93] Mermin asks an important question: How do the media decide when to cover a story out of the many, many stories that could be covered? He suggests two possible answers. First, the media act independently and "independent journalistic initiative"[94] puts stories in the headlines. Mermin cites the story of one NBC correspondent who decided on his own to publicize forgotten stories. He single-handedly put the story of the 1984 Ethiopian famine on the airwaves (a story covered by the BBC but not American media), prompting an outpouring of U.S. aid to Ethiopia. But this independent journalistic initiative is the exception rather than the rule.

The second possible explanation for how the American media come to cover what they cover is that "American journalists turn to politicians and government officials for guidance in deciding what constitutes news."[95] American journalists—and arguably journalists from around the globe on issues of broad importance—take their cues from Washington for practical reasons. Mermin offers three. First, given limited budgets and staff, reporters are assigned to newsworthy places[96]—Washington, D.C., would rank among the top newsworthy places on almost anyone's list. Second, on foreign policy issues, Washington generates a plethora of information every day.[97] Third, "considerations of the need to establish the legitimacy of information reported and the need for protection against the liability for inaccurate reports also encourage the use of official sources."[98]

At the same time that Washington makes practical sense for budget- and personnel-strapped media outlets, Washington also produces far too much news for the media to cover. As Mermin puts it, "Far more stories are pitched to reporters than end up making the news."[99] Members of the media, then, do exercise some independent judgment about which stories to cover. Mermin suggests this about what ultimately is reported: "The news agenda in this view is a joint production of sources and journalists."[100]

Mermin supports his conclusions with evidence of news coverage of the famine and conflict in Somalia in the eleven months leading up to the U.S. humanitarian intervention that started in November 1992. U.S. intervention in Somalia was not the result of the CNN effect, but instead

> journalists worked closely with governmental sources in deciding when to cover Somalia, and how to frame the story, and how much coverage it deserved. The lesson of Somalia is not just about the influence of television on Washington; it is equally about the influence of Washington on television.[101]

But "Washington" involves a large number of actors—within the U.S. government, as well as a multitude of domestic and foreign lobbyists—and so which of these act with the media to set any given foreign policy agenda? Mermin's answer, in brief, involves politics. In July 1992, key senators in both parties—Nancy Kassebaum (R-Kan.) and Paul Simon (D-Ill.)—each of whom at one time chaired the Senate Foreign Relations Committee Subcommittee on Africa, began a public campaign to force the George H. W. Bush (Bush 1) administration to do something about the dire situation in Somalia.[102] Senators Kassebaum and Simon were joined in their efforts by the House Committee on Hunger. These key actors found a sympathetic ear at ABC News, which, according to Mermin, "appears to have observed a rule of deference to government officials, in this case the top Senate experts on Africa in terms of institutional position, in deciding that events in Somalia constituted news in the United States."[103] ABC

News elected to cover the story, on this Mermin is clear, but without critical voices urging such, ABC might not have looked toward Somalia.

Mermin's description of the politics of setting the news agenda, with the media at once dependent on and independent of Washington, is echoed in Patrick Haney's study of the U.S. "discovery" in September 1970 of a Soviet missile base in Cuba. As Haney describes this case, then U.S. National Security Adviser Henry Kissinger perceived the discovery of the Soviet missile base to be a major security threat that necessitated a strong and immediate response. President Richard Nixon disagreed with Kissinger's interpretation of the problem and ordered him to keep the issue low profile because Nixon did not want the subs to *become* a crisis. Kissinger then set about orchestrating opinion in favor of his interpretation, including leaking the news over breakfast with a *New York Times* columnist. Not ten days later the story broke in the *New York Times*, at which point Nixon was forced to upgrade the situation in favor of Kissinger's "crisis" interpretation.[104] In this example we see how policy makers attempt to drive the media and use the media to win their own intragovernmental political disagreements. The *Times* columnist could have chosen to ignore the story, but ignoring a "leak" from the powerful Kissinger would have been professionally foolish.

When considering the "joint" agenda setting between government officials and media, can we say the balance of influence leans more toward one side or the other? We might conclude with some degree of certainty that the "power" tilts in favor of those with information—officials—although not overwhelmingly so.

We can find support for the idea that the media are driven more by policy makers than policy makers are driven by the media outside the case of the United States. For example, Tony Shaw examines the British popular press coverage of the early Cold War period in order to learn how the press contributed to the consensus that developed between policy makers and the British public. At the immediate conclusion of World War II, Shaw notes, the British press were diverse in terms of political ideologies and portrayals of the Soviet Union, the United States, and the United Nations.[105] In 1947, Shaw asserts, the British press exhibited widely different views on the Truman Doctrine, the Marshall Plan for the reconstruction of Europe, and whether Soviet troops were correct to stay throughout Eastern and Central Europe.

The British government came to a different opinion regarding the Soviet Union and the United States and, Shaw explains, it decided that the press would need to be brought around to the correct view:

All heads of Foreign Office political departments were instructed on ways to make "subtler use of our publicity machine" to ensure the publication of anti-Soviet material, including various ways of leaking information to friendly diplomatic correspondents and inspiring questions that the Foreign Office could pretend it did not want to answer.[106]

Similarly, the Foreign Office orchestrated a pro-U.S., pro–Marshall Plan campaign aimed at changing press views. The aptness of the government's view regarding the Soviet Union was "demonstrated" by the Soviet-inspired communist takeover of Czechoslovakia in 1948. By 1949—just two years into a concerted government effort to manage the press message on the Cold War—the British press was unified in its portrayal of the emerging Cold War, and this portrayal was in line with the government's view.

A related idea is that policy makers can find ways to ignore events that are covered by the media when those policy makers have already decided not to "do something." Encouraged by humanitarian nongovernmental organizations on the scene, the media *did not* ignore the unfolding genocide and refugee crisis in Rwanda in the summer of 1994. Despite media attention, with the exception of France and to a lesser extent Canada, no major powers called for any type of intervention and, in fact, the major powers worked within the U.N. Security Council to *cut* the presence of U.N. peacekeepers weeks before the genocide started. The French call for action, it should be said, was in *opposition* to any U.N. operation. Media coverage made no difference because policy makers in important countries had decided that intervention would be difficult with little likelihood of success.

Similarly, international media coverage of Russian human rights violations in Chechnya during the first and second Chechen wars evoked little formal condemnation (and no action) by the United States. U.S. humanitarian aid workers[107] attempted to cajole or shame the American government into a more forceful stand on Chechnya, but U.S. policy makers had determined already that they would not jeopardize U.S.-Russian relations on behalf of the people of Chechnya.

Ultimately, the role media play in setting the public agenda is primarily determined by "the conditions that officials themselves . . . create," according to journalist Warren Strobel.[108] Strobel examines the impact of media on the United States' decision to participate in peacekeeping and **peace enforcement** operations, operations in which media have freer access and thus might be able to generate more pressure among publics for the government to act. Strobel proposes that push and pull factors might be at play: the media might push governments into launching peace operations, or the media might pull governments away from certain courses of action or even cause the termination of participation in peace operations. From his study, Strobel concludes,

Images and written accounts of the horrors of the post–Cold War world that stream into the offices of government officials do not dictate policy outcomes. Sometimes they suggest policy choices, but there is ample reason to believe that officials can reject those choices if they feel it necessary. At other times, media reports become an ally for an entire administration, or individual members of it, seeking to pursue new policies.[109]

Media, like other societal actors, can take control of a government's policy only when that government loses control:

If officials let others dominate the policy debate, if they do not closely monitor the progress and results of their own policies, if they fail to build and maintain popular and congressional support for a course of action, if they step beyond the bounds of their public mandate or fail to anticipate problems, they may suddenly seem driven by the news media and its agenda.[110]

This discussion is not meant to suggest that media have no power to mobilize opinion against a government's policy and cause some change to occur to that policy. Recall from our discussion of the first Chechen war earlier in this chapter, Russian media and other interest groups were instrumental in forcing the Russian government to end the war. Similarly, U.S. media played a crucial role in mobilizing antiwar sentiment in the United States during the Vietnam War by offering interpretations on events that did not fit the "official" presentation. Strobel cautions that we should refrain from making blanket statements about the balance of power between media and government in wartime, since the United States has not yet fought a war that involved a high number of casualties in the era of real-time television coverage.[111] The first Chechen war may be instructive here, since Russian media provided real-time coverage of Russian casualties and failed policies. The issue, though, is whether media can drive foreign policy beyond the exceptional cases, and the answer seems to be that policy makers—once set on or against a foreign mission—usually can control or ignore the media when they stay in charge of the policy-making process. The American air campaign against the Taliban and Al Qaeda in Afghanistan in late 2001 seemed informed by this conclusion.

Review

The scope of this chapter demonstrates the many kinds of topics and questions that might be explored at the state level of analysis. We did not cover the full range of foreign policy study here but only sampled the field at this level of analysis. This chapter also demonstrates the blurred lines between the levels of analysis, as scholars at this level borrow generously from concepts and theories cast at the individual and system levels. As we move to the next chapter, remember that the lines we've drawn between the levels help us manage what we study, but these lines are somewhat misleading. Individuals, governmental and societal actors, and system-level dynamics blend to create foreign policy.

Some Key Ideas from This Chapter

- National self-image and culture drive the kinds of foreign policy roles countries play and foreign policy behaviors in which countries engage.
- National self-image and culture directly influence the types of institutions used to govern the nation.
- According to the theory of the democratic peace, both culture and institutions of governance interact to create a foreign policy marked more by cooperation than by conflict.
- Countries undergoing democratization appear to be more likely to resort to war than countries undergoing no regime change. The mix of **political opening,** unrestrained demands on government, and weakening central authority combine to create a volatile situation in which ruling regimes may resort to war in order to maintain political power.
- In all types of political systems, retaining political power and building policy coalitions can create dynamics that can propel countries into risky foreign policy behaviors.
- Partisan politics within or between branches of government as well as within party differences complicate the nested game played by national leaders.
- Public opinion seems to have an indirect but significant impact on foreign policy making, even in nondemocratic systems.
- Public opinion gains greater political weight when it is channeled through interest group activity.
- The "CNN effect" appears to be real in the minds of some policy makers, but media do not appear to be able to set the public agenda in the face of leaders who lack interest in a certain foreign policy direction. Media can be used by leaders to promote a selected foreign policy course, but the relationship between officials and media is more likely one of shared interests and "joint" agenda setting.

For Further Study

On state type and foreign policy behavior, see Maurice A. East and Charles F. Hermann, "Do Nation-Types Account for Foreign Policy Behavior?" in

Comparing Foreign Policies: Theories, Findings, and Methods, ed. James N. Rosenau (Wiley/Sage, 1974); David W. Moore, "National Attributes and Nation Typologies: A Look at the Rosenau Genotypes," in Rosenau, *Comparing Foreign Policies;* and Maurice A. East, "National Attributes and Foreign Policy," in *Why Nations Act: Theoretical Perspectives for Comparative Foreign Policy,* ed. Maurice A. East, Stephen A. Salmore, and Charles F. Hermann (Sage, 1978).

On image, culture, and foreign policy, see Kenneth E. Boulding, "National Images and International Systems," *Journal of Conflict Resolution* 3 (1959): 120–31; and John C. Farrell and Asa P. Smith, *Image and Reality in World Politics* (Columbia University Press, 1967).

On domestic institutions and foreign policy, see Peter J. Katzenstein, *Between Power and Plenty: Foreign Economic Policies of Advanced Industrial States* (University of Wisconsin Press, 1978); Jack S. Levy, "Organization Routines and the Causes of War," *International Studies Quarterly* 30, no. 2 (1986): 193–222; and Barbara Salmore and Stephen Salmore, "Political Regimes and Foreign Policy," in East, Salmore, and Hermann, *Why Nations Act.*

On domestic politics and foreign policy, see Joe D. Hagan, *Political Opposition and Foreign Policy in Comparative Perspective* (Lynne Rienner, 1993); Patrick James and John R. O'Neal, "The Influence of Domestic and International Politics on the President's Use of Force," *Journal of Conflict Resolution* 35, no. 2 (1991): 301–32; Stephen D. Krasner, *Defending the National Interest: Raw Materials Investments and U.S. Foreign Policy* (Princeton University Press, 1978); and Theodore J. Lowi, "Making Democracy Safe for the World: National Politics and Foreign Policy," in *Domestic Sources of Foreign Policy,* ed. James N. Rosenau (Free Press, 1967).

On the democratic peace proposition, see Steve Chan, "Mirror, Mirror on the Wall . . . Are Freer Countries More Pacific?" *Journal of Conflict Resolution* 28, no. 4 (1984): 617–48; William J. Dixon, "Democracy and the Management of International Conflict," *Journal of Conflict Resolution* 37, no. 1 (1993): 42–68; Bruce M. Russett, *Grasping the Democratic Peace: Principles for a Post–Cold War World* (Princeton University Press, 1993); and Erich Weede, "Democracy and War Involvement," *Journal of Conflict Resolution* 28, no. 4 (1984): 649–64.

On public opinion and foreign policy, see Ole R. Holsti, "Public Opinion and Foreign Policy: Challenges to the Almond-Lipmann Consensus," *International Studies Quarterly* 36, no. 4 (1992): 439–66; Bruce M. Russett and Thomas W. Graham, "Public Opinion and National Security Policy: Relationships and Impacts," in *The Handbook of War Studies,* ed. Manus Midlarsky (Unwin Hyman, 1989); and Eugene R. Wittkopf, *Faces of Internationalism: Public Opinion and American Foreign Policy* (Duke University Press, 1990). On the linkage between public opinion and interest groups, see David Skidmore and Valerie M. Hudson, eds., *The Limits of Autonomy: Societal Groups and Foreign Policy Formulation* (Westview Press, 1993).

On the media and foreign policy, see Bernard Cohen, *The Press and Foreign Policy* (Princeton University Press, 1963); Daniel C. Hallin, *The "Uncensored War": The Media and Vietnam* (University of California Press, 1986); and Douglas V. Johnson II, *The Impact of the Media on National Security Policy Decision-making* (U.S. Army War College, Strategic Studies Institute, 1994).

4

The System Level of Analysis: Power, Position, and Foreign Policy Behavior

123

In mid-April 2001, the U.N. Human Rights Commission began its annual two-month meeting in Geneva, Switzerland. The Human Rights Commission is a fifty-three-member body elected out of one of the six organs of the United Nations, the Economic and Social Council (ECOSOC). It has met annually since its founding in 1947 to discuss violations of human rights among U.N. member states, issue condemnations, and otherwise attempt to uphold the Universal Declaration on Human Rights. States come together in this **international organization** to wage their foreign policy campaigns against their political opponents using the issue of how these states treat *their own* citizens. The annual meeting of this commission pits states against states at the system level—the level of interstate relations and global politics—on issues that arguably are domestic in nature.

Some of the expected "big" items on the commission's agenda in April 2001 were to be Russia's use of force in Chechnya, Israel's treatment of Palestinians in the West Bank and Gaza, and China's restrictions on religious and political freedoms, including its treatment of Tibetans.[1] Each case should be familiar to the readers of *The New Foreign Policy*. The biggest story at this meeting, however, came at its start. The United States was standing for reelection to a seat on the commission, having held a seat since 1947. Yet, in a secret ballot, the United States was not reelected. China, one of the primary targets of U.S. resolutions every year in Geneva, reacted "gleefully," suggesting that the U.S. loss was a victory for China.[2]

How did the United States—the only global superpower—lose its seat? Media interviews of various international representatives at the meeting suggested that **linkage** politics were at play. *The Times* (London) reported:

> Some diplomats said they believed the [George W.] Bush administration's opposition to the Kyoto climate change treaty as well as its insistence on building a missile defence system contributed to its failure. Other nations may have been trying to punish Washington for failing to support the abolition of landmines, or recognise an International Criminal Court, and its opposition to cheap drugs being made available to Aids sufferers in the Third World. The U.S. may also have lost support from Arab countries during the Israeli conflict with the Palestinians.[3]

Just as the United States had used Human Rights Commission meetings over the years to pursue its own displeasure with the foreign and domestic *non–human rights* policies of some states, this time around the United States was the target of linkage politics.

From the beginning of this book we have talked about linkages across issues and across levels of analysis, and about the blurring lines between foreign and domestic politics, especially in this era of globalization. This example from the start of the 2001 U.N. Commission on Human Rights meeting displays all these elements at play. As already noted, the task of the analyst is made easier by isolating issues at particular levels of analysis. As discussed in chapter 1, sometimes we want to photograph the single flower, but sometimes we want to set the flower in its context on the plant or in the garden. In this chapter, we will be examining the entire "garden"—studying foreign policy at the system level of analysis. Yet we will find it much harder to stay *just* at this level when trying to explain countries' foreign policies. Globalization—the internationalization of economics and culture—necessitates a two-level, or **nested game,** approach to studying foreign policy. The next chapter takes up this theme.

At the system level of analysis, we study state–state relations that occur bilaterally or multilaterally, regionally or globally. This is the level of analysis that is used most commonly in media reports of global affairs ("Today Brazil proposed that it would support a Western Hemisphere free trade zone, if its concerns regarding the use of natural resources . . ."), and thus it will seem more familiar to the reader. This level of analysis might also seem more familiar because the discussion is focused more on policy outcomes—particularly behaviors—than on policy process. The primary purpose of analysts using this level is to get "outside" national borders in order to discuss the interactions of states with other states and **transnational actors,** and within international organizations.

It is not enough to just describe relationships between actors. We want to understand the bases of relations, the different goals being pursued by different actors, as well as the motivations behind actions. There are two fundamental questions (or two sides to a single, fundamental question) underlying much of foreign policy scholarship. Do states act the way they act in the world because of who they are (as defined *within* the state)? Or do states act the way they do because of where they sit in the world (as defined by their relationships with other states in the **international system**)? Scholars studying foreign policy at the system level stress the latter but cannot escape from the former. Foreign policy makers, too, confront this reality, as they play what Putnam, Hagan, and other scholars call the two-level, or nested game, of foreign policy making.

Our discussion at the system level begins with traditional explanations of how position is related to foreign policy, or how foreign policy is related to where a country sits or is ranked among other countries. In this discussion, we will explore what some scholars have proposed about the foreign policies of great, secondary, and small powers. Then we will go into an extended examination of middle powers—a special group of secondary powers—in order to demonstrate that a full understanding of foreign policy requires multiple perspectives and multiple analytical levels. In this discussion, we'll consider how middle power foreign policy is driven *both* by state-level understandings of a state's identity *and* system level understandings of its international position. This discussion will make extended use of an alternative analytical lens in international relations theory—constructivism.

Position, Power, and Foreign Policy

In realist system-level accounts, the focus is on how a state's position in the international system is related to its foreign policy. Sometimes the suggested relationship is causal—a country's position is said to determine its foreign policy—but, most typically, the suggested relationship is a matter of explaining which options are open to states in certain positions and what those states must and/or will do to preserve or enhance their status.

To realists, the nature of the international system conditions and encourages certain foreign policy behaviors, although it does not determine specific behaviors. A classic statement on the impact of the system level on a state's foreign policy comes from neorealist Kenneth Waltz. Waltz writes,

> With many sovereign states, with no system of law enforceable among them, with each state judging its grievances and ambitions according to the dictates of its own reason or desire—conflict, sometimes leading to war, is bound to occur. To achieve a favorable outcome from such conflict a state has to rely on its own devices, the relative efficiency of which must be its constant concern.[4]

And

> In anarchy, there is no automatic harmony. . . . Because each state is the final judge of its own cause, any state may at any time use force to implement its policies. Because any state may at any time use force, all states must constantly be ready either to counter force with force or to pay the cost of weakness. The requirements of state action are, in this view, imposed by the circumstances in which all states exist.[5]

In a realist world, **anarchy** requires a foreign policy stance that is always vigilant for encroachments on one's **security** and power and is always vigilant for opportunities to advance one's security and power. This applies to all states no matter their type or position in the system, although more powerful states can "manage" and have more impact on anarchy than less powerful states can.

The last statement is important because realists place their primary, if not exclusive, emphasis on the study of powerful states. The system level of analysis is the level of choice for realism, and the subject of choice is that group of states that have some shaping impact on the system. This is true for classical realists as well as for those neorealists who study international relations through the lens of **international political economy**. These scholars focus on the states at and near the top of the power hierarchy. For instance, Charles Kindleberger contends that a state's size determines its ability to stabilize or disrupt the international economic system. "Large" countries have the capability to stabilize the system, "middle" countries can damage or disrupt the system, and "small" countries have no impact at all on the system.[6] Because the focus is on expected systemic impact, the study of small countries yields no interesting lessons and thus lacks analytical value to scholars such as Kindleberger. Other foreign policy scholars would not take this position, but all who study foreign policy at this level admit that position in the system opens opportunities for some states—the more powerful—and closes opportunities for others.

The terms used here—large, middle, and small countries, or great, middle, and small powers—can be misleading. For example, when foreign policy scholars speak of "small states," they are not *necessarily* suggesting anything about the geographical size of the state, its population, or the level of the institutional development of its governance structures. Instead, something is implied about how the country's size, population, economy, and so forth position the state in respect to other states. Similarly, foreign policy discussions of "weak states" may not necessarily suggest anything about the internal features of countries and their governments (as is suggested by the terms **failed state** and failing state, for example). Instead, the state is weak in relation to other state actors. System-level analysis focuses on the relationships between international actors.

Another knotty aspect of the use of categories such as great, middle, and small is that there is rarely agreement among scholars or policy makers about which states fit which categories because the categories themselves are often a little "fuzzy." For instance, recall the "pre-theory" of foreign policy proposed by James Rosenau and discussed in earlier chapters. In Rosenau's pre-theory, he offered eight ideal nation-types that he developed from a simple "large country" versus "small country" starting point. Rosenau's purpose, remember, was to get the ball rolling on systematic, comparative foreign policy research, and so he did not offer—nor did he need to offer—any definition of large and small. He had in mind that the United States, Soviet Union, India, and China were large countries, while Holland (Netherlands), (the former) Czechoslovakia, Kenya, and Ghana were small countries. Unfortunately, other analysts have been content to offer similarly impressionistic designations of state type without any greater definitional precision.

The Elusive Concept of Power

Much of the imprecision in categories of states derives from a problem that resists resolution: there is no agreement among analysts about the elemental, fundamental concept of "power." Power is one of the defining features of international politics, according to realists, liberals, and Marxists. But none of these three dominant perspectives has ever reached consensus *within* their ranks about this critical concept. This failure is not limited to international politics; one of the more prominent international relations scholars, Robert Gilpin, noted that this is endemic to the broader study of politics. Gilpin declared that the "number and variety of definitions (of power) should be an embarrassment to political scientists."[7]

When Rosenau divided states into large and small, developed and underdeveloped, and open and closed, he had in mind the idea that we can array states based on measurements made of certain attributes or resources. More powerful states, for instance, are those with larger, more industrialized national economies and larger, better equipped, better trained national militaries. We might also add that more powerful states have healthier, better fed, better educated citizenries. Indeed, we could keep adding different measurable attributes to this list, depending on what we as analysts believe to be important. From this, we can say that power derives from or is the summation of the tangible resources of the state. These tangible aspects of power create a certain level of state capability.

But capability does not translate directly into influence. A highly capable state may not be able to influence the foreign or domestic policies or behaviors of another state. How states translate capability into the ability to make other states modify their behavior is a long-standing puzzle.[8] Contributing to this puzzle is the fact that history provides many examples of very powerful states that "lost" in some way to far less powerful actors. The U.S. failure in Vietnam during the 1960s and early 1970s and the Soviet failure in Afghanistan in the 1980s are two prominent, noteworthy examples. To be sure, powerful states sometimes can have *their* behavior changed by actors whose power capabilities seem miniscule in comparison. For example, consider the "Battle of the Black Sea," which took place in October 1993 between U.S. "peacekeepers" and "civilians" of various loyalties in Mogadishu, Somalia.

On the afternoon of October 3, 1993, U.S. Rangers and commandos from the mysterious Delta Force set out on a routine "snatch and grab" operation in the capital of the failed state of Somalia. The Americans were part of a U.N. **peacekeeping** operation whose mission was to restore law and order to Somalia in order to facilitate humanitarian food relief deliveries. Somalia's government had collapsed in 1991, leaving the country without any commonly accepted central political authority—thus its "failed state" designation. Various armed factions competed for control, with none having sufficient power to conquer the others. In the midst of political disarray and civil war, a famine of enormous proportions hit Somalia. International food relief efforts were stymied and then hijacked by the armed factions, causing humanitarian assistance groups and international media to call for international intervention.

A brief presentation of the three international interventions that occurred in Somalia demonstrates some of the political problems inherent to the use of power, particularly military power. In April 1992 the United Nations dispatched a peacekeeping operation—the United Nations Operation in Somalia (UNOSOM I)—to assist **nongovernmental organizations (NGOs)** with humanitarian relief activities. Traditional peacekeepers carry small weapons for self-defense, but they have no authority to enforce order or compel anyone to stop undesirable behavior. Local compliance with "rules" established by U.N. peacekeepers is totally voluntary. Having no authority to use power in Somalia, UNOSOM I was unable to effect a cease-fire, ensure the delivery of food relief, or even protect itself from hostile fire. By the end of 1992, it was clear that the mission was a failure.

The humanitarian disaster in Somalia had only deepened, so the U.N. peacekeeping operation was replaced by a U.N.-approved, more muscular **multinational force** called the United Task Force (UNITAF) in December 1992. This force was under U.S. command and control and was composed of twenty-eight thousand U.S. troops and seventeen thousand troops from other countries. UNITAF, acting under liberal rules of engagement that permitted the use of force to compel acceptable behavior, was able to impose temporary calm and order, helping NGOs get food relief into about 40 percent of the country. After several successful months, UNITAF was disbanded and a second U.N. peacekeeping operation (UNOSOM II) followed in May 1993. This peacekeeping mission operated under similar, mostly limited rules of engagement, much as the first U.N. mission but was mandated to perform disarmament and reconciliation tasks. Violence reemerged, and once again relief efforts and peacekeepers were threatened.[9]

The violence escalated in Somalia and eventually the U.N. peacekeepers became targets. In one ambush in early June in Mogadishu, twenty-four Pakistani peacekeepers were killed by the Habr Gidr armed faction (the Somali National Alliance army) led by General Mohamed Farah Aidid. In another episode, a U.S. Black Hawk helicopter had been shot at and disabled. The head of the U.N. mission, retired U.S. Admiral Jonathan Howe, ordered a drastic change in some of the peacekeepers' orders in response to this violence. Because peacekeeping troops are volunteered by their national governments, U.N. military and civilian commanders hold precarious and shifting power/authority over these troops. Howe could not issue orders to *all* of the U.N. peacekeepers in Somalia, but he could "order" the U.S. contingent to modify its mission and behaviors. The Clinton administration, commanders in the field, and Howe determined that the violence against peacekeepers could not be tolerated and so U.S. troops were ordered to capture General Aidid and his top advisers. This order was to be accomplished through the use of military force. The U.S. forces, ostensibly part of the U.N. peacekeeping operation, were under U.S. command and control for this new mission.

In the late summer 1993 and into the fall, U.S. Rangers and Delta Force members, using armored vehicles and Black Hawk attack helicopters, conducted many "snatch and grab" operations against the leaders of Habr Gidr. These snatch and grab raids were conducted with massive force and resulted in the deaths of many Somalis and considerable destruction in Mogadishu. General Aidid, however, eluded capture—while his local popularity soared. On October 3, 1993, an afternoon snatch and grab operation went badly awry when the people of Mogadishu decided to fight back against the Americans. (A gripping account of the battle of the Black Sea can be found in Mark Bowden's excellent book *Black Hawk Down.*[10]) Using rocket-propelled grenades, combatants loyal to Aidid shot down two of the Black Hawk helicopters. The 120 elite soldiers and surviving Black Hawk crew members were pinned down in a firefight in the Black Sea area of Mogadishu until early the next morning. Eighteen American soldiers were killed and seventy-three were wounded. Approximately five hundred Somalis were killed and over a thousand were wounded. Somalis celebrated their victory by dragging the dead and mutilated bodies of several American GIs through the city streets. Images of this were broadcast around the world.

In terms of the number of deaths and casualties sustained by each side in the Battle of the Black Sea, the Americans did not lose. In fact, the snatch and grab operation was a success, as two senior Aidid advisers and others from Habr Gidr were arrested and detained, and the pinned-down American troops were rescued successfully by dawn on October 4. We might conclude, then, that American power was flexed successfully over the far less powerful Habr Gidr clan. In terms of tangible, measurable power capabilities, the accounting sheet would clearly present a favorable balance for the Americans. Yet we must look beyond this battle—but not very far beyond it—in order to ascertain whether this flexing of overwhelming U.S. military capability translated into observable changes in the target's behavior or circumstances. The Battle of the Black Sea did not contribute in any way to the ultimate capture of Aidid and the pacification of Somalia. Instead, the battle of the Black Sea caused the immediate reversal of U.S. policy such that Aidid was no longer a pursued criminal, his senior advisers were released, and within months the U.S. military was tasked with providing protective transport for Aidid as he traveled to a U.N.-sponsored peace conference. This change in U.S. policy took effect the day after the battle of the Black Sea, at which time the

United States also announced that it would withdraw completely from Somalia by March 1994.

Ultimately, American interests in Somalia were limited and could not be balanced against American casualties. With limited interests and limited tolerance for casualties, we can conclude that American resolve was also limited. The Somalis, on the other hand, were completely resolved against the American military presence. In terms of *this* accounting sheet, the United States was far less powerful than the Somalis. Analysts are in agreement about this: power is both tangible and intangible. Tangible power can be listed and tallied—the number of well-armed and well-trained elite troops, the number of Black Hawk helicopters and related supporting air cover, the number of armored personnel carriers, and so on—but intangible power cannot be listed and tallied nor even understood or estimated until the firefight occurs. This points to another critical characteristic of power: power is contextual and situational. Analysts can make educated guesses about how powerful one actor might be over another, but the elusive nature of intangible power and the importance of context means there can be no *final* word on which actors are more powerful and which are less until after an event has occurred.

This example pitting the power of the United States against the power of a faction within a failed state offers some insight into the "new kind of war"[11] engaged at the start of the twenty-first century and the situational nature of power. The terrorists who attacked the United States on September 11, 2001, offered a new definition of power when they turned hijacked commercial aircraft into weapons of mass destruction. Without the use of traditional weapons of any sort, these terrorists were able to launch an unprecedented attack of enormous proportions on the world's largest military power. In late 2001, the United States called up traditional state power resources to counter this attack—but as of this writing it is too soon to know how well one type of power matches up against the other. The readers of *The New Foreign Policy* will have the advantage of hindsight to examine this war between a state and a nonstate actor and determine anew what "power" is.

Early in the U.S. war against international **terrorism,** however, some events already signaled the elusive nature of American power over an informal ally, the Northern Alliance. After the George W. Bush (Bush 2) administration determined that Afghan-based Osama bin Laden and his terrorist network, Al Qaeda, were responsible for the September 11 terrorist attacks, the Bush administration demanded that the ruling Taliban regime in Afghanistan turn over its guest bin Laden. When the Taliban rejected U.S. demands, the United States initiated an air war against the Taliban. Already at war against the Taliban was the loosely organized Northern Alliance, a group that had been fighting for control of Afghanistan ever since the former government was deposed by the

Taliban in 1995. Some members of the Bush 2 administration had been reluctant to join forces with the Northern Alliance because of American-ally Pakistan's strong anti–Northern Alliance sentiments. Further, human rights organizations warned about supporting the Alliance, given its known disregard for and abuse of human rights. Indeed, when the leaders of the Alliance ruled Afghanistan from 1992 to 1995, lawlessness and instability reigned, causing the Afghan people to embrace the Taliban as a better alternative. Strong voices from many locations—inside the Bush administration, at the United Nations, and in the international community—suggested that the United States should not ally itself with this notorious group.

After several weeks of holding back air support for the Northern Alliance while it sought direction for a broad-based alternative, the Bush administration came under criticism for letting politics control its military effort. In response, the administration began coordinating air strikes with the Northern Alliance against the common enemy, the Taliban. After several weeks of this bombing, a series of cities in northern Afghanistan fell to the Northern Alliance—surprising all observers by the suddenness of the fall of the Taliban. The Bush 2 administration, aware of strong Pakistani, international, and Afghani opposition to the Northern Alliance, instructed the Northern Alliance not to enter the capital city of Kabul as the Taliban retreated from it. The American administration had decided that the military progress of the Northern Alliance needed to be slowed in order to construct a broad-based coalition of Afghanis to assume control of Kabul and, ultimately, Afghanistan. Despite the clearly expressed U.S. demand that the Northern Alliance not take control of Kabul, the Northern Alliance rolled into Kabul on November 12–13. In its seven-year fight against the Taliban, the Northern Alliance had never been able to win control of more than 10 percent of Afghani territory. But after sustaining considerable damage from U.S. air strikes, the ruling Taliban negotiated a series of surrenders with the Northern Alliance. In less than a week, the Alliance managed to take control of nearly half of the country. Despite its clear reliance on U.S. power to accomplish this task, the Northern Alliance felt under no obligation to heed the desires of the Bush administration regarding Kabul. U.S. power was instrumental to the Northern Alliance's quick victory, but the United States held no ultimate power over the Northern Alliance.

Who Gets to Be a Great Power?

Despite the previous discussion of the elusiveness of power, we continue to define great, middle, and small powers in terms of measurable power capabilities, albeit acknowledging the significance of immeasurables.

Beyond categorizing states using power capabilities, how else might we construct a ranking of more and less powerful states?

We might be inclined to use membership in certain "elite" international organizations as proof of a country's ranking and position. But such an inclination would need to be tempered by the recognition that membership may reflect the institutionalization of an historical "reality" that may no longer hold. For example, we might decide that the permanent members of the United Nations Security Council—the United States, Russia, Great Britain, France, and China—are the states that should properly be designated "great powers." These states were the victors of World War II (with the French resistance earning France its title as victor), and created for themselves a privileged position in the new United Nations with the special power of the veto. Some modifications within this group have been allowed *by the group*. For instance, the China seat was held by the Republic of China or Taiwan until 1971, when the People's Republic of China assumed that seat. Similarly, the Soviet Union was an original member of the "Big Five," but upon its dissolution its seat went to Russia and not to any of the other fourteen independent countries created out of the former Soviet Union.

These self-made modifications notwithstanding, the possibility of *adding* permanent members has been and remains a controversial topic. Other countries have become powerful actors on the world stage—and certainly are great powers using some definitions—yet remain outside permanent membership. Japan is the second largest financial contributor to the United Nations, yet it is only periodically a member of the Security Council sometimes occupying one of the ten two-year, rotating, nonpermanent seats. India is the world's largest **democracy** by population, a major participant in U.N. peacekeeping activities, *and*, just like the Big Five, it possesses nuclear weapons. Indonesia is the world's fourth largest country by population and the largest Muslim country. We could continue to name strong candidates for permanent membership and great power designation— none of which are ever likely to achieve the same status as the Big Five. Why? Because adding permanent members to the Security Council requires a change to the U.N. Charter, and all changes to the U.N. Charter require the approval of three-quarters of the General Assembly membership *and* the agreement of the Big Five. Each of the Big Five maintains opposition to the possibility of admitting certain other states to the permanent membership, and all maintain opposition to sharing the veto with any other state.

The Big Five clearly aren't the only states that could qualify as great powers, but if we determined great power status by Security Council permanent membership, this rank would be closed to others regardless of qualifications. What if we decided to use other criteria for great power designation? For example, what if possession of nuclear weapons "earns" a

Table 4.1. Some Indicators of National Wealth and Well-Being, and Nuclear
Weapons Possession, for Selected States

Country	GNP/Cap (U.S.$) 2000*	Adult Illiteracy 1999**		Nuclear Weapons
		Male	Female	
Afghanistan	178	48.1	78.1	No
Brazil	3,525	14.9	14.6	No
China	798	8.3	23.7	Yes
France	24,267	Not available		Yes
India	453	31.6	54.6	Yes
Israel	17,564	2.1	5.8	Yes
Japan	34,276	Not available		No
Pakistan	487	40.1	68.9	Yes
Russia	1,257	0.3	0.6	Yes
United Kingdom	24,323	Not available		Yes
United States	32,778	Not available		Yes
Zimbabwe	436	7.2	15.3	No

Source: U.N. Statistical Department, online:
*http://www.un.org/depts/unsd/social/inc-eco.htm
**http://www.un.org/depts/unsd/social/literacy.htm

state great power status? Then the great powers would include the United
States, Russia, Great Britain, France, China, India, Israel, and Pakistan. Yet
Pakistan—like India—is a developing country whose national wealth and
well-being are decidedly unlike *some* of the other great powers. Table 4.1
presents selected national statistics of selected states to illustrate this point.
According to Table 4.1, Pakistan's gross national product per capita in 1999
was only US$487, similar to Zimbabwe at US$436, and much unlike France
at US$24,267. Similarly, 40.1 percent of Pakistani males and 68.9 percent of
Pakistani females over the age of fifteen were considered illiterate in 2000,
comparable to its neighbor Afghanistan with 48.1 percent male illiteracy
and 78.1 percent female illiteracy. Pakistan may have the bomb, but it rates
very poorly on other tangible measures of national wealth and well-being.
    When we look at where the Big Five rank on these same indicators,
though, we run into some difficulty understanding why all of them might
be considered "great." Russia's gross national product per capita for 1999
was only US$1,257, while China's was even lower at US$798. By contrast,
Germany—a country blocked by the British for permanent Security
Council membership—had a gross national product per capita for the
same period of US$25,749, slightly higher than Britain at US$24,323.
    Ranking countries in terms of who possesses nuclear weapons or in
terms of national wealth can create more questions than may be resolved.
Should Russia and China be ranked among the great powers? The stan-

dard answer is yes, although these countries are not so "great" by economic indicators. Should India, Pakistan, and Israel be ranked among the
great powers? The standard answer is no, although these countries belong
to the exclusive club of nuclear weapons states. This leaves us again with
a certain amount of imprecision whenever we use state categories to explain related foreign policy behaviors. This imprecision is unavoidable
and nonproblematic, given that our focus at this level of analysis is more
on power *relations* than on absolute power.

Great Powers

Realists, liberals, and Marxists—with some disagreement over the
specifics—agree that the international system is defined by the number
and actions of great powers, especially their actions vis-à-vis other great
powers. What is a "great power?" The *Penguin Dictionary of International
Relations* offers this round-about description:

> In addition to military and economic strength, great powers normally
> have global if not universal interests and are usually characterized as
> possessing the political will to pursue them. The United States, for ex-
> ample, although long regarded by others as a great power, has not al-
> ways displayed the political will to behave like one, especially during
> the period until 1917 and between 1921 and 1941. It was only after the
> Second World War that the United States consistently and self-
> consciously adopted this posture.[12]

We are also told this about the origins of the concept:

> The term itself can be traced back to fifteenth-century Italian politics
> but the first time it was adopted as an orthodox diplomatic concept was
> with the signing of the Treaty of Chaumont in 1817. As a result of the
> Congress of Vienna (1815) five states, Austria, Britain, France, Prussia
> and Russia, had informally conferred on themselves great power sta-
> tus. The intention was that these states acting in concert would adopt a
> managerial role in relation to the maintenance of order in the European
> state system.[13]

Great powers, then, are states with both (extraordinarily) large military
and economic capabilities, global political interests, *and* the will to protect
and maintain those interests. The Concert of Vienna great powers named
themselves to this designation in mutual recognition of the power they
held, and they linked this designation to the job description of maintaining the European state system. These great powers did not act out of al-

truism but out of their own self-interests. Yet these interests were defined more broadly than those of other states. The desired order served their interests and required their maintenance.

Great powers use force to promote goals beyond their immediate national self-defense, and this sets them apart from the small powers. Consider Edward Luttwak's description:

> To struggle for mere survival was the unhappy predicament of threatened small powers, which had to fight purely to defend themselves and could not hope to achieve anything more with their modest strength. Great powers were different; they could only remain great if they were seen as willing and able to use force to acquire and protect even non-vital interests, including distant possessions or minor additions to their spheres of influence. To lose a few hundred soldiers in some minor probing operation of a few thousand in a small war or expeditionary venture were routine events for the great powers of history.[14]

Moreover, Luttwak adds,

> Great powers are in the business of threatening, rather than being threatened. A great power cannot be that unless it asserts all sorts of claims that far exceed the needs of its own immediate security, including the protection of allies and clients as well as other less-than-vital interests.[15]

Luttwak defines "great powers" as those states with overwhelming power resources who display "a readiness to use force whenever it [is] advantageous to do so and an acceptance of the resulting combat casualties with equanimity, as long as the number [is] not disproportionate."[16] Further, Luttwak explains that "great powers [are] strong enough to successfully wage war without calling on allies."[17]

Syndicated columnist and renowned realist Charles Krauthammer defines a major power as a state "with the military, diplomatic, political and economic assets to be a decisive player in any conflict in whatever part of the world it chooses to involve itself."[18] States that possess such power but do *not* choose to use it or only use force as part of a coalition organized and led by another state are dismissed by Krauthammer as "second rank" states.

Krauthammer also asserts that great powers do not let the interests of others, including and *particularly* allies, interfere with the pursuit of their own interests. Early in the U.S. bombing of Afghanistan designed to compel the ruling Taliban to turn over Osama bin Laden, Krauthammer loudly criticized U.S. policy on this very issue. He complained,

The war is not going well and it is time to say why. It has been fought with half-measures. It has been fought with an eye on the wishes of our "coalition partners." It has been fought to assuage the Arab "street." It has been fought to satisfy the diplomats rather than the generals.[19]

Bush military officials, perhaps in agreement with Krauthammer's sentiment, resisted using the military forces of allies in punishing the Taliban, believing that this would "hamstring" war planning and execution. Meanwhile, U.S. State Department officials and key European allies insisted that the Bush 2 administration accept the military contributions of interested allies in order to prevent the loss of international support for the Bush war on international terrorism.[20] The Krauthammer/Pentagon side would argue that great powers should not and do not let themselves be tied down by the wishes of others; the State Department side would argue that great powers need to look beyond the immediate issues of the day toward what is necessary for broader political goals.

This disagreement in the Bush 2 administration threatened to undermine the "nested game" of America's closest ally, the government of British Prime Minister Tony Blair. In mid-November 2001, Blair put four thousand to six thousand troops on forty-eight hours notice for deployment to Afghanistan to provide security in areas abandoned by the Taliban, especially Kabul the capital. This announcement caused Northern Alliance officials to voice strong disapproval of and warnings about the implications of foreign troops on Afghan soil.[21] At the same time, and more to the present point, British plans were no sooner announced then squashed by American military planners.[22] An apparent split between British and American planners about how and whether to deploy a substantial security presence in Afghanistan surfaced in the British press. This in turn prompted Blair and British Foreign Secretary Jack Straw to expend some energy denying any disagreement between the allies. The British officials made it clear that they, and French officials, believed a large security operation was necessary to facilitate humanitarian relief in Afghanistan. Yet these same officials admitted that, ultimately, it was the American commander's call to make.[23] British reputation internationally and Blair's reputation domestically were bruised by this exercise in American singular power.[24]

Not only are great powers defined by their willingness to use force, but great powers *arise* through the use of force. The great powers of the twentieth century, explains Ian Lustick, engaged in large-scale state-building wars in their formative years. Lustick expands on Charles Tilly's description of **state building** in the West, a description summarized in the idea that "war made the state, and the state made war."[25] In the European state-building experience, political units were engaged in an ongoing fight to survive. The need to raise money to field armies, necessary for basic protection and the defeat of opponents and ultimately for the acquisition of increasing amounts of territory, led the early European states to institutionalize. Taxation and conscription could only be successfully accomplished through the consolidation of internal control, and both were necessary for the consolidation of external power. Lustick asserts that European and North American states were free of international constraints such as U.N. Charter prohibitions against the use of force, and thus they were able to amass the necessary power capabilities to be strong internally and externally. The unrestricted use of force was necessary for building great power capabilities and achieving great power status. By the twentieth century, international prohibitions against such use of unrestricted force—prohibitions designed by the existing great powers—kept other great powers from rising in places such as the Middle East.[26]

This last idea is critical to understanding the foreign policy behavior of great powers. Great powers use force not only to become great powers but also to guard against the possibility of other great powers arising. Recall from above Luttwak's proposition: "Great powers are in the business of threatening, rather than being threatened."[27] Great powers employ what scholars call "grand strategies" to manage threats, actively perusing the global system to identify potential threats and proactively constructing the means to protect vital interests.[28]

Such grand strategy often entails denying potential great powers the means to launch a significant challenge, and traditionally a policy of denial entails the use of force. Unique to great power behavior in the twentieth century, however, was the use of force in tandem with the construction of *global* international organizations such as the United Nations. These institutions and their attendant principles locked other states into "antibelligerency norms" that, in turn, limited the ability of these states to amass sufficient power capabilities to challenge the established great powers.[29] Thus, while the European and North American great powers, as well as China and Japan to some extent, used war to increase their land and resource holdings and make them great powers, the norms and institutions established by the (Western) great powers in the twentieth century denied other countries this same route to greatness.

Indeed, twentieth-century institutions and norms, particularly those embodied in the U.N. system, have been used *to justify* the use of force by great powers against potential challengers. For example, Iraq's invasion of Kuwait in 1990 resulted from the inability of the two countries to reach agreement on key points of contention. Central to their dispute were terms of the repayment of debts incurred by Iraq to Kuwait during the decade-long Iraq-Iran war. When the Iraqi leader Saddam Hussein could not persuade Kuwait to more agreeable repayment terms, he decided to settle differences with Kuwait through invasion and occupation. Perhaps

A PLAN TO ERASE THE MODERN MAP OF THE MIDDLE EAST

In the aftermath of the terrorist attacks on the United States on September 11, 2001, many analysts have attempted to understand what motivated the man who was charged with responsibility for them, Osama bin Laden. *Los Angeles Times* diplomatic correspondents Ronald Brownstein and Robin Wright present an analysis of bin Laden that echoes important points in Ian Lustick's explanation of why there are no Middle Eastern great powers.

Brownstein and Wright explain that bin Laden "may dream of erasing the modern map of the Middle East." The existing map was designed by the Western countries as a way to divide the Middle East "into small and little countries." The reason for such division was to prevent the reemergence of a Middle Eastern great power. Bin Laden's goal is to re-create the "modern equivalent of the caliphate that provided an early form of Islamic government after the death of the prophet Muhammad in the 7th century."

The current governments of the Middle East are both weak and corrupted by the West, and so their removal is essential to bin Laden's grand dream. But bin Laden has not aimed his primary attacks against the Arab regimes because these regimes are propped up by the power of the United States. In a 1996 *fatwa*, bin Laden argued that war with the Arab regimes would have only one end result because the "occupier forces will control the outcome of the battle." The only way to establish an Islamic great power is to first eliminate the presence of the United States in the Middle East. The 1998 bombings of the American embassies in Kenya and Tanzania, the 2000 attack on the USS *Cole* in the Yemeni port, and the September 11 attacks were aimed at driving out the Western power that maintains illegitimate Middle Eastern regimes, thereby preventing the rise of an Islamic great power.

References
Brownstein, Ronald, and Robin Wright. "Toppling of Arab Regimes Called Wider Goal of Terror." *Los Angeles Times*, October 5, 2001, A1.

the Iraqi leader had in mind the U.S. invasion of Panama in December 1989 after the U.S. government could not get the Panamanian leader Manuel Noriega to comply with American wishes. The Iraqi invasion of Kuwait, however, was condemned by the members of the United Nations as a violation of key principles of the U.N. system. When Iraq refused to comply with U.N. demands to vacate Kuwait, the U.N. Security Council gave its blessing to the United States and a multinational coalition to use force against Iraq to compel it to act by the established rules.

This description of great powers thus far is essentially derived from realist accounts, but we need only modify it slightly to make it read as a Marxist account or an account positing that economic interests are primary to understanding foreign policy choices. Marxists would argue that states described as great powers are the product of global elite economic interests. Global economic elites—acting through their agents the states—form a global **core** or **centre** that protects established wealth and assists in the acquisition of even greater wealth. International institutions are built by this rich club to impose restrictions on others that serve to keep them in a dependent relationship with the elite. Any time states on the **periphery** attempt to challenge this system—or gain entrance into the rich club—international organizations are used to punish the challengers. The use of U.N. principles to justify the war against Iraq is an example of this in play.

Similarly, great powers impose relationships on lesser powers that serve to undermine the consolidation of power and **legitimacy** *within* those states, thereby establishing the need for the continued presence of powerful external actors in the domestic affairs of those weak regimes. To protect British access to Kuwaiti oil, Britain formed a patron–client relationship with the Kuwaiti monarchy in 1899 that lasted off and on until the early 1960s. In this, Britain secured its oil interests and British troops guaranteed the security of the Kuwaiti regime from *both* external and internal threats.[30] The **cliency relationship** between Britain and Kuwait is discussed in detail below under the heading "Small Powers."

The patron–client relationship between the United States and Saudi Arabia serves as another example, one with serious implications for September 11, 2001, and beyond. The cliency relationship between these two states goes back to World War II when the Franklin Delano Roosevelt administration sought to secure access to Saudi oil supplies. Michael Klare suggests that this relationship constitutes the "roots" of the terrorist attacks of September 11. This relationship was also seen as crucial to American post–World War II power:

> American strategists considered access to oil to be especially important because it was an essential factor in the Allied victory over the Axis powers. Although the nuclear strikes on Hiroshima and Nagasaki ended the war, it was oil that fueled the armies that brought

Germany and Japan to their knees. Oil powered the vast number of ships, tanks and aircraft that endowed Allied forces with a decisive edge over their adversaries. . . . It was widely assumed, therefore, that access to large supplies of oil would be critical to U.S. success in any future conflicts.[31]

Roosevelt administration planners scanned the globe for sufficient oil reserves to guarantee U.S. and European needs and future prosperity. They decided that Middle East oil reserves fit the bill. As Klare describes,

In one of the most extraordinary occurrences in modern American history, President Roosevelt met with King Abd al-Aziz Ibn Saud, the founder of the modern Saudi regime, on a U.S. warship in the Suez Canal following the February 1945 conference in Yalta. Although details of the meeting have never been made public, it is widely believed that Roosevelt gave the King a promise of U.S. protection in return for privileged American access to oil—an arrangement that remains in full effect today and constitutes the essential core of the U.S.-Saudi relationship.[32]

In return for such access, the United States extended a security guarantee to the House of Saud, promising protection from external and internal challengers. The Iraqi invasion of neighboring Kuwait posed a serious external military threat, which the United States answered with a massive military response known as the Gulf War. Internal threats to the Saudi government are managed by the Saudi Arabian National Guard. The National Guard "protects the kingdom from its internal enemies and guards important strategic facilities, such as oil installations."[33] Training the National Guard, as of 2001, was the job of a Virginia-based U.S. military consulting firm, whose paid advisers included former President George H. W. Bush and his secretary of state, James Baker.[34] Through the use of private U.S.-based military and security firms, the United States promotes continued Saudi dependency.

This dependency is further demonstrated in Saudi arms imports from the United States. According the journalist Aram Roston, as of 2001, Saudi Arabia was the world's largest arms importer; weapons constituted some 40 percent of Saudi import dollars.[35] Roston asserts, "The U.S. philosophy is to guarantee the kingdom's safety while also making sure the Saudis buy the best of everything, at top dollar." The deepening military entanglements with the United States and the growing external debt of the Saudi regime is said to cause deep resentment among the Saudi people, including former Saudi citizen Osama bin Laden. Following a pattern used by Britain in its relationship with Kuwait, Iraq, and Iran until mid-twentieth century, the United States and Saudi Arabia find themselves in a mutually advantageous and mutually troublesome relationship.

From a perspective that privileges economics as the primary explanation of all international relations, the cliency relationship between the United States and Saudi Arabia is a clear demonstration of how great powers will use whatever means necessary to maintain their wealth, with clear disregard for the implications such a policy has on others. The internal legitimacy of the Saudi regime—as measured in popular support—is of no consequence to the United States; what counts is U.S. access to Saudi oil. After September 11, this argument is given further support: even an attack on U.S. territory whose roots can be found in the U.S.-Saudi relationship has not altered that relationship in any way.

One need not believe that money is behind all foreign policy choices to agree with the observation that core countries exploit the internal and external weaknesses of the periphery and constantly watch for new avenues through which to maintain the dependency of weaker states. Middle Eastern scholar Fouad Ajami describes a persistent suspicion held in the Arab world regarding the Gulf War and its aftermath:

All around Iraq, the region was poorer; oil prices had slumped, and the war had been expensive for the oil states that financed it. Oil states suspected they were being overbilled for military services and for weapons that they could not afford. The war's murky outcome fed the belief that the thing had been rigged all along, that Saddam Hussein had been lured into Kuwait by an American green light— and then kept in power and let off the hook—so that Pax Americana would have the pretext for stationing its forces in the region.[36]

To sum up our discussion thus far, great powers are states with enormous power capabilities and the demonstrated willingness to use those capabilities whenever necessary. Great powers are especially attuned to potential threats to their status and constantly guard against rising powers. Even allies might restrain great powers from doing what they must do, and so a watch must be kept on allies as well as challengers. Allies and challengers alike are constrained by the web of institutions used by great powers that lock countries into a status quo that feeds the military and economic power of these great powers.

The Unique Case of the United States

From 1945 to approximately 1989, the international system was described as a **bipolar system**. Prior to 1945, the international system was described as a **multipolar system**. When we describe these international systems in these ways, we assert that the number of and relationships between the major or central powers defines global politics. A bipolar system has two great centers of power led by two major powers. A multipolar system has three or more major powers—classical realists would say such a system must have five powers to be a properly functioning balance of power system. With an understanding of the number of major powers, one can make assumptions about the roles and foreign policy behaviors of these states *and all other states* within the system.

At the conclusion of the Cold War that characterized the 1945–1989 bipolar system, foreign policy makers and foreign policy scholars began deliberating what the shape of the "new world order" would be. There was agreement that, after the collapse of the Soviet Union, there was only one superpower remaining in the world. The emerging issue was what would be the nature of the relationship between the single superpower and the other international actors, especially between the United States and the great powers (who were relegated to secondary status by the rise of the United States and former Soviet Union to "superpower" status). One view was that the United States would not stay on top of a **unipolar** world system, but that the system would become multipolar. The view that multipolarity would be reestablished derives from the neorealist assumption that great powers will attempt to balance the power of any state that seeks to achieve predominance. This assumption is examined with reference to the foreign policies of the United States, the Western states collectively, France, Germany, Russia, Japan, and China in a volume entitled *Unipolar Politics: Realism and State Strategies after the Cold War*. The editors of this volume, Ethan Kapstein and Michael Mastanduno, conclude that in the assembled assessments there is "little evidence of military balancing by the major powers of Europe and Asia against the world's only superpower."[37] Instead, they note:

> What is most striking, in the context of neorealist balance-of-power theory, is the reluctance of other major powers to engage in an individual or collective strategy of balancing against the preponderant power of the United States in an effort to create an alternative international order.[38]

Thus, they conclude, "a principal foreign policy challenge for each of the states analyzed, including the United States, is to adjust their strategies to the emergence and possible endurance of a unipolar distribution of power."[39]

Understanding the foreign policy of major powers requires understanding the **grand strategy** they employ. A grand strategy is a global vision and set of operating principles framing a major power's foreign policy. According to Christopher Layne,

> Grand strategies must be judged by the amount of security they provide; whether, given international systemic constraints, they are sus-

tainable; their cost; the degree of risk they entail; and their tangible and intangible domestic effects.[40]

To understand the strategic options available to the United States as the single superpower, we must understand American grand strategy pursued in the previous international system. One part of the American grand strategy post-1945 was defined by the Cold War competition with the Soviet Union. This should be familiar to the reader, and I will not discuss it in detail here, but move on to explore the other part of American grand strategy post-1945. American foreign policy elites concluded that World War II, like World War I, arose because of restrictive trading policies among major actors that impeded the collective ability to "grow" economies and amass wealth. American policy makers undertook to eliminate the causes of major power war by creating a global **liberal economic regime** to support a **global free trade system**. The assumption behind this policy was clear—every country could do better *together* and avoid great power war if they traded freely and openly with other countries. The American grand strategy that focused on the Soviet Union and the Communist threat was embedded in a realist framework, but the American strategy devoted to the construction of a global free trade system was embedded in a liberal worldview. These are not necessarily contradictory impulses. The liberal view is that states can and should pursue their own national interest, *but* these interests are *best* pursued in cooperation with other states. The United States can "win" and other countries can "win" by participating in a global free trade system. The causes of previous great power wars are thus eliminated as the major powers (and others) grow rich together and are ever more bound together through free trade. At the same time, those who threaten this vision of global free trade—during the Cold War the Soviet Union and its communist allies—need to be treated as unfriendly obstacles.

Benjamin Schwarz argues that building and maintaining a global free trade system required the United States to convince the major powers (on the Western side of the Cold War) that their interests could be blended profitably together. Germany and Japan were special targets for U.S. policy, as these countries had waged wars on other countries *because* they had been excluded from the fruits of previous international systems.

Schwarz posits that American policy makers "knew that an open world economy demanded an even more ambitious American project: transforming international relations."[41] This transformation meant dealing with the threat of (re)nationalization. Working on realist assumptions, policy makers believed that

in its efforts to ensure the distribution of power in its favor and at the expense of actual or potential rivals, a state will "nationalize"—that is, pursue autarkic policies, practicing capitalism only within its borders or among countries in a trading bloc.[42]

Creating a liberal world order meant guarding against the possibility that one or more major powers might turn away from the cooperative union in pursuit of narrow national interests. Schwarz contends that the United States decided that if it were to pay the costs of security for the major powers—especially Germany and Japan, but all the others as well—it would be able to keep these powers happy with the system *and* keep them in the system. The United States would "relieve" these countries of the burden of high defense costs, thereby "relieving" them of the military capacity to return to individualistic great power behavior. In Schwarz's words, the United States would "protect the interests of virtually all potential great powers so that they need not acquire the capability to protect themselves—that is, so those powers need not act like great powers."[43]

This grand strategy would entail clear costs for the United States, but it would gain in the long run as the global economy flourished. In Europe, the foreign policy behavior associated with this strategy was the establishment of a strong U.S. military presence in Europe through the North Atlantic Treaty Organization. NATO would constrain the European states from pursuing unilateral foreign policies, while pulling Germany firmly into the fold. In Asia, the United States established a significant military presence in Japan, while the Japanese government developed a national security policy that was founded primarily on a U.S.-Japanese defense arrangement. Christopher Layne—a critic of this strategy—sums up it up this way: "The logic of the strategy is that interdependence is the paramount interest the strategy promotes; instability is the threat to interdependence; and extended deterrence is the means by which the strategy deals with this threat."[44]

In a post–Cold War continuation of this American grand strategy, American policy makers declared that American predominance was still necessary to maintaining the liberal economic order, and even an end goal in and of itself. Key to this continuing grand strategy was keeping the world's other major powers from "ever aspiring to a larger regional or global role," as Schwarz quotes from a 1992 Pentagon Defense Planning Guidance paper.[45] The American role would be to guard against anything that would threaten international relations, while providing "adult supervision" to the other major powers.[46]

Both Schwarz and Layne warn that this grand strategy is too costly to maintain for very long. Schwarz worries about the expense of a strategy that allows and encourages other states to grow economically at the expense of the superpower. Layne worries about both expense and the problem of "strategic overextension." That is, this grand strategy requires the United States to actively address threats to the international order whether these occur in the core or periphery.[47] The danger of this is twofold: (1) the United States could become engaged militarily in far too many peripheral areas, stretching itself too thin and draining its resources; or (2) the United States might falsely promise extended **deterrence** and then fail to become involved in problem zones, thereby undermining its credibility to become involved anywhere.

After the terrorist attacks of September 11, Schwarz and Layne—writing together—suggest that a third danger in this grand strategy had revealed itself: "Those who undertook [the terrorist attacks] acted with cool calculation to force the United States to alter specific policies—policies that largely flow from the global role America has chosen." Schwarz and Layne intone,

> We need to come to grips with an ironic possibility: that the very preponderance of American power may now make us not more secure but less secure. By the same token, it may actually be possible to achieve more of our foreign policy goals by means of a diminished global presence.[48]

The lesson they take from the attacks of September 11: the United States does not need to remain predominant and engaged in the world. Instead, the United States should disengage and "pass the buck" for maintaining the international system to others.

Not all analysts have reached the same conclusions—before or after September 11. The dissolution of the Soviet Union and the resurgent U.S. economy of the 1990s suggested to other analysts that this American grand strategy was not impractical after all. The demise of Soviet-led communism as the only significant challenger to the American liberal economic vision, the rush of Communist China to join the World Trade Organization, and the strength of the U.S. economy vis-à-vis all other national economies helped consolidate the U.S. vision of a global free trade system at the end of the twentieth century. The post-1945 American grand strategy paid off and its vision—what we now call globalization—had become reality by century's end.

The pace of globalization, its apparent inevitability, and the nature of U.S. global predominance at century's end led some analysts to propose that U.S. unipolarity might not be transitory or even perceived as threatening by the other major, but less powerful, countries. For example, Josef Joffe argues that U.S. policy aimed at creating a global free trade system has manufactured an enduring state of affairs in which the United States will be able to maintain its position as sole superpower. Joffe proposes that American foreign policy has created a situation in which other major powers may not want to challenge the United States. "America is different," Joffe writes.

It irks and domineers, but it does not conquer. It tries to call the shots
and bend the rules, but it does not go to war for land and glory. . . .
Those who coerce or subjugate others are far more likely to inspire
hostile alliances than nations that contain themselves, as it were.[49]

Borrowing Joseph Nye's phrase, Joffe proposes that the United States has
a monopoly on **soft power**. "This type of power—a culture that radiates
outward and a market that draws inward—rests on pull, not on push; on
acceptance, not on conquest. Worse, this kind of power cannot be aggre-
gated, nor can it be balanced."[50]

Much of U.S. foreign policy activity since 1945 was devoted to international institution building. These institutions were, for the most part, independent of the Cold War American grand strategy. Instead, these
institutions were fundamental to the building of the world order envisioned by the United States. Even the institutions that had been directly
tied into the Cold War strategy—NATO particularly—survived the Cold
War era and transformed themselves into promoters and protectors of the
globalization project. Joffe's position is that "the genius of American diplomacy in the second half of [the twentieth] century was building institutions
that would advance American interests by serving others. Who can count
the acronyms made in the USA—from NATO to GATT, from the OECD to
the PfP?"[51] At the start of the twenty-first century, what bothers other major powers like Russia is not that NATO exists but that Russia has not been
invited to join. Similarly, Communist China, unlike the former Soviet
Union, has not offered an ideological alternative to international capitalism
but has worked hard to gain membership in the World Trade Organization
(WTO). Globalization—the realization of American post–World War II liberal grand strategy—reinforces the American vision and maintains American dominance. The best U.S. foreign policy position in such a situation,
according to Joffe, is to maintain support for the institutions that facilitate
globalization, while maintaining "better relations with all possible con-
tenders than they do among each other."[52]

American Foreign Policy under George W. Bush

This prescription to remain engaged with the world, giving firm support to the institutions created by the United States, characterized the
George H. W. Bush (Bush 1) and Bill Clinton administrations. But the
pre–September 11 George W. Bush (Bush 2) administration appeared to be
following a much different regimen. This administration announced that
it would review a number of "flawed" international treaties and agreements, unilaterally withdrawing from those that did not fit an America-
first worldview. The Kyoto Protocol on global warming was one of the
first from which the Bush administration extricated the United States.

Protocols on biological and chemical weapons were also to be reviewed with the goal of "untying" the hands of the United States—and this remained the policy after the terrorist attacks of September 11, 2001. The 1972 Antiballistic Missile (ABM) Treaty between the United States and Soviet Union/Russia was also to be abrogated, regardless of Russian views on the subject. The administration wanted to proceed with building a missile defense that many critics proclaimed both a practical impossibility and a move that would destabilize mature **nuclear deterrence.** Even after these critics pointed out that the September 11 attacks could not have been prevented by missile defense, the Bush 2 administration stayed wedded to the program and announced in December 2001 that the six-month notice for American withdrawal would begin in January 2002.

Similarly dismaying allies, the Bush administration announced early on that it would withdraw troops from Europe, especially from NATO peacekeeping operations there. This announcement was tempered by qualifications offered by Secretary of State Colin Powell, although into the fall 2001 the administration had yet to name anyone to manage peacekeeping issues in the State Department or National Security Council. In mid-December 2001, Secretary of Defense Donald Rumsfeld indicated that a withdrawal from peacekeeping operations in Europe was still on the agenda and now critical to the war on international terrorism. Rumsfeld criticized NATO peacekeeping efforts in Bosnia, calling the use of military forces for such "not an effective use of NATO's valuable military assets, putting an increasing strain on both our forces and our resources when they face growing demands from critical missions in the war on terrorism."[53] The goal remained the same for the Bush 2 administration—withdraw U.S. troops from Europe—but the reasoning took on a different shape after September 11.

Similarly, the Bush 2 administration put a damper on (some would say derailed) Korean unification talks—a blow to ally South Korea—when it repudiated and denigrated North Korean peace efforts in the spring and summer 2001. On the Israeli–Palestinian divide, Bush officials announced that the United States wanted peace in the Middle East but would not remained engaged in diplomatic efforts as long as the parties themselves made no progress; meanwhile, the violence between the sides grew worse. The Bush 2 administration would only begin to reengage in the Middle East in late fall–early winter 2001 when the conflict threatened to disrupt the larger war on terrorism, and then its reengagement had no discernible results. And the administration left the United Nations waiting for more than half a year to learn who the new U.S. ambassador would be.

The September 11, 2001, terrorist attacks on the United States caused the Bush 2 administration to take another look at the world. As of this writing at the start of 2002, we can say that the terrorist attacks did not cause the administration to become any more committed to **multilateral-**

ism, but it did shift from being an almost entirely inward-focused presidency to one almost exclusively focused on the war on international terrorism. **Unilateralism** remained the key operating mode, although the United States would fully expect others to fall in line behind it. The United States would call the shots of any "international" policy and those who were or wanted to be friends would need to line up in support.

This new foreign policy orientation was made clear in two public addresses given by George W. Bush in the aftermath of September 11. First, in his September 20, 2001, address to a joint session of Congress, Bush declared:

Figure 4.1.   Facing the Global Threat

Before the terrorist attacks of September 11, 2001, the Bush 2 administration had been following a "go-it-alone," isolationist foreign policy. This policy was met with dismay around the world. After September 11, George W. Bush declared that other countries were either with the United States or against it in the American-led war on international terrorism. In this cartoon, Tom Toles depicts a change in perspective in the Bush 2 White House.

Every nation, in every region, now has a decision to make. Either you are with us, or you are with the terrorists. From this day forward, any nation that continues to harbor or support terrorism will be regarded by the United States as a hostile regime.

In an address to the U.N. General Assembly on November 10, 2001, Bush warned:

In this war of terror, each of us must answer for what we have done or what we have left undone. After tragedy, there is a time for sympathy and condolence. And my country has been very grateful for both. The memorials and vigils around the world will not be forgotten. But the time for sympathy has now passed. The time for action has now arrived.

We're asking for a comprehensive commitment to this fight. We must unite in opposing all terrorists, not just some of them. In this world, there are good causes and bad causes, and we may disagree on where that line is drawn. Yet there is no such thing as a good terrorist. No national aspiration, no remembered wrong can ever justify the deliberate murder of the innocent. Any government that rejects this principle, trying to pick and choose its terrorist friends, will know the consequences.

Although the Bush 2 administration clearly threatened punishment for not cooperating with the United States, it was also ready to reward states that did cooperate. In a variation on the realist-based, early Bush 2 administration theme of freeing the United States from international commitments, two weeks after the terrorist attacks Bush

asked Congress to waive all existing restrictions on U.S. military assistance and weapons exports for the next five years to any country if he determines the aid will help the fight against international terrorism.

The waiver would cover those nations currently ineligible for U.S. military aid because of their sponsorship of terrorism, such as Syria and Iran, or because of their nuclear and offensive-weapons programs or lack of commitment to democracy, which would include Pakistan and China.[54]

The allies to be rewarded for their participation in the war against international terrorism would *not* be long-term allies, though. Long-term commitments were not envisioned in the Bush 2 grand strategy even after September 11. Instead, the administration wanted to be free to pick allies to fit particular operational aspects of what Secretary of Defense Donald Rumsfeld called "a new kind of war." In a *New York Times* op-ed piece of the same name, Rumsfeld announced:

This war will not be waged by a grand alliance united for the single purpose of defeating an axis of hostile powers. Instead, it will involve floating coalitions of countries, which may change and evolve. Countries will have different roles and contribute in different ways. Some will help us publicly, while others, because of their circumstances, may help us privately and secretly. In this war, the mission will define the coalition—not the other way around.[55]

The "floating coalitions" used to prosecute the war on international terrorism (the Bush 2 war) would not resemble the celebrated multinational coalition of the Gulf War (the Bush 1 war). In the Gulf War, the coalition was carefully pieced together and the war was conducted with the full consent and advice of key allies. Bush 1 was a multilateral-minded administration. Not only would coalitions be formed to fit the operational needs of the United States in the Bush 2 war, but allies would be restricted in their contributions and full authority would retain in U.S. command.

How might we explain Bush 2 foreign policy in terms of grand strategy if this administration did/does not seem to be following the post–World War II American strategy? Writing in 1997, Christopher Layne argued that American foreign policy should embrace a different grand strategy,[56] one that expressly rejected the notion of global predominance and the costs of playing the role of "adult supervisor." In the post-September 11 reassessments of American foreign policy, Layne reasserts his argument in conjunction with Benjamin Schwarz.[57] The grand strategy that Layne and Schwarz advocate appears to be the grand strategy of the Bush 2 administration: offshore balancing.

The strategy of offshore balancing is based on the assumption that multipolarity is inevitable and that ultimately other great powers will attempt to balance against the power of the United States. The use of U.S. power to deny incentives to other great powers to develop their own great power capabilities is self-defeating and thus the United States should abandon its half-century-old policy of protecting the interests of other significant actors around the world. Instead,

because of its insularity, the United States can stand aloof from others' security competitions and engage in "bystanding" and "buck-passing" behavior, thereby forcing others to assume the risks and costs of antihegemonic balancing. When an offshore balancer shifts to others the dangers entailed by "going first," it can reasonably hope that it may never have to become involved.[58]

Layne proposes that such a strategy involves the narrow definition of U.S. national interests "in terms of defending the United States' territorial integrity and preventing the rise of a Eurasian hegemon."[59] Narrow national interests would allow the United States to disengage from its military commitments in Europe, Japan, and South Korea. Bush 2 feelings about U.S. troops in Europe have already been discussed; similarly, before September 11, the administration had been putting enormous pressure on Japan to assume more of its own defense burden *and* to participate in the development of the administration's favorite defense project, national missile defense. The Korean peninsula appeared to be the only "regular" troop deployment favored by the Bush 2 policy planners.

Layne further contends that offshore balancing "would abandon the ideological pretensions embedded in the strategy of preponderance"[60]—a statement that mirrors the Bush 2 campaign statement that the United States needed to be more "humble" in its foreign policy. As part of this abandonment of pretensions, the offshore balancer "would not assertively export democracy, engage directly in **peace enforcement** operations, attempt to save 'failed states' (like Somalia and Haiti), or use military power for the purpose of **humanitarian intervention.**"[61] George W. Bush's disdain for **nation building** was famous in his campaign for the White House and persisted in terms of U.S. policy in post-Taliban Afghanistan.

The goal of offshore balancing is to amass and retain resources for the benefit of the United States and not for the benefit of some broader U.S.-inspired vision for the world. Rather than keep other great powers dependent on the United States, the United States should allow the European Union, Germany, Russia, Japan, and China to develop their own great power military capabilities. The promotion of national missile defense (NMD) by Bush 2 was based on the strong suggestion that these countries would not be threatened by NMD. For example, in the beginning of September 2001, National Security Adviser Condoleezza Rice explained that the administration needed to be realistic about Chinese nuclear policies, that "modernization" was already under way and that some buildup in the Chinese arsenal and even Chinese testing of nuclear weapons would be acceptable to the administration. This "realistic" policy stand would help to overcome Chinese opposition to the administration's proposed NMD.[62] Although loud criticism of this policy caused some "restatement" by the administration within days, the administration insisted that it was only "recognizing the strategic reality."[63]

Offshore balancing does not require **isolationism,** but it is founded on the importance of retaining a "free hand strategically: although it might need to enter into temporary coalitions, the United States would disengage from permanent **alliance** relationships."[64] Here Layne's idea seems to be the basis for the Rumsfeld notion of "floating coalitions" discussed above. Indeed, the Bush 2 grand strategy fits exactly the strategy of offshore balancing offered in 1997 by Layne and by Schwarz and Layne post-September 11. These analysts argue that this is precisely the strategy for security needed by the United States in this new kind of world. They write, "America will sacrifice some of the awe with which it is viewed by the world. But less awe and less influence will bring the United States more security."[65]

A Cautionary Word on American Foreign Policy in the Twenty-first Century

We should not turn this discussion of American foreign policy in the twenty-first century into a more generalized discussion of major power foreign policy. Before the September 11 attacks on the United States it was correct to say that the global system had become unlike anything encountered before historically: the "rules" of the system had changed too fundamentally, and no state in the history of the world had ever become so singularly predominant.

Given the events of September 11, 2001, and beyond, we also must note that the discussion presented here about the unique case of the United States is somewhat limited in its focus. This discussion has been premised on the idea of an international *state* system in which states and their supported international forums and organizations are the primary international actors of note. The terrorist attacks on the United States remind us that the world contains other actors, some of which do not play by the same rules nor even play the same "game." How different is the "game" demonstrated by September 11? Since the Japanese attack on Pearl Harbor on December 11, 1941, no state has determined that attacking the territory of the United States would be worth the costs that such an attack would ultimately incur. Yet, on September 11, a loosely knit terrorist organization did what no state would consider doing and attacked civilian and military targets on U.S. territory. Further, this group carried out this amazingly brazen act by turning commercial aircraft into weapons of mass destruction. States are still the dominant actors in the world post–September 11, 2001, but it would be foolish to consider nonstate actors as peripheral to the main stage of world politics any longer.

Just as the terrorists seem to have rewritten global politics, the lone superpower is also rewriting its interests and behaviors in this "new world order." As of this writing, it is too soon to say what form post–September 11 American foreign policy will take, although America's dominance in standard categories of state power and its predominantly unilateral use of such power will figure prominently into this shifted international landscape. What we cannot say at this time with any degree of certainty is whether standard power resources match up well against the "power" of nonstate actors who do not seem bound by the standard rules. These same actors may not even be "playing the game" with the same endpoint in mind, since it comes as no surprise to anyone that the United States, having been attacked, will attempt to annihilate the source of that attack. State actors, we can safely say, avoid foreign policy actions that might lead to annihilation. The terrorists who attacked the United States appear to be unconcerned with this potential endgame. In the next chapter of *The New Foreign Policy*, we'll return again to the foreign policy challenges posed by nonstate actors.

Secondary Powers

The category of secondary powers is amorphous and instantly presents us with some conceptual problems. We'll use "secondary powers" to designate countries who have sufficient resources and power to sit near the top of the international hierarchy of states but, for different reasons, do not sit precisely at the top. Since the rise of the United States and the former Soviet Union as "superpowers," this secondary category has included some very powerful states—such as Great Britain and France, two nuclear weapons states with permanent membership in the U.N. Security Council—and some relatively powerful states—such as Canada and Australia. The inclusion of Great Britain and France suggests that this category includes all the great powers *except* the United States, as well as includes some countries that have never been characterized as "great powers." All of this makes our use of the term "great power" in the previous section problematic but not something easily resolvable in this book! Instead, keep in mind the previous discussion of "great power" politics applies to great powers historically as well as to current great powers, as conceptualized in abstract, general terms. Admittedly, these are not intellectually satisfying categories.

Secondary states, we might say, are the ones that occupy a middle range between superpowers and the smallest powers. As indicated above, we can include great powers in this category. Secondary powers also include what we might call regional powers and middle powers. Secondary powers sometimes lack the complete "bundle" of power requisites to be central, major, or "super" powers—such as Japan, whose military capacities are limited by its Peace Constitution, or Russia, whose internal instability and economic weakness relegate it to secondary status.

What foreign policies are associated with secondary status? Charles Krauthammer suggests that in foreign policy, secondary powers stand behind the great powers—or the relevant single great power with which they are aligned. Standing behind the great power can mean being a good supporter, but Krauthammer's view is less kind as he depicts the secondary powers as passive about international affairs, needing to be threatened and bribed by the United States to take an active role in international problem solving, as in the days leading up to the 1991 Persian Gulf War.[66] In other words, given the choice, Krauthammer's secondary powers are or would choose to be free riders in the international system.

Scholars who study "middle powers" would disagree strongly with this assessment. Later in this chapter we take up an extended discussion of middle powers, so suffice it now to say that middle powers are secondary powers whose primary foreign policy behaviors are aimed at maintaining international order. Middle powers, like Krauthammer's second-rank powers, follow the relevant great power, but they do so willingly and with alacrity.

Some secondary powers are countries that have decided to forgo the pursuit of great power status for a variety of reasons. For example, Japan is a country of considerable economic strength but limited military capacity. This imbalance of power results from Japan's 1956 Peace Constitution, in which Japan renounced the use of force in the pursuit of foreign policy goals. Politically, Japan has been content to play key follower to the United States in global affairs. Militarily, Japan relies on its special defense arrangement with the United States and on the U.N. collective security system for protection. Although political and military avenues to great power status are closed off to Japan (or closed off *by* Japan, depending on one's perspective), it does pursue economic great power status. This is particularly manifested in Japanese trade policy vis-à-vis the United States. Eric Heginbotham and Richard Samuels suggest that, in its pursuit of economic goals, Japan poses a significant challenge to the United States, as other commentators have warned.[67] Politically and militarily Japan agrees to occupy a secondary status, but economically it pursues great power status.[68] Scholars have some difficulty categorizing a state such as Japan because of its split personality on standard power indicators.[69]

France and Germany provide more examples of states that have accepted secondary status, primarily as a way to check the great power aspiration of one another and perhaps to achieve some extraordinary status *together*. Michael Loriaux proposes that both countries pursued a policy of geopolitical **internationalism** in the aftermath of World War II and on the path to European Union. Essentially, Loriaux's idea is that both countries pursued realist policies based on geostrategic interests, but both decided that the best way to pursue power politics was through cooperation, or internationalism. This geopolitical internationalism bound Germany and France into a supranational Europe, thereby denying either or both singular great power status, while ensuring their mutually supported pursuit of key national interests and collective status enhancement. As Loriaux explains:

> The Germans showed generally strong support for [European] multilateralism, but only because those arrangements provided the most expeditious way to regain the equality of status with the victorious

powers and curry Western support for territorial reunification. France, however, continued to work to institutionalize its cartel relationship with Germany and to construct a viable European rival to the Atlantic alliance, because this was the most expeditious way to maximize control over the way Germany used its resources.[70]

For France, especially, the pursuit of European integration was seen as the most effective way to keep a watch on its enduring rival, Germany. For both countries, European integration or union was a means by which great power status could be achieved collectively when individual great power status was unachievable. From this, we might say that secondary powers are countries that cannot singly achieve great power status and so are willing to (permanently?) trade away that goal in exchange for collective empowerment.

Japan, France, and Germany pursue limited realist goals because of the different constraints that deny them individual great power status. This limited, prudent realism does not result in behavior that threatens the major power's—in this case American—interests. Russia, on the other hand, might serve as an example of a secondary power that does threaten the United States and the international system *in order to* **leverage** greater status than its power capacities merit. Secondary states may challenge the great powers (or the single superpower as is the present case) and the international system in order to gain admission into the great power ranks (as in the example of Iraq's invasion of Kuwait in 1990 or Japan's wars with Russia at the dawn of the twentieth century),[71] or in order to obtain disproportionate influence in international or regional affairs. Neil MacFarlane explains the confrontational foreign policy of Russia in the late 1990s as an effort by Russia to assert itself as a great power even as its many internal weaknesses would suggest that it was no more than a paper tiger. This strategy worked—more or less—for Russia because of those very internal weaknesses. Western fears of a total Russian collapse caused the West to placate and otherwise attempt to support the Russian government. Knowing how much fear the West held about a failed Russian state gave Russia inordinate leverage over the West and allowed it to pursue unsavory policies in its own region without worry of condemnation, punishment, or impediment.[72]

From this discussion it should be clear that there is no commonly accepted definition and pattern of behavior attributed to secondary powers. In many ways, this conceptual incompleteness results from the realist preoccupation with great powers and the Marxist preoccupation with those states composing the powerful core. This discussion should also suggest that some of the countries we might call "secondary" are really members of the great power rank or the core.

British, French, German, Japanese, Russian, Canadian, and Australian foreign policy makers have far more in common with American policy makers than they do with states in less privileged economic circumstances. Like the United States, these secondary powers have far greater control over the direction of their foreign and domestic policies than do smaller powers as a direct result of their individual and collective wealth and power. We might imagine a line separating these powerful states from most of the world's states (designated below as "small powers"), a line that divides greater from lesser wealth, greater from lesser power, and greater from lesser control over foreign and domestic policy. On one side of the line, policy makers play a more or less distinct nested game between domestic and international politics even in this era of globalization. On the other side of the game, policy makers cannot afford to ignore international issues and concerns in order to concentrate most of their resources on domestic politics because their "game" occurs in what has been called a penetrated political system. This reality is the starting point for our discussion of the next category of states.

Small Powers

James Rosenau defines "penetrated political systems" in his foundational "pre-theories" work:

A penetrated political system is one in which *nonmembers of a national society participate directly and authoritatively, through actions taken jointly with the society's members, in either the allocation of its values or the mobilization of support on behalf of its goals.* The political processes of a penetrated system are conceived to be structurally different from both those of an international political system and those of a national political system.[73]

As Rosenau offers in a footnote to this definition, denoting a system as "penetrated" does not suggest anything about its legitimacy or type of government. Indeed, his assumption is that "penetrated processes are conceived to be legitimate and authoritative for the society in which they unfold."[74]

Rosenau theorizes that all "national societies can be organized as penetrated political systems with respect to some types of issues—or issue-areas—and as national political systems with respect to others."[75] That is, on some issues, all countries must accommodate the participation of non-nationals in policy making. Rosenau made this observation in 1966; in the twenty-first century this seems all the more the case given globalization. Clearly some countries—in 1966 and the twenty-first century—have far greater control over the degree and type of participation of nonnationals than do other countries. Here we will think of small powers as countries in situations of near total penetration, penetration that spans the range of political issue areas, both domestic and foreign. How policy makers might find some room for independent policy making in this penetrated position is a topic for students of small powers.

In the same way that Neil MacFarlane portrays Russia as using its weakness to leverage power against the West in order to pursue Russian national interests (as discussed above), small power foreign policy is examined in terms of whether and how small powers may find openings to pursue independent foreign policies. Most of the scholarship on small power foreign policy comes from the liberal and Marxist schools, as realists are largely dismissive of small states. Realists only focus on states that can make an impact on the international system; small states, according to realists, cannot individually or collectively have such an impact and thus can be disregarded.

The starting point for any observer of small power foreign policy is the acknowledgment that the range of opportunities for independent, self-interested behavior is more limited than that of any of the more powerful states. Small powers are boxed in by virtue of their relative weakness, but they are not *powerless*. Maria Papadakis and Harvey Starr contend that small states have *some* power over their foreign policy choices and ultimate fates, but this power is contingent on the *opportunities* present in the international system and the *willingness* of the leaders of small states to take advantage of those opportunities.[76] In this way, small states are like secondary states and great powers; international conditions must be ripe for action and leaders must be inclined to act.

Davis Bobrow and Steve Chan assert that some small powers have greater ability than other small powers to create opportunities for themselves. Distinguishing among small powers is necessary for analysts since this category—like the related categories "Third World" or "developing countries"—contains the majority of the world's countries. Except in the most abstract sense, it would be impossible to generalize about the foreign policy behavior of this classification of states, since so many different states "belong" here. Bobrow and Chan contend that some small states are more powerful than others because they "have been able to carve out for themselves a special niche in the strategic conceptions, political doctrines, and domestic opinions of their chief ally."[77] These states derive power from manipulating the very relationship in which they are the dependent partner. Israel and South Korea are small powers that have been especially successful in defining their importance to the United States and taking great advantage from this.

Let's examine how a small power might manipulate its relationship with a great power by examining the scholarship of Mary Ann Tétreault on Kuwait and of Martin Sampson III on Libya. Tétreault defines a small state as one whose small territory, population, and resource base make it virtually impossible for it to defend itself against external attack.[78] Defense is the first, most basic duty of any government. A government that cannot defend its country against external threats is a government that lacks fundamental legitimacy. It is also a government that will not be in charge of a country for very long. Other national goals are important, but without basic defense, all other goals fall by the wayside.

In order to guarantee Kuwait's external security against the Ottoman Empire, and to prop it up internally as well, the Kuwaiti Mubarak regime (1896–1915) entered into a cliency relationship with Great Britain in 1899.[79] Tétreault defines cliency as a "strategic relationship between a strong state and a weak one."[80] Although the power relationship is asymmetrical, cliency is *reciprocal*. Great Britain, the *patron*, gained a secure base in the Persian Gulf region from which to check expanding German presence in the Middle East and, in 1913, all rights to the "rumored" Kuwaiti oil reserves. Kuwait, the *client*, gained external security from the Turks and internal order through the presence of British troops. Cliency "placed a severe limitation on Kuwait's sovereignty, but it preserved the existence of Kuwait."[81] Cliency did not preserve *all* of Kuwait, though, as its size would ultimately be pared down through various treaties designed and mediated by, ironically, the British.[82] That the Kuwaiti regime was able to engage such a relationship indicates that Kuwait was not a completely powerless small state.

The cliency relationship remained relatively stable until the early 1940s, about the time that Kuwait's oil production took off. Tensions between client and patron over the division of oil revenues and British control of the Kuwaiti economy and entanglement in Kuwaiti political affairs led the Kuwaiti regime to begin seeking another patron around 1950.[83] The "patron" eventually found was oil and economic interdependence.

Tétreault posits that the Kuwaiti **leadership** placed its faith in oil and economic interdependence, rather than a strategic interdependence. She explains:

> Substituting oil for cliency seemed to be a reasonable strategy from the perspective of Kuwaiti rulers. If the primary domestic goal of cliency was to acquire instruments enabling the government to meet domestic demands with a minimal loss of autonomy, oil was even more useful than cliency for obtaining such instruments. Oil revenues not only enabled the ruler to buy off domestic elites quite openly and to retain his independence from domestic society as the source of state income, but they also expanded his resources so astronomically that he could create a huge constituency supporting the regime by making the whole population of Kuwait dependent on the state. In the external realm, the shift from cliency to oil was trickier, but the same strategy applied. Oil revenues were used to buy off the most

dangerous of the state's external enemies, also quite openly. In addition, they were used to mobilize an international constituency of supporters of Kuwait by creating foreign aid dependencies.[84]

Kuwait's new "patron" was soon to be tested. The British-Kuwaiti cliency relationship ended in 1961 with the full and formal independence of Kuwait. Almost immediately, Iraq declared Kuwait part of Iraq and moved troops into place to back this claim. This prompted the quick return of British troops. Then British troops were replaced with Arab League troops as a condition to Kuwait's membership in this organization. Thus Kuwait's Arab neighbors became its protectors, just as Kuwait was the financial benefactor of the Arab states.[85] Kuwait made the shift from a military patron to an economic "patron" at a time when international institutions such as the Arab League and the United Nations were being formed, binding states into a series of agreements on acceptable and unacceptable foreign policy behavior. At the same time, the booming, oil-hungry world economy ensured Kuwait adequate resources to maintain loyal friends in the Arab world. Beyond the Arab world, growing Western oil dependence sealed Kuwait's importance.

The international political and economic environments were also important variables in two different Libyan regimes' efforts to set an independent foreign policy course. Libya became an independent state in 1951, just as global politics entered the Cold War era and the postwar industrial appetite for oil exploded. As described by Martin Sampson, Libya faced three constraints on independence. First, Cold War politics imposed a nonchoice on the Libyan monarchy, as Middle Eastern monarchies generally aligned with the United States. Second, Western multinational corporations—Exxon, Mobil, Texaco, Standard Oil, Gulf, Shell, British Petroleum, and French Campagnie—held near total control of the oil wealth of the region. These multinational corporations (MNCs) operated together to limit new oil production in order to maintain the petroleum price structure and their own profits. Third, the monarchy had little internal support or legitimacy and a poor resource base to draw on for governing. Sampson concludes:

> In 1951 Libya would seem to have been as dependent and powerless a country as one could imagine—a country that had few foreign policy choices and virtually no possibility of affecting the systems and structures of the outside world. This was not a country from which one would expect foreign policy innovation, or even a foreign policy that would have much impact.[86]

The Libyan monarch, King Idris, *did* engage in foreign policy innovation, or, to put it differently, he read the opportunities in the system and was willing to attempt to exploit them. Libya was not an oil producer at independence, but it was thought to possibly possess significant oil reserves. King Idris wanted to tap into the potential oil riches, but without giving oil MNCs too much control of the Libyan fields. Politically, Idris was constrained by Cold War politics, but he turned these constraints into opportunities that in turn were put toward the service of transforming Libya into a wealthy oil producer and exporter.

Idris's policy contained two elements: he would pursue a conventional political/military strategy that would enable him to pursue an unconventional economic strategy. First, Idris signed agreements with the United States and Britain allowing both countries to build military bases in Libya. The American base was built within a short distance of Idris's palace, ensuring internal protection for Idris if needed. This base, Sampson reports, was the largest U.S. base outside U.S. territory with the exception of the base in Danang, South Vietnam.[87] This conventional political–military strategy gave Idris "cover" to pursue his second, more important strategy.

Because Libya's oil industry was still in its nascency, Idris was able to exert strong control over its development. In 1955, the Petroleum Law divided Libya into many small oil exploration zones, which were opened to the oil MNCs for bidding. Winners of bids had to begin exploration within a specified time frame, and, if oil was found, the MNC's control over the field would be reduced over a period of ten years until ownership was returned to the Libyan state.[88] This caused oil MNCs to rush into the exploration and exploitation of the oil reserves, which in turn caused Libya to jump from a nonplayer in oil production in the 1950s to the third largest Middle Eastern oil producer by the mid-1960s.[89] Additionally, Idris opened the Libyan economy to all who wanted a part of the action, including Eastern bloc countries and China. The Libyan economy thus was developed rapidly by a diversity of foreign investors, with little cost and much gain for Libya's economic independence.

King Idris saw clear opportunities in the situation confronting Libya in the 1950s and clear constraints. He used the political constraints of the Cold War as opportunities to buy protection and insulation for his economic goals. U.S.-Libyan relations were so secure and comfortable for the United States that the American government felt no threat in Libyan economic policies. Ultimately, though, Idris was not immunized against internal opponents who disagreed with the trade-offs he made. In September 1969, a group of young nationalist military officers deposed Idris in a bloodless coup. Their chosen leader was Colonel Muammar Qaddafi.

Sampson's reading of the Qaddafi era is that it was made possible by the innovations of Idris. Libya's economic independence and new wealth ultimately empowered those opposed to political dependence on the West. The Qaddafi regime negotiated an end to the American and British military presence in Libya in 1971 and set Libya on a socialist-Islamic path by 1973. In time, Qaddafi moved Libya to the Soviet side of the Cold War while supporting a strongly anti-Western, pro-Arab, pro-Islamic foreign policy stand. Qaddafi set Libya's political-military foreign policy on its head, *yet he maintained Idris's economic policies.*[90] In particular, Qaddafi used the 1955 Petroleum Law to pressure individual oil MNCs into paying Libya higher and higher revenues from oil production. This had a multiplier effect throughout the region, as Sampson explains:

> [Qaddafi] soon had the oil companies paying Libya more revenue per barrel of oil than other countries were receiving. Libya's success encouraged leaders of other Middle Eastern oil states to demand an increase in the royalties the [oil] monopoly consortia paid to them—to which the companies eventually agreed. Libya would then pressure the companies for even higher prices, would receive them, and then the other oil states of the Middle East would renew their quest for higher royalties. In a very real sense the 1970 to 1972 maneuvering in the Middle East among oil companies and oil exporting states over higher royalty payments was made possible by the independent oil policy that the Libyan monarchy had left to [Qaddafi]. What appeared to be an aggressive and innovative foreign policy change by the [Qaddafi] regime was in fact grounded in the policy of [Qaddafi's] predecessor; he had only extended the exploitation of the structural seams that was initiated by King Idris.[91]

In a brief span of twenty years or so, Libyan leaders saw opportunities and took full advantage of them, revising Libya's position in the region and world. Sampson concludes, "Under two different regimes Libya's foreign policy change has made it important out of all proportion to what would have been expected from structural predictions of Libya's foreign policy."[92]

The examples of Kuwait and Libya demonstrate how small powers can manipulate their circumstances in order to gain greater—even disproportionate—power. Yet not all small powers are presented with the same opportunities and endowed with the same resources. Libya and Kuwait possess a critical natural resource and insightful leaders in each country found ways to leverage this resource and external relations in ways that served their own independent foreign policies. Small powers without such an economic resource need to look elsewhere for ways to exploit the system and gain greater independence. Some small states can draw on their geostrategic location for such leverage—as in the cases of Israel and South Korea mentioned in brief earlier. But many small states possess neither an economic resource nor geostrategic importance that can be manipulated to their advantage. These small states better fit the notion of "powerless" states.

Even the "success" stories have within them cautionary tales. Idris was secure from international threats because of the deal he struck with the United States. Yet this deal was the source of Idris's fall from power. The terms and extent of American penetration of Libyan politics gave rise to the 1969 nationalist-socialist-Islamist coup. Around the time that Britain and Kuwait embarked on a cliency relationship, Britain forged a similar relationship with Iran. Subsequently, the United States assumed the role of Iran's patron. This relationship ultimately generated a popular uprising in Iran, resulting in the 1979 revolution and the founding of the first Islamic republic in modern history. Certainly for the old ruling monarchies in Libya and Iran, cliency had enormous short-term gains and enormous long-term drawbacks.

And then there is the case of Saudi Arabia in the post-September 11 political environment. As discussed earlier in this chapter, the American and Saudi governments established a patron–client relationship at the close of World War II. This relationship is one of the three "props" of the House of Saud—the ruling monarchy—alongside oil and the Wahhabi sect of Islam.[93] This relationship is also one of the primary reasons that Osama bin Laden and the Al Qaeda terrorist network declared war on the United States and sought to overthrow the House of Saud. The "power" that the ruling regime of a small state derives from a cliency relationship, we might conclude, is finite, and potentially fatal on one or both sides of the nested game.

A Complex, Multilevel Game: The Case of the Middle Powers

"Middle power diplomacy" involves international mediation, peacekeeping, consensus building within international organizations, and other similarly cooperative behaviors. According to some analysts, middle power diplomacy (i.e., the foreign policy behaviors of the middle powers) derives from a moral imperative *found in the cultures* of the middle powers (Canada, Australia, Sweden, Norway, Denmark, and so forth). This moral imperative is to serve as international "helpful fixers," extending their own social policies on the redistribution of wealth, peaceful conflict resolution, and so on, outward. To other observers, middle powers play their roles because of their *position in the international distribution of power, especially vis-à-vis the major powers*. Middle powers are not capable of directing the system—as are the great or major powers—but neither are they the weakest members of international society. Thus their foreign policy derives from their in-between status.

An in-depth examination of middle powers demonstrates that position alone cannot explain foreign policy behavior. We will use this examination to reassert the importance of multilevel analysis, as well as to introduce the critical theoretical framework known as constructivism.

"Middle power" is a self-identification taken up by Canadians, Australians, Swedes, Norwegians, Dutch, and Danes, and as of the 1990s, (South) Koreans, to explain their own country's roles and position in the world. The self-identification goes back to the interwar period; "middle power" was a designated category within the League of Nations system (1920–1946), but not a particularly popular one. Brazilian delegates threatened to end their participation in League activities if Brazil were designated as being in the middle of anything. Indeed, Brazil quit the League in 1926, only a few years into its existence.

At about the half-century mark, Canadian diplomats set their sights on carving out a role for Canada in the architecture of the post–World War II era. "Middle power" would designate both what certain states had contributed to the Allied war effort—important, albeit secondary, resources and energies—and what these states would contribute to maintaining the postwar international system. As the United Nations took shape, Canadians and Australians began promoting the codification of middle power status into the U.N. Charter based on this functional criteria. The great powers—the soon to be Big Five or "Perm Five" (the United States, Soviet Union, Great Britain, France, and China)—had no particular interest in delineating categories for non–great powers. And countries relegated by the self-described middle powers to small power status had no interest in seeing another layer constructed atop them.[94] This functionally based, status-seeking claim by the Canadians, Australians, and others, was rejected, but the notion of the middle power was not.

The self-identified middle powers did not go back to stand among the ranks of the non–great powers—not entirely. Instead, they internalized the idea of the middle power and began conforming their external behaviors to role expectations. In time, middle power diplomacy became defined as the "tendency to pursue multilateral solutions to international problems, [the] tendency to embrace compromise positions in international disputes, and [the] tendency to embrace notions of 'good international citizenship' to guide . . . diplomacy."[95] In line with this, middle powers were self-defined as states that committed their relative affluence, managerial skills, and international prestige to the preservation of international peace and order. Middle powers were the coalition builders, the mediators and go-betweens, and the peacekeepers of the world. Middle powers, according to the diplomats and scholars of these states, performed internationalist activities because of a moral imperative associated with being a middle power—middle powers were the only states that were able and willing to be collectively responsible for protecting the international order, especially when smaller states could not and greater powers would not.[96]

How did this moral imperative get imported into what, in the first instance, was a status-seeking project? One quick answer is that the "imperative" was already present. The self-declared middle powers already possessed a sense of moral superiority and certitude that required a unique foreign policy stance. For instance, J. L. Granatstein suggests the following origins of the Canadian notion of Canada as the world's "helpful fixer":

Probably the idea emerged out of the missionary strain in Canadian Protestantism and Roman Catholicism that saw Canadian men and women go abroad in substantial numbers in the nineteenth and twentieth centuries to bring the word of God to India, Africa, and China. . . . the "do-good" impulse that they represented was a powerful one, and it had its strong resonances in the Department of External Affairs.[97]

Granatstein goes on to explain that many in the early Canadian diplomatic corps (1930s–1940s) were the children of missionaries or clergy and had been born abroad.[98] Similarly, Peter Baehr attributes Dutch moral leadership on human rights issues to a cultural imperative to "do good all over the world," to be a "guiding country."[99]

Going hand in hand with this do-gooder impulse was the equally strong impulse to demonstrate to the world that middle powers *were like* great powers, *but were not* great powers. As Granatstein explains in regard to Canada:

Canadian policy in the postwar world would try to maintain a careful balance between cooperation with the United States and independent action. This was especially true at the United Nations. And peacekeeping, while it often served U.S. interests, to be sure, nonetheless had about it a powerful aura of independence and the implicit sense that it served higher interests than simply those of the United States, or even the West.[100]

The packaging of middle power diplomacy in a moral wrapping was not intended to obfuscate the essentially interest-based, status-seeking nature of the middle power project. Middle power scholars, particularly, never shied from this element of middle power diplomacy. Middle powers were devoted to the preservation of international norms and principles because they clearly benefited from a routinized international system. Further, middle power internationalism earned these states much deserved prestige. Even as middle powers proclaimed that their internationalism made them different from the great powers, middle powers also acknowledged that they generally were *active followers* of the great powers. Middle power scholars Andrew Cooper, Richard Higgott, and Kim Richard Nossal have coined a term to describe this behavior: "followership." This phrase is chosen to both be similar and dissimilar to the term "leadership."[101]

"Middle power," then, is a self-declared role that contains both status-seeking, self-interested behavior (securing a coveted international position) and moralistic/idealistic elements (being a good international citizen). Thus both realist and liberal elements characterize this role. Post–World War II efforts to attain international recognition for the middle power label failed, yet the middle powers maintained the identity and elaborated on the role expectations attendant to it. It is not difficult to find statements from the prime ministers or foreign ministries of middle powers saying: Middle powers act in certain ways, and therefore we must act in certain ways. Yet the middle power imperative did not blind these states to real-world constraints and dangers, and so it also is not difficult to find statements that take the following form: Middle powers act like this, we are a middle power so we naturally want to act like this, but unfortunately, this is not a prudent time for such actions. Imperative—a sense of duty coming from within the country's national culture to do some good in the world—and position—where one is positioned or where one desires to be positioned in the international hierarchy of states—have long been two sides of the middle power coin, equally at play in explaining middle power diplomacy.

It is important to stress here that the self-identified middle powers—all Western states—were never "revisionist" states for all the efforts they made to distance themselves from the relevant great power (i.e., the United States). From the start of the post–World War order, these states were content with the status quo and were more concerned that this order would be upset by the great powers through nuclear war than they ever were concerned about their secondary status in it.

Another key point is that middle power studies all have emphasized middle power vulnerability to changes in the central great power relationship. The central great power relationship defines the system, and establishes the range for permissible actions *particularly* for states closest to the top. Middle powers understand this constraint and carefully negotiate their own positions and behaviors within the tolerable range. As the central relationship changes, so too do the possible roles and behaviors of the middle powers. Carsten Holbraad gives an example of expected middle power behaviors under conditions of cold war between the central powers:

> Not always willing and only in certain conditions able to reduce tensions and promote agreement between the camps, middle powers in a cold war alliance are no more than occasionally to be found in the role of mediators. Their real part in relation to the central conflict is as supporters or lieutenants of the alliance leader.[102]

Thus middle powers are comfortable with both their self-elected position in the world and with the leadership at the top.

Problems arise for middle powers when changes occur in the relations between the central great powers, or when the central great powers themselves change. For example, central power détente—a period of reduced tensions between traditional competitors—is a period of considerable anxiety for middle powers. Holbraad depicts the period of detente between the United States and Soviet Union (mid-1960s to late 1970s) as a time when the central powers turned their attention away from their competitive relationship and focused on their own blocs. The Cold War did not disappear during the period of détente, but the United States and Soviet Union were not directly confronting each other during this time. When the central powers focus on their own blocs, bloc members must be careful not to engage in activities that might be seen as too independent or threatening to the major power's domination of the group. Any such challenging act would be met with swift "policing" by the major power. The Soviet invasion of Czechoslovakia in 1968 can be seen in this way. The government of Czechoslovakia was attempting to implement internal reforms that were perceived to be a threat to Soviet-led communism there. The Soviet Union and its Warsaw Treaty Organization allies stepped up to the threat by invading Czechoslovakia and deposing the reformers. This police action stopped the Czechoslovak threat and was designed to deter future challenges coming from anywhere within the Soviet bloc. The United States, it should be noted, did little more than protest the Soviet invasion, an acknowledgment by one central power that the other has the right to keep its bloc members in line.

Holbraad suggests that the safest mode for middle powers during détente is multilateralism because any apparent independent activity by the middle power might be met with suspicion by the relevant great power. Multilateralism—working within international organizations such as the United Nations or within a coalition of states—can "conceal" a country among many others so that it does not stand out and draw attention to itself. The on-again, off-again, stop-and-go competitive Cold War that reemerged after the period of U.S.-Soviet detente (roughly 1979 until 1988) was also troubling for the middle powers, as they were unsure about what the great powers would require or demand of the faithful lieutenants during this time.

The end of the Cold War and the collapse of the Soviet Union caused anxiety among the middle powers that has yet to be resolved. Several prominent scholars from middle power countries were invited to a conference in Canada in 1993 to discuss their country's roles in the "new world order."[103] This conference was sponsored by the Canadian foreign ministry, a clear demonstration of the interplay between middle power scholars and government. The consensus of the conference's participants was that uncertainty over the shape of the emerging world order—particularly whether the new order would be unipolar or multipolar—meant insecurity for middle powers. The safe bet for middle powers was to go on "extended holiday" until a new order presented itself. Middle powers should not be too ambitious or adventurous in their foreign policies until the uncertainty over the shape of the international system was resolved.

When we think about middle powers in international politics, then, we consider a group of states that have self-elected themselves to a status and defined its attendant behaviors. This self-election comes out of some moral imperative based in national culture. This self-election also derives from satisfaction with the international system and the middle power's position within it, and a desire to use relative affluence and power to maintain the essential elements of the status quo. "Middle power" is a liberal construct because of the dedication of middle powers to performing important system- and peace-maintenance roles: the middle powers take the role of "good international citizen" seriously. Middle power is also a realist construct in that it entails claims on a special status and role in the international state system.

Let's step away from our discussion of middle powers briefly to consider an alternative "lens" in international relations theory that we can use to explore the notion of "middle power" at a theoretical level. This lens—constructivism—is not just a framework for studying middle powers, but the study of middle powers seems especially well-suited for constructivism.

Constructivism: An Alternative Lens

Realists, liberals, and Marxists all think about states as self-interested actors responding to an established reality. The "reality" differs for these three grand theoretical frameworks, but "it" is somewhere "out there" and somewhat distinct from the international actors. Constructivists take a different view of reality. There is no more or less objective reality; instead, reality is constructed from people's perceptions of it. James Dougherty and Robert Pfaltzgraff explain:

> social reality is what people construct or constitute as reality. Those activities that are deemed to be the most important to the interests of the members of a social unit such as a state are by definition political in nature. When such activities extend beyond the immediate locale or boundaries of the unit, they become international relations.[104]

Discussing the work of constructivist scholars, Dougherty and Pfaltzgraff emphasize the important point that

> the terms *construct* and *constitute* are synonymous in the theoretical sense that people and society construct, or constitute, each other. Thus, there is an interactive process in which people constituting a group or a unit continuously construct in their individual and collec-

tive mind the reality that forms the basis for and is shaped by the decisions made.[105]

The primary target of constructivism is the realist and liberal characterization of international politics as anarchic. The realists respond to anarchy by explaining that in an environment of uncertainty in which no overarching authority exists to govern relations between states and in which all states are motivated to survive by whatever means necessary, power politics and conflict are the natural results. Even liberals start with the idea of anarchy, but they explain that states are able to order anarchy through the cooperative development of guiding institutions that preserve the collective good. Constructivists take on this idea of anarchy as a given reality, especially the realist view of anarchy and the inevitability of power politics and conflict. Alexander Wendt argues "that self-help and power politics do not follow either logically or causally from anarchy, but that if today we find ourselves in a self-help world, this is due to process, not structure."[106] Because states (as the collective voice of people) *perceive* international reality as anarchic and *interpret* that in anarchy states must ultimately engage in self-help, they construct their own identities and role behaviors to conform to this constructed view of reality. States "make" the system (anarchic) and then the system they create "makes" the states (self-interested and predatory by necessity). Ideas about the state system, identities for states within this system, norms, principles, and expected behaviors are combined in an interactive, mutually constitutive, mutually maintaining process.

One implication of the constructivist argument is that if states make the system, then states can remake the system. If reality is constructed by people, people can emancipate themselves from the dominant reality by reconstituting, rethinking, and reshaping it. As Dale Copeland puts it:

> If Wendt is correct, and "anarchy is what states make of it," then realism has been dealt a crushing blow: States are not condemned by their anarchic situation to worry constantly about relative power and to fall into tragic conflicts. They can act to alter the intersubjective culture that constitutes the system, solidifying over time the nonegoistic mind-sets needed for long-term peace.[107]

"Middle Power" as a Constructed Role

Returning now to middle powers, it should be clear from the earlier discussion that "middle power" is a constructed identity that was intended to have a shaping impact on the nature of international society. The self-construction of the middle power identity and role should be evident from our earlier discussion. Even middle power scholarship began with the memoirs and philosophizing of middle power diplomats. These statespersons so dominated the national debates and/or were so representative of the public's view on the proper role of their states in world affairs that the middle power identity was internalized quickly. Within this national identity, academics began to describe the ways in which their states acted like middle powers. These scholars were deeply integrated into the governance and ideational structure of their societies, and they served to reinforce the middle power identity through their work. Thus the common understanding of the self-perception and foreign policy behavior of middle powers has been shaped by a dialogue conducted within the middle powers between statespersons and scholars. Within this dialogue, the country's role and behavior as a middle power were constantly reevaluated and reexamined for inconsistencies as well as for possibilities for evolutionary change.

The construction of middle power identity should not stop at their borders, however, if constructivists are correct. Recall that the self-identified middle powers were attempting to shape the structure of the United Nations system through the codification of middle power status. The goal was to carve out a special place for the middle powers to ensure a privileged position in the postwar order. As Adam Chapnick explains in regard to Canada: "The history of middlepowerhood uncovers a tradition of Canadian rhetoric crafted to justify the attainment of disproportionate influence in international affairs."[108] Middle powers attempted to shape their environment in a way that would institutionalize their special identity.

The middle power investment in this identity has not come without costs. Sometimes middle power commitment to maintaining the U.N. system and to playing the good international citizen and loyal coalition member traps middle powers into activities that they would rather forgo. The constructivist position would be that these states can emancipate themselves from costly circumstances because, after all, they have a role in shaping the existing "reality." Furthermore, the uncertainty over the nature of the post–Cold War (and post–Soviet Union) international system offers a wide-open opportunity for *all* states to recraft their identities and the world.

The Case of Australia

We can "test" constructivist expectations by tracing the foreign policy strategies and choices made by the middle powers since the dawn of this "new world order." Australia presents an interesting example of a middle power searching for its new role at the end of the Cold War. Australian foreign policy makers decided to plot two courses. First, they argued in favor of strengthening the United Nations and continuing internationalist commitments into the new world order. At the same time, Australian leaders determined that they needed to redefine Australia as Asian in anticipation of a changing international order. Richard Higgott and Kim Nossal contend,

Few countries have as self-consciously sought to "relocate" themselves in international politics—economically, diplomatically, and militarily—as Australia did in the 1980s and 1990s. Between 1983 and 1996, the Australian Labor Party (ALP) governments of Bob Hawke and Paul Keating pursued an undisguised "push into Asia" . . . there can be little doubt that the ALP was seeking to "move" Australia from being a European-American-oriented community to being a nation in, and of, the Asia Pacific.[109]

Before the mid-1980s, Australians considered their state a European state not in Europe. Until the early 1970s, Australia had a "whites only" immigration law that Asian states saw as intended to keep Asians out of Australia. Given this history, why would Australian leaders begin to focus on Asia? Although the calculation was a complex one having to do with changing security dynamics as the Cold War began to wane, economic considerations drove this reorientation. One feature of the transforming global picture of particular importance to Australia was the growing economic power of East Asia. To accommodate the changes occurring in the international system, Alexander Downer, Minister of Foreign Affairs, declared a new foreign policy framework for Australia in a speech in November 1996:

The Government has a vision for Australia in the 21st century as a cooperative, economically competitive and secure nation, fully engaged with the East Asian region, while maintaining and developing important links with countries beyond the region. . . . Our policy has as its core a commitment to advance Australia's national interests in a focused, practical, realistic and above all, a principled manner.[110]

In the same speech, Downer declared that Australia's commitment to Asia would be its "highest foreign policy priority for one very simple and enduring reason: It is the vital sphere of our economic and strategic interests." Strengthened bilateral relations with Indonesia would be the cornerstone of Australia's new Asian policy.

One problem confronting Australia as it tried to make itself an Asian middle power was that in its relationship with Asian states Australia had bordered on being overly critical. During the Cold War, Australia saw itself as a global champion for universal human rights and often voiced criticism of Asian states for their treatment of their own citizens. Australian policy makers, by the mid-1990s, needed to disconnect issues of regional relations from Australia's global promotion of human rights in order to establish Australia as an Asian middle power.

Just as Australian foreign policy was being recast in the mid-1990s to reflect the shape and rules of the new international order, the system experienced great changes in fortunes and direction. The 1990s brought phenomena that were not fully anticipated by many observers. During the 1980s, the world prepared for a coming "Asian century," with the United States recast as a declining great power. The Gulf War of 1991 and the dissolution of the Soviet Union in December of that same year, the Asian economic meltdown starting around 1997, the resurgent and predominant U.S. economy from the mid-1990s, and—for Australia—the completely unexpected Australian economic boom all came as great surprises.

The falling fortunes of Indonesia and the clear resurgence of U.S. power caused Australian policy makers to decide, once again, to recast Australia. Policy makers did an about-face on Australia's newly acquired Asian skin and awkwardly attempted to link Australia to the United States. The violence in East Timor in the fall of 1999 provided the occasion to announce Australia's newest middle power project.

In the 1970s, Indonesia annexed the former Dutch colony of East Timor. Many of the East Timorese protested this and called for the independence of their nation from Indonesia. In 1999, the Indonesian government agreed to conduct a referendum on whether East Timor should be independent or not. This decision came about after decades of claims and evidence of human rights abuses by Indonesian troops and government officials against the East Timorese. A referendum is like a vote, but not a vote. A referendum is the opinion of a people on a key political issue. The Indonesian government did not have to honor the results of the East Timorese independence referendum, but it was expected to do so in order to maintain international status. With the Indonesian government's consent, the United Nations dispatched a peacekeeping operation to East Timor in late spring 1999 to prepare for the referendum.[111]

As the time for the U.N.-sponsored independence referendum in East Timor approached in early September 1999, violence between pro- and anti-independence forces rose sharply. Anti-independence forces (including the police and militia) tried using violence to stop people from voting in the referendum. The U.N. peacekeeping operation was unable to prevent the mounting violence.[112]

In late summer, as acts of "ethnic cleansing" against the East Timorese mounted, neighboring New Zealand called for military support to back the U.N. East Timor mission and restore law and order. New Zealand called for the United States, Australia, Japan, and members of ASEAN (the Association of South East Asian Nations) to deploy a peace support mission. This call was rejected loudly by the Australians as well as by the U.N. secretariat. *The Times* (London) quoted an Australian foreign ministry spokesman as saying, "Just for everyone who still has not got the message, Australia has no intention of invading Indonesia."[113] Within a week of this statement—after the September 6 referendum that demonstrated over-whelming support for independence and after anti-independence forces began a campaign of destruction—Australia was leading the call for mili-tary intervention in East Timor.

The explosion of violence in East Timor coincided with two events in Asia—the Asian Pacific Economic Cooperation (APEC) forum being held in New Zealand and a joint U.S.-Australian military exercise called "Crocodile 99." At the time the international community was being en-couraged by Australia to do something about the violence in East Timor, the American president was in New Zealand and some six thousand American troops were gathering on the north coast of Australia.[114]

The APEC meetings and important side discussions occurring there in regard to China's place in Asia and in world trading and economic insti-tutions remained the focus of the Clinton administration. While Australia promoted a peace enforcement mission of possibly seven thousand inter-national troops, the United States stayed aloof and would only commit to a possible logistical support role and airdrops of food and emergency sup-plies.[115] The Australians needed to convince the United States that East Timor was a direct threat to U.S. interests to get President Bill Clinton to come out more strongly behind Australia's plan for intervention. On September 13 Clinton signaled a somewhat more active U.S. involvement in the proposed operation—in response to *Asian calls* for U.S. involve-ment. Clinton explained that if the Asian countries requested U.S. help, the United States might provide "some command and control."[116]

U.S. command and control was not exactly what the Australians had in mind. Putting the correct spin on the Clinton statement, a report the next day in *ABIX: Australasian Business Intelligence* claimed,

> The United States has changed its position on East Timor from pres-suring Indonesia to supporting Australia. U.S. President Bill Clinton was willing to offer substantial logistical support to peacekeeping forces in East Timor, after Australia took the lead on the issue, setting a precedent of the U.S. allowing an ally to take the lead in a regional crisis to stop human rights abuses.[117]

Other countries were not as sanguine about an Australian-led, U.S.-sup-ported enforcement mission, especially Indonesia. Indonesia had been ac-tively opposing any peace enforcement operation that would include Australia and the United States, claiming that "Asian faces" would be "more palatable" to the Indonesian (and presumably East Timorese) peo-ple.[118] Despite earlier Australian aspirations to hitch Australia to Indonesia's rising star, Indonesia had kept Australia at arm's length.

Ultimately, a British-proposed Security Council resolution was acceptable to Indonesia once Australia was no longer named as the leader of the U.N.-approved operation.

By September 15, the American president—now officially on a state visit to New Zealand—suggested a more elaborate U.S. vision for the East Timor operation. Forces would come together from the United States, Australia, New Zealand, and "other nations" and hold training exercises to prepare for the mission. Threatening rapid deployment after training exercises, Clinton reminded the government of Indonesia that it had a responsibility to prevent violence in East Timor. Thus Clinton's announced preference was to use the threat of joint exercises as a way to compel Indonesia to reassert order in East Timor.

Australian Prime Minister John Howard acted quickly to *discredit* the Clinton plan. Despite the fact that Australian and U.S. forces were already engaged in joint exercises, Howard dismissed the plan to hold pre-Timor deployment exercises: "I do not think that [the Clinton proposal] is going to be feasible. . . . I think if you tried to do that you would be delaying the [Timor mission] considerably."[119]

The following day, the "Howard doctrine" was announced in the Australian magazine *Bulletin*. The Howard doctrine would entail a change in Australia's relations with Asia, deemphasizing previous efforts to establish "special relations" in the region. Instead, Australia would embark on an activist foreign policy as "deputy" to the "global policeman role of the United States." To facilitate this new role, defense spending would be the first priority of the government.[120] Howard explained the reason behind this policy shift as being one of near moral imperative, in classic middle power style. Australia, Howard stated, "has a particular responsibility to do things above and beyond in this part of the world," and further, Australia would be a "participant on our own terms" in Asia.[121]

Howard claimed that Australia's suitability for this role in the East Timor **crisis** was recognized by others as well:

> We have been seen by countries, not only in the region but around the world, as being able to do something that probably no other country could do, because of the special characteristics we have, because we occupy that special place—we are a European, Western civilization with strong links with North America, but here we are in Asia.[122]

Leading the way in East Timor as deputy to the United States would establish a precedent for Australia's future role, continued Howard, "Despite the inevitable tensions that are involved (in East Timor) and some of the sensitivities, this has done a lot to cement Australia's place in the region."[123]

Truer words may not have been spoken, but the result was paradoxical to what Howard intended. The Howard doctrine was widely condemned throughout Asia as arrogant and racist. Malaysia's *New Straits Times* equated the Howard doctrine to the Malaysian myth of "mata mata" coming, a myth of a bogeyman used by parents to control wayward children. Malaysian officials condemned Australia and the United States for declaring themselves the proper ones to "discipline" those who did not live up to Western standards. The influential newspaper noted that Australia had once been a "collaborator" on the Indonesian annexation of East Timor, but now was playing the "liberator." Finally, the *New Straits Times* concluded that the countries of ASEAN had always managed their own affairs without the need for Western police.[124]

In the wake of the Howard doctrine and Asian condemnations of it, and as the Australian-led peace enforcement mission (INTERFET) deployed, the United States limited its role to minimal, off-site support, assigning only some two hundred troops to the operation. At this point—coming almost ten days after the notorious doctrine was first published—the Australian government made some efforts to recast what Howard had said to bolster U.S. support and tone down Asian criticism. Howard went before the Australian parliament to assert that he had been misquoted in his use of the word "deputy." The next day Howard insisted that he had not used the word "doctrine" and that it was not true that Thailand was scaling back its commitment to INTERFET because of the Howard doctrine.[125]

It is important to note that none of the retractions changed the essence of the doctrine. This was not lost on observers in Australia or in the region. Despite the fact that the Australian-led INTERFET was successful in restoring security to East Timor, media in neighboring countries—including New Zealand—were sounding the call to put distance between their countries and Australia,[126] while the American profile in INTERFET was kept decidedly low.

The Australian-led INTERFET peace enforcement operation lasted a few short months and then was disbanded in favor of a traditional U.N. peacekeeping force. This stood in direct contrast to U.N.-approved peace enforcement operations in Bosnia and Kosovo, which remained in place years after they were started. The brevity of INTERFET suggests that members of the international community had different comfort levels on Bosnia and Kosovo than on East Timor. A safe conjecture is that Australia caused this through the awkward efforts of the Howard government to construct and play the role of American deputy in Asia. The United States and its Asian friends (even New Zealand) put distance between themselves and Australia and offered very limited support for the Australian-led INTERFET. The East Timor episode succeeded in undermining past Australian efforts to be a helpful Asian middle power and demonstrated that the United States had no particular interest in Australia's loyal follower act in policing Asia.

Does Constructivism Help Us Understand Middle Power Diplomacy?

Middle power Australia's search for its foreign policy stance in the 1990s and beyond demonstrates both domestic and international factors influenced Australia's choices and efforts. Australian leaders—invested in the notion of Australia as a middle power well suited to play a key follower role—went searching for the "appropriate" powerful country to follow and assist. Australian foreign policy was directed by a self-concept or **national self-image** that we might properly attribute to state-level factors. With this self-concept in hand, Australian leaders forged a role and set of behaviors for their state; Australia's leaders and government acted as autonomous agents in constructing and executing Australian foreign policy. To understand *why* Australian leaders selected the course they did, we would need to look *within* Australia—at its history, its people, its collective view of the world.

On the other hand, Australia's idea of itself in the world was absolutely tied to its relationship with other states. Australia's ability to act in any significant way was (and is) limited by what the structure of international politics would allow. Further, Australia's ability to alter this structure was limited by its secondary position—arguably its *tertiary* position—in the structure.

Can middle power behavior—whether now or in the Cold War era—be explained by a constructivist argument? Middle power scholars Higgott and Nossal explain Australia's efforts to "relocate" itself in Asia through a constructivist lens that emphasizes the agency of middle power decision makers:

> Australian policy, especially in its Asian regional guise, constitutes an exercise in the inducement of change by active *intellectual* and *ideational* intervention, a significant departure from the usual historical reading of Australia's regional relations as a realist exercise.[127]

Australian foreign policy elites made the decision to recast Australia's role in Asia and by this conscious act the elites exerted control over the shape of and framework for thinking about Australia's place in Asia. Then because of related changes in Australian foreign policy, to follow the constructivist line, the nature of regional relations should change, thereby supporting and reinforcing the Australian elite's portrayal of Australia's (new) Asian role. Australian leaders could redefine Australia's position in Asian society and thereby redefine Asian society. This change in Asian society would in turn shape future Australian foreign policy.

On one level the constructivist argument seems intuitive—states are affected by and affect their international environment. It is not difficult to make this argument for all but the states with the fewest international ties to the global economy and political hierarchy. The constructivist argument restates an older proposition made by Maria Papadakis and Harvey Starr:

> The state is an entity in an environment, and the environment may be divided into different levels with different sets of variables characterizing each level. The environment defines the context within which a state may act, but how the state *actually acts* or deals with its environment depends upon a number of factors: the set of opportunities that the characteristics of the sub-environments "objectively" provide the state, how the state perceives its environment, its willingness to take a particular course of action, and so on.[128]

What happens to the constructivist position when key actors within the international environment are not just resistant to but dismissive of a particular state's efforts to shape the environment and its place in it? Malaysian opposition leader Lim Kit Siang reportedly said that the "burial" of the Howard doctrine by the Asian response to it should be a lesson to the Australian government "that it has not yet developed the mindset to be accepted as an Asian nation." Twenty years of active, concerted efforts on the part of Australian foreign policy elites, coupled with real and significant Australian contributions to the maintenance of regional forums, and a real and significant contribution to security in East Timor, did nothing to reshape the views of the Malaysian and Indonesian elite, and perhaps no one else's views as well. Moreover, later Australian efforts to reconstruct Australia's role in the world again were dismissed by the dominant global shaper and mover, the United States.

There is a debate in international relations and the study of foreign policy called the **agent-structure problem**. This debate goes back to a basic difference over which level of analysis is the most likely to yield helpful insights into foreign policy making. Constructivism takes up this debate as well when it proposes that states/agents make international society and international society/structure makes states. Which part of the constructivist model—or which level of analysis—is more powerful or determinative? In terms of the case at hand, do the middle powers engage in the actions they do because they think of themselves as middle powers or because of where these states sit in the hierarchy of states?

Foreign policy scholars will continue to debate which level of analysis is the most useful for studying any particular problem, as the constructivists similarly take sides and argue that agent or structure is more important. What is critical to the constructivist account, though, is that ultimately agent and structure are *mutually* constituted. Some constructivists put primary emphasis on the agent side of the argument, especially when they argue that states can actively reshape their identities and foreign policy behaviors and thereby cause changes to occur in the structure of international society. In emphasizing agency, arguably, states can emancipate themselves from costly identities and role expectations first within their own national political arenas and then in terms of their global relations.

Using the case of Australia as our working example, we can see that there are limits to how much *some* states can redefine themselves in world politics. We can reasonably speculate that states with more power—economic, military, diplomatic, and so forth—have more ability to redefine themselves and international society than do weaker states.

This limited applicability of constructivism to the situation of smaller or weaker states suggests that we need other tools to examine why states act the way they act in the world. For example, we could offer realist or Marxist arguments about the limited applicability of constructivism. A realist might assert that constructivism offers an interesting account of how *major* powers shape the international system and are also shaped by it. Major powers construct international organizations to facilitate their interests, and then agree to limit their own foreign policy behaviors in conformity to the rules established in these IOs. Although East Timor was not considered a direct threat to U.S. interests and the United States had more pressing concerns in the broader Asian region, once the U.N. Security Council approved the peace enforcement mission, the United States made a token contribution. Ultimately, a realist might add, the United States conformed to U.N. resolutions on East Timor. But this was because the United States would not have to do much to conform, and the United States could rest assured that the United Nations would never ask too much of it, since the United States had been a primary architect of the U.N. system.

Similarly, a Marxist argument would accept the basic setup of the above explanation of how major powers structure the international system to fit their own interests. A Marxist perspective would privilege the role that mutual economic interests played in bringing major powers together to build international institutions. Still, realists and Marxists would agree that the interests and power of the major powers shape international structures. Further, both would agree that to the extent that major powers do limit their actions in compliance with structural constraints, these constraints are more apparent than real because the structures themselves only promote long-term major power goals. To paraphrase and put a different spin on a famous constructivist dictum with which neither realists nor Marxists would argue: *Anarchy is what major powers make of it, and what major powers make it.* Weaker powers are shaped by exogenous forces much more than they shape the outside world, its ideas and structures.

Thinking back to efforts to establish a middle power category within both the League of Nations and the United Nations, we see the limited ability of weaker states to shape international structures. The "middle" category was established within the League, but some "middle" states so resisted the imposition of the term and its related identity that they left the forum altogether. Within the U.N. system, middle powers were never able to get their self-defined identity legitimized through codification in the U.N. Charter. The middle powers of the time, affluent states that had made significant contributions to winning World War II and offered their affluence to the new U.N. system but on their own terms, were denied the ability to shape the single most important political body of the international system. The dominant states had already constructed a vision of the new system that was translated into a United Nations controlled by the military and political power of the Big Five of the Security Council. Everyone else had to accommodate their own actions, their own roles, their own ideas to this reality. In this regard, middle and small powers were not and are not participants in a set of "mutually constitutive" relations with major powers and international institutions and norms, but instead are the weaker parties in a dependent relationship.

Dale Copeland asserts that constructivism has even more limited usefulness than suggested above:

Constructivism is inherently an argument about how the past shapes the way actors understand their present situation. By its very nature—its focus on historical processes—constructivism has trouble analyzing how rational, prudent leaders deal with the pernicious problem of future uncertainty. And this uncertainty is given by the human condition. Human beings are not born with the ability to read the minds of other actors, and they have only limited means for foreseeing the future. Moreover, human beings, as constructivists emphasize, are mutable—they can be changed through interaction. Yet if much of this interaction takes place at the domestic level and is independent of diplomatic interaction, then prudent states must be worried. They know that the other may become aggressive despite all diplomatic efforts to instantiate other-regarding values and to communicate their own nonaggressive intentions. The material distribution of power then becomes critical to their calculations. It represents the other's potential to do harm in the future. Hence, if power trends are negative, a declining state must worry that the other will turn aggressive after it achieves preponderance, even if it seems peaceful right now.[129]

Copeland thus does not deny the fundamental constructivist argument about the social construction of identities, but he worries that this understanding does nothing to help foreign policy makers know how to deal with other actors in the system. To paraphrase his argument presented above, the constructivist framework adds a dangerous element into the mix of an already potentially dangerous international system. *If* national identities (and goals) are "mutable" *and* states ultimately have limited influence on this essentially internal process, *then* states need to be concerned about the distribution of power resources that might be harnessed to pursue the goals of the state undergoing identity change.

By way of example, consider the case first discussed in chapter 1 and then taken up again briefly in this chapter's introduction—the case of Chinese-U.S. relations. The single George H. W. Bush (Bush 1) administration and then the two Bill Clinton administrations pursued **constructive engagement** with China. Despite warnings by some military analysts and realist observers that China's intentions toward the United States were aggressive and competitive, these U.S. administrations acted on the notion that staying engaged with China would do more to make China a good international citizen—that is, would do more to reinforce the value of Chinese cooperation with the existing rules of the international system and thereby produce "good" Chinese behavior—than would a more confrontational and punishing policy mode. Yet Chinese–American relations turned sour and potentially dangerous in spring 2001, as China engaged in increasingly hostile foreign policy actions toward the United States despite the many efforts by American diplomats over some dozen or so years to foster good relations and a cooperative China. A constructivist would not have been able to predict this dramatic shift in Chinese foreign policy.

Similarly, a constructivist might have some difficulty explicating the dramatic shift in U.S. policy toward China in the George W. Bush (Bush 2) administration. The Bush 2 administration, packed with political appointees who also served in the Bush 1 administration, established a confrontational policy toward China, aggravating the worsening relations. The foreign policy team in the Bush 2 administration was drawn from the same group of foreign policy elites who were some of the architects of the "constructive engagement" policy pursued for twelve years by the U.S. government. A realist could explain that constructive engagement fit U.S. purposes before, but a different policy mode better suited U.S. interests in 2001. A constructivist might have some difficulty explaining why *these elites* would throw off so abruptly the constructive engagement mantle of which many of them were the architects.

Let's return to the middle powers. What if states do not wish to "emancipate" themselves from costly roles and behaviors? What if the middle powers persist in their role as good international citizens even if that role is pared down somewhat? Neither realism nor constructivism can explain the continuation of behavior that does not seem to serve any identifiable state interests. We might explain some of the foreign policy of middle powers by reference to constructivism, realism, even Marxism, but we would not be able to offer a fully satisfactory explanation. To do so, we need to go back into the state and consider the durability of national image and national values and how these determine foreign policy orientation. Then we need to pit the state-level picture against the system-level picture, to understand the totality of the circumstances. That is, we need to explore the "nested game" of foreign policy between the state and system levels, between domestic and international politics.

Review

In this chapter, we examined foreign policy from the system level of analysis, although the other levels—particularly the state level—could not be left behind. Two questions (or two sides to a single question) framed our discussion here: Do states engage in certain foreign policy behaviors because of *who* they are (defined at the state level), or do states engage in certain behaviors because of *where* they sit in the world (defined at the system level)? A complete answer to this requires attention to both sides of the nested game, although scholars at this level of analysis emphasize the relationship between a state's international position and its foreign policy options. Additionally, we reviewed an alternative lens through which to examine foreign policy, constructivism, and the levels-of-analysis problem, or the so-called agent-structure debate.

Some Key Ideas from This Chapter

- At the system level of analysis, we study state–state relations that occur bilaterally or multilaterally, regionally or globally.
- The discussion at the system level is focused more on policy outcomes—particularly behaviors—than on the policy process.
- The primary purpose of analysts using this level is to get "outside" national borders in order to discuss the interactions of states with other states and transnational actors, and within international organizations.
- In realist system-level accounts, the focus is on how a state's position in the international system is related to its foreign policy; the suggested relationship is a matter of explaining which options are open to states in certain positions and what those states must and/or will do to preserve or enhance their status.
- There is considerable imprecision in the use of categories of states—for example, great, middle, and small powers. This imprecision derives from a problem that resists resolution: there is no agreement among analysts about the elemental, fundamental concept of "power."
- The imprecision regarding who gets to be designated a great, middle, or small power is intellectually dissatisfying but not too damaging to our pursuit in this chapter, since our focus at this level of analysis is more on power *relations* between countries than on absolute power.

- Great powers are states with enormous power capabilities and a demonstrated willingness to use those capabilities whenever necessary. Great powers are especially attuned to potential threats to their status, and they stay on constant guard against rising powers.
- Since the collapse of the Soviet Union in December 1991, the United States has held the position of the single remaining superpower. American predominance and the cementing of the post–World War II American grand strategy—manifested in globalization—require us to rethink our expectations about how the international system operates.
- Secondary states, we might say, are states that occupy a middle range between superpowers and the smallest powers. Secondary powers sometimes lack the complete "bundle" of power requisites to be central, major, or "super" powers.
- "Middle power diplomacy" involves international mediation, peacekeeping, consensus building within international organizations, and other similarly cooperative behaviors. Middle power foreign policy derives from both the culture and society of the middle powers as well as their privileged position in the international distribution of power, especially vis-à-vis the major powers.
- The starting point for any observer of small power foreign policy is the acknowledgment that the range of opportunities for independent, self-interested behavior is more limited than that of any of the more powerful states. Small powers are boxed in by virtue of their relative weakness, but they are not *powerless*.

For Further Study

One of the most eloquent statements of how the international system influences the foreign policies of states is Kenneth N. Waltz, *Man, the State, and War* (Columbia University Press, 1959). This important book still stands as one of the best explanations of the three levels of analysis.

To read more about the expected behaviors of the United States and the important powers of Great Britain, France, Germany, Russia, Japan, and China, see the volume discussed earlier in this chapter, Ethan B. Kapstein and Michael Mastanduno, eds., *Unipolar Politics: Realism and State Strategies after the Cold War* (Columbia University Press, 1999).

To explore some of the arguments about the shape of American grand strategy, see the articles discussed at length in this chapter, as the arguments there are far richer than can be portrayed in these pages: Christopher Layne, "From Preponderance to Offshore Balancing: America's Future Grand Strategy," *International Security* 22, no. 1 (1997): 86–124; Benjamin Schwarz, "Why America Thinks It Has to Run the World," *Atlantic Monthly*, June 1996, 92–102; Josef Joffe, "'Bismarck' or 'Britain'? Toward an American Grand

Strategy after Bipolarity," *International Security* 19, no. 4 (1995): 94–117.

To explore American grand strategy after the terrorist attacks of September 11, 2001, an excellent starting point is the entire January 2002 issue of *Atlantic Monthly*, entitled "The Hard Questions." This issue features Benjamin Schwarz's and Christopher Layne's combined arguments, "Must the United States Remain a Superpower?" As well as Bernard Lewis's intriguing multilevel discussion, "What Went Wrong with Muslim Civilization?"

Far more books have been published on the foreign policies of great powers than on the foreign policies of non–great power states. Two new edited volumes offer case studies on the foreign policies of great and emerging great powers: Steven W. Hook, ed., *Comparative Foreign Policy: Adaptation Strategies of the Great and Emerging Great Powers* (Prentice Hall, 2002); and Ryan K. Beasley, Juliet Kaarbo, Jeffrey S. Lantis, and Michael T. Snarr, eds., *Foreign Policy in Comparative Perspective* (CQ Press, 2002). Two excellent volumes that systematically examine the impact of system-level factors on non–great power foreign policy are Jerel A. Rosati, Joe D. Hagan, and Martin W. Sampson III, eds., *Foreign Policy Restructuring: How Governments Respond to Global Change* (University of South Carolina Press, 1994); and Edward E. Azar and Chung-in Moon, eds., *National Security in the Third World: The Management of Internal and External Threats* (Edward Elgar, 1988).

To read more about middle power diplomacy, see these two representative works: Carsten Holbraad, *Middle Powers in International Politics* (St. Martin's, 1984); and Andrew F. Cooper, Richard A. Higgott, and Kim Richard Nossal, *Relocating Middle Powers: Australia and Canada in a Changing World Order* (University of British Columbia Press, 1993).

Constructivism is, as mentioned above, much more than a framework for studying middle powers. One of the very best places to start an exploration of constructivism is Nicholas Greenwood Onuf, *World of Our Making: Rules and Rule in Social Theory and International Relations* (University of South Carolina Press, 1989).

5

Conclusion: A Nested Game with Many Players

In This Chapter

- A Tangled Tale of Pinochet
- Between Domestic and International Politics in an Era of Globalization
- Nonstate Actors on the Rise
  Global Rage
- Concluding Thoughts

A Tangled Tale of Pinochet

In the summer of 1996, a Spanish group called the Association of Progressive Prosecutors filed a criminal complaint in a Spanish court against Chilean citizen Augusto Pinochet. The complaint alleged that Pinochet was responsible for the murder or disappearance of seven Spanish citizens while he was the military dictator of Chile from 1973 to 1990. The prosecutor of the case expanded the indictment to include charges of genocide, murder, and torture of Chileans and non-Chileans. Spanish Judge Baltazar Garzón issued an arrest warrant for Pinochet.[1]

Twenty-five years earlier, Socialist Party leader Salvador Allende was elected president of Chile. Marc Cooper, a young American who became Allende's interpreter, describes how this came about:

In Chile, the ascension to power of Socialist Party leader Salvador Allende came not as a result of the doffed tenacity of an armed elite. It was rather the culmination of fifty years of massive electoral campaigning for democratic socialism. Socialism was not some novel idea that had to be announced or decreed during a postelection rally. It was, rather, something that millions of Chileans had been demanding for decades.[2]

Not all Chileans were happy with the election; the economic **elite** and the military were particularly opposed to socialist Allende. Some non-Chileans were unhappy with the election as well. U.S. multinational corporations doing business in Chile felt their economic interests threatened, and then U.S. National Security Adviser Henry Kissinger is reported to have made this remark in response to Allende's election: "I don't see why we need to stand by and watch a country go Communist due to the irresponsibility of its own people."[3]

The U.S. Nixon administration undertook a destabilization plan that involved, among other things, CIA support for the Chilean military's orchestration of unrest and lawlessness. In September 1973, General Augusto Pinochet launched a military attack against the presidential palace. Salvador Allende and his closest advisers were killed or committed suicide during the attack. With the Allende government so dispatched, Chile was plunged into seventeen years of military dictatorship led by Pinochet. By official Chilean records, more than three thousand people were tortured and murdered or "disappeared" during these years.[4] In the early years of this brutal regime, Secretary of State Henry Kissinger visited Pinochet in Chile and assured him that he could ignore congressional protests about human rights abuses in Chile. Kissinger's message to Pinochet was encouraging: President Gerald Ford stood firmly behind him.[5]

The domestic politics of Chile were of the utmost importance in the foreign policies of several successive U.S. administrations. Many international and "domestic" actors—Chilean and non-Chilean, state representatives and nonstate actors—get entangled in this tale, as the introductory paragraph to this chapter suggests. The tangled tale of Pinochet will help us return to the primary themes of *The New Foreign Policy*, reinforcing the importance of multilevel foreign policy analysis, while bringing into focus the nonstate actors who play an increasingly critical role in shaping states' foreign policies. Now back to our tale.

The Pinochet government eventually gave way for the return to democratic **governance** in Chile in 1990. Throughout Latin America in the preceding decade or so, there had been a "return to the barracks" as militaries relinquished control and democracy swept over the region. The Chilean military leaders, like military leaders elsewhere, negotiated "golden parachutes" to ease their way out of politics. Pinochet's golden parachute came in the form of "senator for life" status, with limited immunity from prosecution and a permanent presence in Chilean politics (albeit a decidedly low-key presence). Although many Chileans and non-Chileans believed that Pinochet's deal meant that justice would be forever denied, Chilean political leaders believed the deal was the best way to move Chile into a democratic future.

In the fall of 1998, Augusto Pinochet underwent back surgery in London. While he was recuperating, the London Metropolitan Police arrested him on the warrant issued by Spanish Judge Garzón. The British police, a domestic institution whose purpose is to uphold British law inside Britain, arrested a former Chilean head of state for crimes allegedly committed in Chile on a warrant issued by a Spanish judge in Spain. Why would the British police carry out an arrest warrant issued by a Spanish judge? Great Britain, Spain, and Chile were/are all signatories to the United Nations Convention against Torture and Other Cruel, Inhuman, and Degrading Treatment or Punishment. The convention became binding for all three countries in 1988. Once ratified at home, international treaties take on the force of domestic law and are upheld within national territory by the same state agents—the police and the courts—that uphold domestic law. Legal proceedings commenced in Britain to extradite Pinochet to Spain.

Spain's extradition request to the British government was joined by Switzerland, Belgium, and France, while Germany and Sweden opened their own investigations into allegations against Pinochet. Chile, on the other hand, protested Pinochet's arrest and requested that he be allowed to return to Chile. Chile's protest was based on the principle that heads of state and former heads of state enjoy state/diplomatic immunity from prosecution. This was the same claim made by Pinochet's lawyers as they attempted to stop his extradition to Spain and win his release from British custody.

The issue of immunity for heads of state and former heads of state (or their representatives) is an extremely contentious one. New millennium efforts to establish the International Criminal Court (ICC) for prosecuting crimes against humanity and war crimes were met with strong opposition by some states who feared the ICC could be turned against them as a political tool. The United States, in particular, opposed the ICC for this reason. (Bill Clinton signed the ICC treaty, but George W. Bush "unsigned" it in spring 2002.) Countries opposed to the ICC argue that their own domestic legal systems are adequate for ensuring justice in cases of true war crimes and that an international legal authority is unnecessary. These states are reluctant to cede traditional state authority to a supranational or international organization.

Six of the European states involved in this tangled tale—Great Britain, Spain, Belgium, France, Germany, and Sweden—are members of the European Union. As EU members, these states already assented to supranational authority on particular issues. For instance, individual rights are privileged in the EU system such that community citizens have legal recourse to challenge *domestic* laws that are claimed to be in conflict with EU legislation.⁶ Community citizens may bring their challenges in domestic courts or within the European Court of Justice (ECJ) framework.⁷ Thus Great Britain, Spain, Belgium, France, Germany, and Sweden erased one important line dividing domestic from international. Their membership in the EU and ECJ *and* their obligations under the U.N. Convention against Torture and Other Cruel, Inhuman, and Degrading Treatment or Punishment *required* them to investigate allegations against Pinochet.

By international accord, diplomatic immunity could not be claimed in cases of human rights violations because even heads of state—*particularly* heads of state—must recognize and protect human rights. In the words of the British Law Lords who ruled on the Pinochet case:

> international law has made plain that certain types of conduct, including torture and hostage-taking, are not acceptable conduct on the part of anyone. This applies as much to heads of state, or even more so, as it does to everyone else; the contrary conclusion would make a mockery of international law.⁸

Chile's argument against the extradition was premised on the idea of state immunity, although the government's real goal was to maintain democracy in Chile against some strong oppositional forces. Chilean leaders were in an uncomfortable nested game. On one side were the European states with whom Chile wanted favorable relations and international public opinion in which Chile wanted to maintain its reputation as a good member in standing of the international community. Chile had entered into voluntary obligations to the international community that the government wanted to uphold: the Chilean government had signed the Rome Statute of 1998, which would bring life to the International Criminal Court and, *under the Pinochet regime,* Chile had signed the U.N. Convention against Torture.

On the other side of this nested game was a divided domestic political arena: many Chilean citizens and citizens' groups demanded that justice be done in the Pinochet case while the military and its supporters wanted the past to remain in the past. As a democracy, the government of Chile was bound to listen to the many voices of its people and to the rule of law—and in both regards, the government was highly conflicted. The possibility of a return to military rule was an unfortunate reality that figured into the calculations of Chile's civilian leaders, as were the legal commitments made to Pinochet and his cadre as the price of returning to democracy.

Chile's leaders appealed to the Spanish government to intercede and save Chile from this difficult situation. Since the early 1980s, Spain had cultivated a special relationship with its former colonies in Latin America, and it was on the basis of that special relationship that the Chilean leaders made their appeal. But the Spanish government did not intercede on Chile's behalf, out of respect for both its own relatively young democratic system and its commitments to the European Union and the U.N. Convention.

Chilean leaders also appealed to another international actor with whom it had a special relationship: the Roman Catholic Church. Since Pinochet's arrest in October 1998, Chilean leaders had appealed to the Vatican—even directly to the pope—to ask the British authorities to allow Pinochet to return to Chile. In Latin American international relations, there is a long history of mediation and arbitration by the Vatican.[9] The Vatican holds religious and historical importance in Latin America, giving it considerable diplomatic power and influence. In February 1999, it was revealed that the pope and his representatives had appealed to the British government for "leniency for humanitarian reasons and in the interests of national reconciliation in Chile."[10] The Vatican also endorsed Chile's claim that diplomatic immunity barred the prosecution of Pinochet on any charges stemming from his rule.

If you have not been keeping a scorecard, one will be provided shortly! This tale became more tangled as the case moved to British court in October 1998.[11] What is important to note in the following discussion is the variety of actors—state, nonstate, and individual—involved. Pinochet's lawyers brought an action of habeas corpus before the London High Court to win Pinochet's release. The London High Court agreed that Pinochet had diplomatic immunity from the charges, but it ruled that he would remain under arrest while an appeal was heard. The Crown Prosecution Service (an agent of the British government) brought an appeal on behalf of the Spanish government. The appeal was heard by a five-member panel convened by the House of Lords. In this hearing, several human rights organizations—Amnesty International, Redress Trust, the Medical Foundation for the Care of Victims of Torture, and Human Rights Watch (in a more restricted fashion)—were permitted to intervene in the case, as was a British doctor who had been tortured in Chile and the family of a British citizen who disappeared in Chile during the Pinochet era. Meanwhile, the Spanish government filed a formal extradition request with British Home Secretary Jack Straw.

The House of Lords rejected the previous court's ruling and declared that Pinochet was not protected by diplomatic immunity. The Law Lords, however, restricted the charges to those that occurred after 1988—the year that the Convention against Torture was incorporated into British law. The Home Secretary, in response, announced that the extradition would go forward. In December 1998, Pinochet appealed the Law Lords' ruling after it was revealed that one of the ruling judges had a formal affiliation with Amnesty International, one of the interveners. The first ruling was set aside and the implicated judge was disqualified from the case. But, in an unprecedented

---

HENRY KISSINGER'S DIFFICULT YEAR, 2001

In the summer of 2001, an Argentine judge issued an order for Henry Kissinger's testimony about Plan Condor, a 1970s plan by South American military dictators to cooperate against their leftist opponents.[1] Then, in August 2001, the Chilean Supreme Court sent a list of questions to the American government inquiring into Kissinger's knowledge of events leading to the death of American journalist Charles Horman. Horman's death at the hands of Pinochet's troops was the subject of the film *Missing*. Said an angry Bush 2 official in response to the Chilean Supreme Court's questions: "It is unjust and ridiculous that a distinguished servant of this country should be harassed by foreign courts in this way." The official issued a warning, "The danger of the ICC [International Criminal Court] is that, one day, US citizens might face arrest abroad and prosecution as a result of such politically motivated antics."[2]

Kissinger's problems were not just coming from abroad, though. On September 10, 2001, Kissinger was sued in U.S. federal court by the family of a Chilean military commander who was killed because of his opposition to a U.S. plan to execute Salvador Allende *before* his election as president. Kissinger, CIA director Richard M. Helms, and other Nixon administration officials were sued for more than $3 million in damages for "summary execution," assault, and civil rights violations.[3]

---

move, Amnesty International was allowed to participate in the oral arguments in a second hearing. The government of Chile was also allowed to make arguments before the court. In March 1999, a seven-judge panel of Law Lords ruled again that Pinochet was not entitled to diplomatic immunity.

Over the course of the next year, the extradition process played out with Pinochet's lawyers and the Chilean government making repeated requests for Pinochet's release, citing his medical condition as the reason. In early January 2000, the Home Secretary declared that a medical review panel had found Pinochet mentally unfit to stand trial, and so he would be released to return to Chile.[12] Belgium and a group of human rights organizations filed an appeal against the ruling, but this only extended Pinochet's stay in London by another month or so. In March 2000, Pinochet was released from detention and returned home aboard a Chilean air force plane. Within a week of Pinochet's return to Chile, in an odd twist of fate, Ricardo Lagos was elected Chile's second socialist president, the first having been Salvador Allende.[13]

But this was not the end of Kissinger's problems. Also in September, the regional parliament of Geneva, Switzerland, was set to authorize an inquiry into Kissinger's part in Pinochet-era crimes.[4] In October 2001, a French judge investigating the deaths of five French citizens in Chile announced that he, too, was seeking testimony from Kissinger.[5]

Journalist Christopher Hitchens, meanwhile, compiled what he claims to be convincing evidence that Kissinger should be brought before the ICC in his book *The Trial of Henry Kissinger*.[6] Hitchens maintains an interesting Web site that includes a dispute between himself and Kissinger's lawyers: <www.enteract.com/~peterk>.

Notes

1. Jan McGirk, "Kissinger Sued over CIA-Backed Kidnap," *Independent* (London), September 12, 2001, 16.

2. Toby Harnden, "US Angry as Chile Asks Kissinger about Death," *Daily Telegraph* (London), August 1, 2001, 13.

3. Bill Miller, "Family of Slain Chilean Sues Kissinger, Helms," *Washington Post*, September 11, 2001, A22.

4. "While America Mourns Geneva Parliament Wants to Sue Henry Kissinger," *Global News Wire (Financial Times)*, September 14, 2001, Lexis-Nexis.

5. "French Judge Issues Arrest Warrants against Ex-Chilean Leaders," *Global News Wire (Financial Times)*, October 25, 2001, Lexis-Nexis.

6. Christopher Hitchens, *The Trial of Henry Kissinger* (New York: Verso, 2001).

Eventually Augusto Pinochet was stripped of his immunity from prosecution and made to stand trial in Chile for crimes committed while in office.[14] Meanwhile, international human rights groups hailed the Pinochet case as an important step forward for the protection of human rights everywhere, despite the fact that Pinochet was not made to stand trial in Spain. The case became the model for similar NGO efforts to bring dictators to justice, as in the case made by Human Rights Watch against Hissene Habre, the former ruler of Chad.[15] The case brought to the forefront one of the U.S. government's worst fears when former Secretary of State Henry Kissinger was asked to give evidence to a French judge investigating the murder of French citizens in Chile during the Pinochet dictatorship.[16] What Kissinger knew about Pinochet's Chile and what Kissinger (and his bosses, Presidents Nixon and Ford) approved or assisted remain of great interest to state and nonstate actors who support an international criminal court.

> ## SLOBODAN MILOSEVIC AT THE INTERNATIONAL CRIMINAL TRIBUNAL FOR THE FORMER YUGOSLAVIA (ICTY)
>
> In 1993, the U.N. Security Council established the International Criminal Tribunal for the former Yugoslavia (ICTY). The ICTY—which sits in The Hague—was given original jurisdiction to hear cases against individuals for war crimes and crimes against humanity committed in the wars that occurred as the former Yugoslavia dissolved.[1] At the start of August 2001, the ICTY issued its first conviction on the charge of genocide against a Bosnian Serb general for his part in the execution of seven thousand unarmed Muslim men and boys in Srebrenica in July 1995.
>
> Awaiting trial in early 2002 on the same charge of genocide stemming from the ethnic cleansing of Srebrenica, as well as charges of genocide and other war crimes in Croatia and in Kosovo, was the former president of Yugoslavia, Slobodan Milosevic. Milosevic was the first former head of state to come before the ICTY after being extradited from Yugoslavia to The Hague in the summer of 2001. Milosevic refused to recognize the authority of the ICTY and refused to accept a lawyer for his defense. He claimed that the ICTY was illegitimate because it was not authorized by the U.N. General

Between Domestic and International Politics in an Era of Globalization

Many questions of domestic and international politics are linked in the tangled tale of Pinochet, including:

- How do the citizens of a country seek protection against human rights abuses by their own government? How do noncitizens seek protection? How might individuals seek redress when their rights have been violated? From whom would individuals seek redress?
- Who is to judge the validity of the claim made by national leaders that acts which appear to be human rights violations are in fact efforts to protect national security against internal threats to the state?
- Should democratic leaders make deals with former dictators in order to protect a fledgling democracy? If such deals are made, does this mean that some citizens have special rights over others? Is this a democracy?

Assembly, an argument that was not explained. According to Milosevic, the ICTY was a proxy of the North Atlantic Treaty Organization (NATO) and would be used by NATO to present false justification for its air war and war crimes committed against Yugoslavia in spring 1999.

Milosevic had legal advisers as he awaited his trial, including former U.S. Attorney General Ramsey Clark (Lyndon Johnson administration), who was a noted human rights activist. Clark expressed clear doubts about the impartiality of the ICTY in an interview with CNN: "This whole trial is a waste of money and a terrible injustice against the traditions of international law. . . . Even Slobodan Milosevic deserves to have a trial in which he is considered innocent until proven guilty, and its hard to find anybody who thinks that way."[2]

In late December 2001, Milosevic filed suit against the Netherlands in the European Court of Human Rights. His suit alleged that the Dutch government violated its own laws when it assisted in his arrest and detention. As of this writing in early 2002, the European Court of Human Rights was considering whether to hear his suit, while Milosevic's ICTY trial got under way.

Notes

1. For more on the ICTY, see its Web site at <www.un.org/icty>.
2. William Drozdiak, "Milosevic to Face Genocide Trial for Role in the War in Bosnia," *Washington Post*, November 25, 2001, A22.

- Should the leaders of a country in democratic transition be allowed to "silence" opponents whose activities pose a threat to the development of the democracy?
- What principles or interests should inform the relationship between democratic and nondemocratic governments?
- What rules should inform the relationship between states and nonstate actors?
- Should countries help other countries undergoing **democratization**? Would such help constitute interference in the state's domestic affairs?
- Should states be held responsible for their obligations under international conventions and treaties such as those within the United Nations system? How? What authority would enforce such obligations?
- Is there a need for an international criminal court if international treaties entered into have the effect of domestic law? How can an international criminal court be structured so as not to become a political instrument used by states against their opponents or used by nonstate actors against states?

Some of these issues are more clearly in the realm of foreign policy and some are more clearly domestic, but all have implications in both. It is the nature of global politics in the new millennium that makes this true. Indeed, consider this description of the Pinochet case written in 1999 by Ricardo Lagos—the second socialist president in Chile's history—and Heraldo Muñoz:

> In recent years, it has become commonplace to think of globalization solely in terms of transnational finance. The economic well-being of countries such as Brazil, Mexico, and South Korea ebbs and rises on the decisions made by international speculators and foreign investors. Recognizing the growing interdependence of national economies, we use terms such as the Tequila Effect and Asian flu to describe the global contagion that allows financial crises to spread unimpeded across borders. But Pinochet's detention in London has shown that globalization has now expanded from economic affairs to the institutions of politics and justice.[17]

Lagos and Muñoz continue, "Chile enjoys the unique status of having been buffeted by both forms of global contagion—with diametrically opposite results."[18] In the 1980s, the Latin American debt crisis and the resulting disruption to economies throughout the region put Chileans on the street protesting their economic distress. In response—and giving way to internal and external critics—Pinochet began to relax political restrictions on opposition. A prodemocracy movement took off at the same time that Chile's economy began to slowly recover, but Pinochet could not recover his iron grasp. Forces at the international and domestic levels combined to compel Pinochet to call a referendum on his rule, which he lost.

The second "buffeting" of Chile involved the arrest of Pinochet. Lagos and Muñoz, writing before Pinochet returned to Chile, note that "in Chile the [arrest] has created strong political tensions and threatens to fracture further a society that remains deeply embittered and divided over Pinochet's legacy."[19] Chile's new democracy was put under a severe test by the same forces of globalization that helped loosen Pinochet's control.

Globalization is much larger, penetrating, and pervasive a project than any previous international systems have offered. Even states that have been the most hostile to a **global free trade system** and to the westernization of world culture have indicated that there are no alternatives to globalization. For example, in May 2001, President Fidel Castro of Cuba and the former Iranian President Ayatollah Akbar Hasemi-Rafsanjani met in Tehran to discuss their mutual interests in the world. In this meeting, they issued the standard declarations against the United States while congratulating themselves for serving as "examples of resistance and independence." Rafsanjani also declared that "the two countries should cooperate to benefit from globalization while preventing its disadvantages."[20]

Iran's domestic political arena and its foreign relations have been profoundly affected by globalization, according to R. K. Ramazani. The election of moderate cleric Sayyid Muhammad Khatami to the Iranian presidency in 1997 was the product of the "quest of young Iranians for an open society at home and a peaceful state abroad."[21] Khatami won his first term as president with 68 percent of the vote in heavy voter turnout. In his reelection bid, Khatami won 77 percent of the vote, while his party dominated the parliament.[22] Younger people and women were among his strongest supporters. Ramazani characterizes the vote for Khatami as part of a wider trend:

> The aspirations for an open society at home and integration into the international community stem from a combined sense of national pride and a growing consciousness of the need to be part of the democratic movement sweeping across the world.[23]

Khatami's new foreign policy orientation "rejects the notion of the clash of civilizations; embraces the principle of dialogue among religions, cultures and nations; believes in the interdependence of societies, cultures and economies; and advocates a 'proactive and firm foreign policy.'"[24] Reflecting the real changes in the world and in direct repudiation of Iran's previous oppositional stance toward the American-dominated Western world, Khatami urged a new understanding of the world on attendees at the global Islamic summit of 1997. That understanding, he suggested, must be based on a critical appraisal of the Islamic nations' "weakness and backwardness," and a corresponding understanding of the fundamental *positive values* of Western civilization. According to Ramazani,

> Khatami spelled out the implications of the essentially democratic nature of his idea of an Islamic civil society, Madinat al-Nabi, for both domestic politics and foreign policy. Domestically, "the government in such a society is the servant of the people and not their master, and in every eventuality, is accountable to the people whom God has entitled to determine their own destiny." Internationally, he said, "our civil society neither seeks to dominate others nor to submit to domination. It recognizes the right of other nations to self-determination and access to the necessary means for an honourable living."[25]

Ramazani calls Khatami's vision a foreign policy of **democratic peace**. A democratic peace, of course, is one of the companions to globalization.

In April 2001, Iran signaled to the world its changing foreign policy stance when it signed a security agreement with Saudi Arabia. American troops were still present in Saudi Arabia, but the Iranian government no longer perceived those troops as a menacing anti-Islamic presence. The foreign ministries of both countries reported that cooperation on security between the two previously hostile countries was the first step to broader regional cooperation on political and economic matters.[26] Iranian leaders took huge steps in changing Iran's foreign policy course in the first half of 2001, even as a new U.S. administration (Bush 2) declared Iran a continuing international threat.[27]

Although Iran's domestic politics at the end of 2001 were still split between the followers of spiritual supreme leader Ayatollah Ali Khamenei (who retains ultimate political authority) and the supporters of the reformist government led by Khatami, the new millennium with its new realities witnessed an Iran reemerging in the international community. Iran, we might say, was being buffeted by globalization—a circumstance that may, ironically, strengthen the hand of the reformers as well as the hard-liners.

India has undergone a similar foreign policy transformation because of the realities of the new millennium. During the Cold War, Indian leaders managed to carve considerable power from India's nonaligned status, insulating India from international as well as domestic criticism. India championed the Nonaligned Movement and its themes of opposition to European colonialism, imperialism, and economic apartheid.[28] According to Sanjoy Banerjee, Indian leaders claimed that fighting colonialism and imperialism required certain government policies, such as strict government control of the domestic economy, to guard against imperialists. Because of the Cold War competition for India's friendship, neither West nor East would criticize India for its domestic or foreign policies. The collapse of the Soviet alternative and the reality of globalization exposed India's domestic and foreign policies to criticisms both domestic and foreign.[29] Criticism from abroad regarding India's decision to test nuclear weapons in the summer of 1998 and its human rights violations in the contested Kashmir put India on the defensive for the first time since its independence. Similarly, with the fight against colonialism over, the Indian government could no longer justify to its own citizens how far its economy had fallen behind the other Asian economies, forcing India to seek economic favors from the very Western states it had scorned previously.[30]

Globalization has caused and will continue to cause major foreign *and* domestic policy restructuring for the world's states. Globalization, with all its faults and promises, is now a conditioning feature of all states' policies. But states are not the only actors affected by globalization. Nonstate actors have been empowered by globalization even as many of them rise up to protest globalization's darker side. Some nonstate actors are rising up to speak out on behalf of people left behind in globalization; the more extreme of these—symbolized by Osama bin Laden's Al Qaeda terrorist network—seek to eliminate globalization and its perceived companion, westernization. We will discuss the rise of global rage shortly.

Nonstate Actors on the Rise

Let's return to the tangled tale of Pinochet to consider the many different actors present in this episode. Like the earlier tangled tale of Tibet, the Pinochet case involves more actors than just states. The international actors involved in the tale of Pinochet include:

- Chile, Great Britain, Spain, France, Belgium, Switzerland, Sweden, and the United States
- the United Nations, European Union, and European Court of Justice (all by implication)
- the Roman Catholic Church/Vatican
- international human rights groups: Amnesty International, Human Rights Watch, Redress Trust, Medical Foundation for the Care of Victims of Torture
- Chilean-based human rights groups
- Spanish-based human rights groups
- British-based human rights groups
- the Spanish Association of Progressive Prosecutors
- the Spanish legal system
- the British legal system/House of Lords
- General Augusto Pinochet
- Spanish Judge Baltazar Garzón
- British Home Secretary Jack Straw
- U.S. Secretary of State Henry Kissinger
- the British doctor tortured in Pinochet's Chile
- the family of the British citizen "disappeared" in Pinochet's Chile
- the other victims of torture and murder in Pinochet's Chile

This list, like the list of issues already mentioned, is far from complete, but it demonstrates a key point: the "stuff" of foreign policy involves many different actors. It would be impossible to try to understand the issues involved in the Pinochet case just from the perspective of the involved states. The issues go beyond state interests and state actors.

Nongovernmental organizations (NGOs) played critical roles in the arrest of, and the case made against, Pinochet. The important roles played by NGOs increased the net power of citizen groups and forwarded the notion of a global citizenry, while diminishing the strong grip of states on their own domestic affairs. Similarly, large and sometimes confrontational interest group protests at the World Trade Organization meetings in Seattle

(1999) and Prague (2000) and at the Summit of the Americas in Montreal (2001) and the International Monetary Fund meeting in Genoa (2001) signaled that citizens will attempt to exert control over the process of globalization in order to minimize its human toll.

Amnesty International, a key player in the Pinochet case, declared in its fortieth anniversary annual report that "globalization is no excuse for states to shirk their human rights responsibilities."[31] The report states that the work of Amnesty International and the *targets* of its work have changed to meet the new era:

> The human rights challenges which arise from globalization have stimulated Amnesty International to expand its work by promoting the human rights agenda within the business community, confronting multinational corporations and insisting that companies engage in protecting human rights—particularly those active in countries where there are massive human rights violations.

Further,

> The potential conflict between the pursuit of profit and the protection of human rights has led Amnesty International to communicate its concerns with the international financial institutions, like the World Bank, which is in a position to exert great influence over national economic and political agendas.[32]

Beyond increasing the power of NGOs vis-à-vis states, globalization also opens the door to greater empowerment of international organizations (IOs). Lagos and Muñoz argue that the empowerment of IOs is critical to ensuring that the globalization of human rights norms not lead to the destabilization of fledgling democracies or to more great power politics. They write,

> With the indictment and detention of Pinochet, it is now clear that the erosion of national borders is fast becoming a fait accompli. But just as economic globalization relies on international institutions such as the World Trade Organization to regulate the system and level the playing field, so too does the globalization of justice require mechanisms to minimize potential chaos.[33]

For Lagos and Muñoz, the International Criminal Court is the mechanism that "meets the dual objective of curtailing impunity on serious human rights violations and, at the same time, of ensuring just and fair processes subjected to clear rules that are accepted voluntarily by all countries."[34]

Globalization—a force that no state can resist—undermines the grip of states on both their foreign and domestic policies while opening the door for NGO and IO empowerment. The tangled tale of Pinochet prompts us to think about the impact of these rising **nonstate actors** on states' foreign and domestic policy making and the strategies these groups employ.

Karen Mingst provides such a framework in her work on **"linkage actors,"** in which she develops a typology of linkage actors and their strategies. Mingst uses James Rosenau's definition of "linkage" to mean "any recurrent sequence of behavior that originates in one system and is reacted to in another."[35] She offers seven categories of linkage actors:

1. Government negotiators engaged in the nested game between domestic and international politics.
2. International organizations, whether acting as agents in their own right or as agents of states.
3. International courts, especially the European Court of Justice, which enjoys supranational jurisdiction.
4. Transgovernmental coalitions between agencies of different states acting cooperatively toward a common goal.
5. Individuals involved in "track two" or informal diplomacy, such as the representative of the Vatican or a former head of state.
6. Nongovernmental organizations.
7. Epistemic communities, which are, as Mingst quotes Peter Haas, "network[s] of professionals with recognized expertise and competence in a particular domain and an authoritative claim to policy-relevant knowledge within that domain or issue area."[36]

Mingst states that linkage actors utilize four strategies to influence state policy. The first strategy is the **power approach.** This entails making diplomatic contacts at the ultimate decision-making levels in a high-stakes game of influence. Because failed efforts can come at a great loss of the linkage actor's credibility, Mingst warns, this strategy should not be overplayed. In our example of the Pinochet case, the Vatican effort to convince the British government to release Pinochet on humanitarian grounds illustrates a nonstate actor utilizing a power approach.

The second strategy employed by linkage actors is the **technocratic approach.** This entails, among other things, the use of the linkage actor's knowledge and expertise of the procedural mechanisms of domestic and international courts to force state compliance with international agreements. In the Pinochet case, a coalition of human rights groups in Chile and Spain led by a group of Spanish prosecutors used those prosecutors' expert knowledge of Spanish law to establish the grounds for the original arrest warrant. Similarly, the human rights NGOs that intervened in the hearings in the British House of Lords used expert knowledge of British and international law to argue against Pinochet's claim of diplomatic immunity.

The third linkage actor strategy is **coalition building.** Building a coalition that contains many different linkage actors and their resources ensures a stronger, more effective tool to change state policies. The coalitions of European governments and human rights organizations and of British human rights organizations and private British citizens who had suffered under the Pinochet regime are illustrations of effective coalition building.

Finally, the fourth strategy is **grassroots mobilization.** This entails building widespread public involvement in the cause, especially when the "public" spans several national borders. Generally such a strategy involves the use of large-scale public education efforts designed to mobilize the public to demand a response from officeholders. Although Pinochet was not made to stand trial in Spain, the case was seen as a victory for the larger cause: publicity generated by the case educated people worldwide on their rights and on the costs of violating those rights. Moreover, the case served to educate global citizens on the notion that heads of state and former heads of state did *not* enjoy unlimited diplomatic immunity on human rights issues, thereby standing this old notion on its head.

As nonstate actors rise in importance and power, foreign policy analysts will need to incorporate them into foreign policy studies. The realist notion that nonstate actors are simply instruments of state interests and the Marxist notion that nonstate actors are simply instruments of economic elite interests do not cover the range of nonstate motivations, behaviors, and power we see displayed in the tangled tale of Pinochet.

Global Rage

Before September 11, 2001, I intended to end this book with a discussion of nonstate actors on the rise, illustrated with a passing discussion of the antiglobalization protests at turn-of-the-millennium world economic meetings. Nonstate actors use features of globalization—such as global communications—to protect individuals against states even while recognizing that globalization itself poses dangers to individuals. Globalization offers such paradoxes—it offers avenues for strengthening the hands of citizens and NGOs against the traditional state structure and against states while also offering more reasons for citizens and NGOs to be alarmed. States, too, may reap the benefits of globalization while also experiencing erosion of sovereignty. States may also engage a darker side of globalization by claiming they cannot act to protect their poor or their environment because the globalization tide is inevitable and overwhelming.

But September 11 presented us with another paradox of globalization that cannot and should not be ignored or dismissed any longer. For many people in the world, globalization seals the indictment against the United States and the West while it also potentially presents the means by which the Western world system can be destroyed. According to the United States,

Osama bin Laden and his terrorist network, Al Qaeda, were responsible for the September 11 attacks. Al Qaeda stands in opposition to the U.S.-dominated world economic and political systems and to the Americanization of world culture. At the same time, Al Qaeda is the full beneficiary of globalization with associated groups, cells, and operatives in some sixty countries who share resources, finances, and expertise globally. As *Washington Post* reporters Karen DeYoung and Michael Dobbs explain,

> A defining characteristic of the movement's development has been its success in combining two seemingly incompatible sources of strength: a conservative interpretation of Islam and a comfort with aspects of the modern world that have given birth to a highly mobile, popular, wealthy, technologically savvy transnational enterprise.[37]

The groups that together form Al Qaeda have become "models of globalization."

The Qaeda network operates in much the same way as any linkage actor, yet its stakes and methods are extreme, as are its goals. Certainly the 1993 bombing of the World Trade Center, the attacks on the U.S. Marine barracks in Saudi Arabia in 1996, the 1998 bombings of the U.S. embassies in Kenya and Tanzania, and the attack on the USS *Cole* in 2000 can all be characterized as extreme versions—even ultimate versions—of the power approach described above. September 11 demonstrated that this particular linkage actor will go where the strongest state opponent of the United States will not. Further, the terrorist attack of September 11 took considerable technocratic expertise—the second linkage actor approach discussed above. How else would the hijackers fly jumbo commercial aircraft into the World Trade Center and Pentagon? Everything about the September 11 attacks required precise, long-term planning and execution, considerable knowledge of building structures and airport security, not to mention absolute commitment to the cause. Coalition building, the third approach, is the way in which Al Qaeda arose. As governments attempt to undermine this terrorist network, they are finding it to be a diverse and knotty web that combines humanitarian assistance groups, governments, terrorist training bases, and various legitimate and illegitimate financial concerns. Finally, the network that took on the United States finds its strength and its next round of frontline troops in grassroots mobilization, or in the "rage, poverty, and hopelessness in neighborhoods throughout the Middle East and sub-Saharan Africa."[38]

Like all other linkage actors, global terror must work within the confines of the international *state* system. This is yet another paradox of globalization: it erodes the importance of states while it accentuates the power of states. In 1991, Saudi Arabia expelled Osama bin Laden because he had issued a *fatwa* against the government, denouncing the regime as illegitimate.

From then until 1996, Osama bin Laden and his entourage of mujahideen (holy warriors left over from the 1980s Afghani war against the Soviets) resided in Sudan. Under some pressure from the United States, Sudan offered to arrest bin Laden and turn him over to American or Saudi Arabian authorities. Amid some confusion in the diplomatic channels between the three states, bin Laden was not arrested. Instead, the Sudanese government asked him to leave, and he chartered a jet and took his entourage and financial assets to Afghanistan.[39]

Osama bin Laden was forced by states to relocate several times. States—fully functional states—retain control over who resides within their borders. Afghanistan was, perhaps, a much better refuge for bin Laden, since the ruling Taliban regime was extraordinarily sympathetic to him, his cause, and his money. Plus, the Taliban did not have full control over the country, so its own position was precarious, giving it less relative power over bin Laden than the Saudi or Sudanese governments had and making it far more dependent on bin Laden's fighters and assets.

Bin Laden had written and spoken about his desire to destroy the state system—no wonder, he and his group were confined by it. Although Afghanistan was not what we might call a **failed state**, it certainly was not a fully integrated or articulated state with full state powers. Indeed, high on the list of potential targets for the United States in the war against **terrorism** at the end of 2001 was another failed state, Somalia—a country familiar to the readers of *The New Foreign Policy*. A meeting of various Somali leaders in 2000 resulted in the election of a parliament and the selection of a president, but these authorities only governed the environs of Mogadishu. Southern Somalia, at the end of 2001, was in the hands of an Al Qaeda–affiliated clan according to the U.S. government. American foreign policy makers faced a situation that challenged the Bush 2 administration's dislike for **nation building:** failed states present a ready-made refuge for people who oppose states in general.

Bin Laden and Al Qaeda were not the only actors in this "war" bound by the state system. The American war against international terrorism was constrained by the power retained by other states. For example, the first arrests in the September 11 attacks came in Spain. In mid-November 2001, eight men were arrested and charged with complicity in the attacks in an indictment released by a Spanish investigative judge, Baltazar Garzón—the same judge who issued the indictment that led to Augusto Pinochet's arrest in London as discussed in the tangled tale of Pinochet. Spanish authorities had been investigating an Al Qaeda cell that had formed in 1994 in Madrid. Phone intercepts indicated that the individuals in the cell had helped plan the September 11 attacks with some of the hijackers.[40]

Although the arrest of the Al Qaeda cell for complicity in the attacks should have been very good news, it actually posed some diplomatic difficulties for the Bush 2 administration. As part of the administration's evolving plans for the war on international terrorism, George W. Bush had announced that he would use military tribunals to try any foreign nationals on charges stemming from September 11. This announcement was met with criticism from all sides of the political spectrum within the United States and as well as from the closest American allies. The rules for the tribunals had not been fully formulated at the start of 2002, leaving critics to worry further about the kind of justice they would meter out.

Within days of the announcement of the arrests of the cell, the Spanish Foreign Ministry announced that "Spain could extradite detainees only to countries that offer defendants the legal guarantees provided by Spanish courts."[41] Military tribunals would *not* offer the same legal guarantees, making extradition to the United States highly unlikely. Moreover, none of the other European Union countries could be expected to extradite suspects to the United States for the same reason. Because the death penalty would be an option in these U.S. tribunals, extradition of suspects from Europe would violate EU policy against the death penalty. Although Spain and the broader EU were supportive of U.S. efforts in the war against international terrorism, they were not prepared to sacrifice their own national and EU laws and principles in the process.

The American war on international terrorism and the investigation into the attacks of September 11 are ongoing as this book is being written. It many ways, it is too early to draw conclusions about this episode. But we can say that globalization created the conditions in which global terror could take on the lone superpower. At the same time, global terror was/is confined within the international state system. Finally, although states retain control over the international system, they would be foolhardy to ignore the rising power and rage of certain nonstate actors.

Concluding Thoughts

Our study of *The New Foreign Policy* began with this list:

- Foreign policy is made and conducted in complex domestic and international environments.
- Foreign policy results from coalitions of interested domestic and international actors and groups.
- Foreign policy issues are often linked and delinked, reflecting the strength of various parties and their particular concerns.
- The *stuff* of foreign policy derives from issues of domestic politics as well as foreign relations.
- Foreign policy analysis needs to be multilevel and multifaceted in order to confront the complicated sources and nature of foreign policy.

This list rightly suggests that foreign policy analysis is an enormous undertaking. If we were to attempt to untangle the many issues and actors involved in any foreign policy tale, we would have a number of tools to assist us, as described in these pages.

For example, we could propose to study the decision-making process of British Home Secretary Jack Straw as he determined whether to release Pinochet and undermine British and international human rights law or extradite Pinochet to Spain and risk destabilizing a fragile Chile. The Home Secretary's responsibilities usually extend over domestic affairs, but this was a nested game nightmare for Straw. How did he arrive at the solution he did? What calculations did he employ or what preexisting beliefs did he hold that shaped his decision making? Foreign policy scholars who pose their research at the individual level offer a variety of tools that might help us understand Straw's role in this tangled tale.

We might want to analyze the bigger picture of British, Chilean, or Spanish politics, and how this influenced these states' policies. For example, we might want to investigate the consolidation of Spanish democracy in order to understand why the judiciary would be so proactive. Spain's own experience under the Francisco Franco military dictatorship of 1936–1975 must have had some influence on the division of powers between branches of government. Further, we might explore whether Spanish public opinion supports a proactive human rights stand, thereby eliminating the "thunder" of any political voices that would preach state interests over universal values. State-level explorations of foreign policy making provide us with the tools to undertake such an investigation.

Staying at the state level and using some of the newer tools offered by Karen Mingst for studying nonstate actors, we might explore the place of Amnesty International in the development of British human rights foreign policy. Amnesty was founded in Great Britain in 1961 and has since risen to global stature and reach. We might examine the politics of coalition building between Amnesty and the British Labour Party in order to understand the prominent position given Amnesty in the Pinochet hearings.

At the system level, we might ask how the transnational coalition developed that worked together so effectively to establish the Pinochet precedent. State immunity has been a bedrock of the international system, yet a transnational human rights coalition was able to dislodge that bedrock. We might construct an explanation for this that uses the insights of scholars on the ways that small states exert leverage over great powers.

Despite the level of analysis we choose to unravel a foreign policy puzzle, we know that the resulting picture remains incomplete without incorporating lessons from the other levels. To manage our task as analysts, we decide to examine some and not other aspects of our subjects. Furthermore, we know that our own worldviews condition the choices we make about what to study, but we stay open to the answers that might be offered by other worldviews.

Foreign policy study *is* an enormous undertaking. Globalization and its attendant blurring of distinctions between foreign and domestic and the opening it provides for the rise of nonstate actors make foreign policy study even more complicated. Yet, with an understanding of the grand theories that shape the existing studies and with the tools in hand that we call the levels of analysis, we can approach this enormous subject with confidence.

Canada –	Mexico
United Kingdom –	Brazil
France –	Chile
Spain –	Argentina
Germany –	Turkey –
Italy –	China –
Poland –	Vietnam
Ukraine –	Taiwan –
Russia –	S. Korea
Israel –	N. Korea –
Syria	Japan –
Nigeria	Australia –
South Africa	
Saudi Arabia	
Egypt	
Libya	
Iran –	
Pakistan –	
India –	

Major	Regional	
Canada	Mexico	Indonesia
United Kingdom	Cuba	New Zealand
France	Brazil	Sweden
Spain	Argentina	Norway
Germany	Chile	
Italy	Denmark	
Poland	Netherlands	
Ukraine	Greece	
Russia	Egypt	
Turkey	Libya	
Israel	Morocco	
Nigeria	South Africa	
Iran	Syria	
Pakistan	Saudi Arabia	
India	S. Korea	
China	Thailand	
Taiwan	Vietnam	
N. Korea	Philippines	
Japan	Malaysia	
Australia	Singapore	

Notes

Chapter 1

1. Jonathan Mirsky, "The Dalai Lama on Succession and on the CIA," *New York Review of Books*, June 10, 1999, 48.

2. Jim Mann, "China Issue: Early Test for Clinton," *Los Angeles Times*, January 25, 1993, D1.

3. John W. Dietrich, "Interest Groups and Foreign Policy: Clinton and the China MFN Debates," *Presidential Studies Quarterly* 29, no. 2 (1999): 285.

4. Daniel Southerland, "U.S. Policy on Tibet Assailed at Hearing," *Washington Post*, July 29, 1992, A18.

5. Southerland, "U.S. Policy on Tibet," A18.

6. Dietrich, "Interest Groups," 286.

7. Nicholas D. Kristof, "Chinese Apparently Halt Rights Talks with U.S.," *New York Times*, November 25, 1992, A12.

8. Mann, "China Issue."

9. Dietrich, "Interest Groups," 288.

10. "Approval Likely on China Trade Status—with Restrictions," *USA Today*, May 26, 1993, 4B.

11. Steven A. Holmes, "World Moratorium on Nuclear Tests Is Broken by China," *New York Times*, October 6, 1993, A1.

12. Dietrich, "Interest Groups," 289.

13. Dietrich, "Interest Groups," 292.

14. In this same year, the Clinton administration changed its policy on humanitarian intervention, backing away from campaign pledges and early administration policy. This change went hand in hand with a redefining of when the United States would assist the United Nations in such interventions, repudiating the earlier policy of being a better, more helpful member of the U.N. community (i.e., a policy committed to multilateralism).

15. Leon Hadar, "Clinton Firm on Delinking China Trade, Human Rights," *Business Times (Singapore)*, December 19, 1995, Lexis-Nexis.

16. "Dalai Lama as [sic] U.N. to Trace Panchen Lama, Protest in New Delhi," *Agence France Presse*, December 2, 1995, Lexis-Nexis.

17. "Senate Passes Measure on Panchen Lama," *Agence France Presse,* December 14, 1995, Lexis-Nexis.

18. "Senate Passes Measure."

19. "China Condemns U.S. Interference in Its Internal Affairs," *Xinhua News Agency,* December 14, 1995, Lexis-Nexis.

20. Kevin Platt, "Why China's Activists Speak Out for Tibet," *Christian Science Monitor,* November 19, 1998, 1.

21. Ralph Jimenez, "Issue Arrives Here from Top of World," *Boston Globe,* January 23, 2000, 1, New Hampshire Weekly section.

22. Office of the Press Secretary, May 9, 2000.

23. Robert D. Putnam, "Diplomacy and Domestic Politics: The Logic of Two-Level Games," *International Organization* 42, no. 3 (1988): 427–69.

24. Karen Mingst, *Essentials of International Relations* (New York: Norton, 1999), 139.

25. James N. Rosenau, "Pre-theories and Theories of Foreign Policy," in *Approaches to Comparative and International Politics,* ed. R. Barry Farrell (Evanston, Ill.: Northwestern University Press, 1966).

26. J. David Singer, "The Level-of-Analysis Problem in International Relations," in *The International System: Theoretical Essays,* ed. Klaus Knorr and Sidney Verba (Princeton: Princeton University Press, 1961).

27. The realist worldview has many variants, particularly neorealism, or structural realism, as well as balance-of-power and balance-of-threat adherents. For an interesting presentation of the variations in realism, see Ethan B. Kapstein and Michael Mastanduno, eds., *Unipolar Politics: Realism and State Strategies after the Cold War* (New York: Columbia University Press, 1999).

28. Liberalism is one of the many labels applied to this worldview. It has been known as idealism, pluralism, and neoliberal institutionalism. For an example of this worldview compared with realism, see Daniel Deudney and G. John Ikenberry, "Realism, Structural Liberalism, and the Western Order," in Kapstein and Mastanduno, *Unipolar Politics.*

29. Marxism has variants of its own: neo-Marxism, structuralism, dependency theory, world-systems theory. For a comprehensive overview of Marxism as compared with realism and liberalism, see Paul R. Viotti and Mark V. Kauppi, *International Relations Theory: Realism, Pluralism, Globalism, and Beyond* (Boston: Allyn & Bacon, 1999).

30. Charles F. Hermann, "Foreign Policy Behavior: That Which Is to Be Explained," in *Why Nations Act,* ed. Maurice A. East, Stephen A. Salmore, and Charles F. Hermann (Beverly Hills: Sage, 1978), 25.

31. Hermann, "Foreign Policy Behavior," 26.

32. Hermann, "Foreign Policy Behavior," 34.

33. Bruce Russett, Harvey Starr, and David Kinsella, *World Politics: The Menu for Choice,* 6th ed. (New York: St. Martin's, 2000), 117.

34. Russett, Starr, and Kinsella, *World Politics,* 117.

35. Deborah J. Gerner, "The Evolution of the Study of Foreign Policy," in *Foreign Policy Analysis: Continuity and Change in Its Second Generation,* ed. Laura Neack, Jeanne A. K. Hey, and Patrick J. Haney (Englewood Cliffs, N.J.: Prentice-Hall, 1995), 18.

36. Deborah J. Gerner, "Foreign Policy Analysis: Renaissance, Routine, or Rubbish?" in *Political Science: Looking to the Future,* vol. 2, *Comparative Politics,*

Policy, and International Relations, ed. William Croty (Evanston, Ill.: Northwestern University Press, 1992), 126.

37. Gerner, "Foreign Policy Analysis," 126.

38. Gerner, "Foreign Policy Analysis," 128.

39. Howard Wiarda, "Comparative Politics Past and Present," in *New Directions in Comparative Politics,* ed. Howard J. Wiarda (Boulder, Colo.: Westview, 1984).

40. Laura Neack, Jeanne A. K. Hey, and Patrick Haney, "Generational Change in Foreign Policy Analysis," in Neack, Hey, and Haney, *Foreign Policy Analysis,* 5.

41. Wiarda, "Comparative Politics," 12.

42. Neack, Hey, and Haney, "Generational Change," 5.

43. Neack, Hey, and Haney, "Generational Change," 6.

44. Gerner, "Foreign Policy Analysis," 130.

45. Richard Snyder, H. W. Bruck, and Burton Sapin, *Decision-Making as an Approach to the Study of International Politics,* Foreign Policy Analysis Series, no. 3 (Princeton: Princeton University Press, 1954); and Snyder, Bruck, and Sapin, eds., *Foreign Policy Decision Making* (New York: Free Press, 1963).

46. Charles F. Hermann and Gregory Peacock, "The Evolution and Future of Theoretical Research in the Comparative Study of Foreign Policy," in *New Directions in the Study of Foreign Policy,* ed. Charles F. Hermann, Charles W. Kegley, and James N. Rosenau (Winchester, Mass.: Unwin Hyman, 1987), 22–23.

47. Snyder, Bruck, and Sapin, *Foreign Policy Decision Making,* 65, as quoted in James E. Dougherty and Robert L. Pfaltzgraff Jr., *Contending Theories of International Relations: A Comprehensive Survey,* 5th ed. (New York: Longman, 2001), 554.

48. Hermann and Peacock, "Evolution and Future of Theoretical Research," 23.

49. Rosenau, "Pre-theories."

50. Rosenau, "Pre-theories," 115–16.

51. Rosenau, "Pre-theories," 124.

52. Hermann and Peacock, "Evolution and Future of Theoretical Research," 23.

53. Neack, Hey, and Haney, "Generational Change."

54. Robert O. Keohane and Joseph S. Nye, *Power and Interdependence: World Politics in Transition* (Boston: Little, Brown, 1977).

55. Neack, Hey, and Haney, "Generational Change," 7.

Chapter 2

1. Margaret G. Hermann and Joe D. Hagan, "International Decision Making: Leadership Matters," *Foreign Policy,* Spring 1988, 124–37.

2. Hermann and Hagan, "International Decision Making," 135.

3. Patrick J. Haney, "The Submarines of September: The Nixon Administration and a Soviet Submarine Base in Cuba," Pew Case Studies in International Affairs, no. 372 (Washington, D.C.: Georgetown University School of Public Service, 1996).

4. Haney, "Submarines of September," 3.

5. Joe D. Hagan, "Domestic Political Regime Changes and Third World Voting Realignments in the United Nations, 1946–84," *International Organization* 43, no. 3 (1989): 508.

6. Hans J. Morgenthau, *Politics among Nations,* brief ed., rev. Kenneth W. Thompson (New York: McGraw-Hill, 1993), 5.

7. Michael D. McGinnis, "Rational Choice and Foreign Policy Change: The Arms and Alignments of Regional Powers," in *Foreign Policy Restructuring: How Governments Respond to Global Change,* ed. Jerel A. Rosati, Joe D. Hagan, and Martin W. Sampson III (Columbia: University of South Carolina Press, 1994), 69.

8. McGinnis, "Rational Choice and Foreign Policy Change," 70.

9. McGinnis, "Rational Choice and Foreign Policy Change," 67.

10. James E. Dougherty and Robert L. Pfaltzgraff Jr., *Contending Theories of International Relations: A Comprehensive Survey,* 5th ed. (New York: Longman, 2001), 553.

11. Richard Snyder, H. W. Bruck, and Burton Sapin, "Decision-making as an Approach to the Study of International Politics," in *Foreign Policy Decision Making: An Approach to the Study of International Politics* (New York: Macmillan, 1962).

12. Graham Allison, *Essence of Decision: Explaining the Cuban Missile Crisis* (Boston: Little, Brown, 1971); Graham Allison and Philip Zelikow, *Essence of Decision: Explaining the Cuban Missile Crisis,* updated and exp. (Cambridge, U.K.: Pearson, 1999).

13. Ben D. Mor, "Nasser's Decision-making in the 1967 Middle East Crisis: A Rational-choice Explanation," *Journal of Peace Research* 28, no. 4 (1991): 359–75.

14. For details on the Suez Crisis, see Michael G. Fry, "The Suez Crisis, 1956," Pew Case Studies in International Affairs, no. 126 (Washington, D.C.: Georgetown University School of Public Service, 1989).

15. U.N. peacekeeping troops can only be placed within a country with the permission of that country's government, if there is one. This consent requirement is necessary because the United Nations recognizes the key principle that all states are sovereign. Sovereignty means that there is no higher authority than a state in its territory. Placing foreign troops in a country without the consent of the government would constitute an invasion or intervention and would only be permissible under certain narrow and relatively untested provisions of the UN Charter.

16. Mor, "Nasser's Decision-making," 371–72.

17. Deborah Sontag, "No Optimism about Mideast Talks," *New York Times,* September 6, 2000, A13.

18. Robin Wright, "Attack on Iraq May Be Outcome Hussein Wants," *Los Angeles Times,* January 31, 1998, A1.

19. Dougherty and Pfaltzgraff, *Contending Theories,* 562.

20. Karen Mingst, *Essentials of International Relations* (New York: Norton, 1999), 68.

21. Robert L. Jervis, "Hypotheses on Misperception," *World Politics,* April 1968; reprinted in *American Foreign Policy: Theoretical Essays,* ed. G. J. Ikenberry (Glenview, Ill.: Scott, Foresman, 1989), 477.

22. Jervis, "Hypotheses on Misperception," 477.

23. Kenneth Waltz, *Man, the State, and War* (New York: Columbia University Press, 1959), chap. 23; Jerel Rosati, "A Cognitive Approach to the Study of Foreign Policy," in *Foreign Policy Analysis: Continuity and Change in Its Second Generation,* ed. Laura Neack, Jeanne A. K. Hey, and Patrick J. Haney (Englewood Cliffs, N.J.: Prentice-Hall, 1995), 51.

24. Jervis, "Hypotheses on Misperception," 461.

25. Jervis, "Hypotheses on Misperception," 462.

26. Irving L. Janis, *Crucial Decisions* (New York: Free Press, 1989); and Janis,

Groupthink: Psychological Studies of Policy Decisions and Fiascoes (Boston: Houghton Mifflin, 1982).

27. Rosati, "Cognitive Approach," 50.

28. For an elaboration on five stereotypical images of outside actors, see Richard K. Herrmann and Michael P. Fischerkeller, "Beyond the Enemy Image and Spiral Model: Cognitive-Strategic Research after the Cold War," *International Organization* 49, no. 2 (1995): 415–50.

29. Ole R. Holsti, "Cognitive Dynamics and Images of the Enemy: Dulles and Russia," in *Image and Reality in World Politics*, ed. John C. Farrell and Asa P. Smith (New York: Columbia University Press, 1967), 17, as discussed in Rosati, "Cognitive Approach," 55.

30. Jack S. Levy, "Learning and Foreign Policy: Sweeping a Conceptual Minefield," *International Organization* 48, no. 2 (1994): 283.

31. Janice Gross Stein, "Political Learning by Doing: Gorbachev as Uncommitted Thinker and Motivated Learner," *International Organization* 48, no. 2 (1994): 172.

32. Stein, "Political Learning," 172.

33. Matthew S. Hirshberg, "The Self-Perpetuating National Self-Image: Cognitive Biases in Perceptions of International Interventions," *Political Psychology* 14, no. 1 (1993): 80.

34. Hirshberg, "Self-Perpetuating National Self-Image," 85.

35. Hirshberg, "Self-Perpetuating National Self-Image," 91.

36. Keith Shimko, "Foreign Policy Metaphors: Falling 'Dominoes' and 'Drug Wars,'" in Neack, Hey, and Haney, *Foreign Policy Analysis*, 73.

37. Phil Reeves, "Sharon Appeals to America Not to 'Appease' Arabs," *Independent* (London), October 5, 2001, 15; Alan Sipress and Lee Hockstader, "Sharon Speech Riles US," *Washington Post*, October 6, 2001, A1.

38. Reeves, "Sharon Appeals to America," A1.

39. Alexander George, "The 'Operational Code': A Neglected Approach to the Study of Political Leaders and Decision-making," in *American Foreign Policy: Theoretical Essays*, ed. G. John Ikenberry (Glenview, Ill.: Scott, Foresman, 1989), 486. Reprinted from the original article, which appeared in *International Studies* 13, no. 2 (1969).

40. Stephen G. Walker, Mark Schafer, and Michael D. Young, "Presidential Operational Codes and Foreign Policy Conflicts in the Post-Cold War World," *Journal of Conflict Resolution* 43, no. 5 (1999): 613.

41. Ibrahim A. Karawan, "Sadat and the Egyptian-Israeli Peace Revisited," *International Journal of Middle East Studies* 26, no. 2 (1994): 249–66.

42. Karawan, "Sadat and the Egyptian-Israeli Peace," 252.

43. Karawan, "Sadat and the Egyptian-Israeli Peace," 252.

44. Allison Astorino-Courtois, "The Cognitive Structure of Decision-making and the Course of Arab-Israeli Relations, 1970–1978," *Journal of Conflict Resolution* 39, no. 3 (1995): 420.

45. Peter Suedfeld, Michael D. Wallace, and Kimberly L. Thachuk, "Changes in Integrative Complexity among Middle East Leaders during the Persian Gulf Crisis," *Journal of Social Issues* 49, no. 4 (1993): 183–84. See also Philip E. Tetlock, "Integrative Complexity of American and Soviet Foreign Policy Rhetoric: A Time-Series Analysis," *Journal of Personality and Social Psychology* 49 (1985): 1565–85.

46. Astorino-Courtois, "Cognitive Structure of Decision-making," 420; Stephen G. Walker and George L. Watson, "Integrative Complexity and British Decisions during the Munich and Polish Crises," *Journal of Conflict Resolution* 38, no. 1 (1994): 3–23.

47. Astorino-Courtois, "Cognitive Structure of Decision-making," 421.

48. For this insight, I thank Amanda Bulick, a student in my undergraduate foreign policy class at Miami University, Oxford, Ohio, fall 2000.

49. Dorothy V. Jones, *Code of Peace: Ethics and Security in the World of the Warlord States* (Chicago: University of Chicago Press, 1991).

50. J. Ann Tickner, *Gender in International Relations: Feminist Perspectives on Achieving Global Security* (New York: Columbia University Press, 1992); Christine Sylvester, *Feminist Theory and International Relations in a Postmodern Era* (Cambridge: Cambridge University Press, 1994); and V. Spike Peterson, "The Politics of Identity and Gendered Nationalism," in Neack, Hey, and Haney, *Foreign Policy Analysis*.

51. Tom Princen, "Camp David: Problem-Solving or Power Politics as Usual?" *Journal of Peace Research* 28, no. 1 (1991): 58.

52. Princen, "Camp David," 59.

53. Princen, "Camp David," 59.

54. Jeffrey Hopkins, ed., *The Art of Peace: Nobel Peace Laureates Discuss Human Rights, Conflict, and Reconciliation* (Ithaca, N.Y.: Snow Lions, 2000), 116.

55. Jones, *Code of Peace*.

56. With thanks to Dr. Susan Penksa, Westmont College, Santa Barbara, California, for help with this list of suggested readings.

Chapter 3

1. Ulf Hedetoft, "National Identity and Mentalities of War in Three EC Countries," *Journal of Peace Research* 30, no. 3 (1993): 295.

2. Hedetoft, "National Identity," 292.

3. Hedetoft, "National Identity," 295.

4. Peter R. Baehr, "Trials and Errors: The Netherlands and Human Rights," in *Human Rights and Comparative Foreign Policy*, ed. David P. Forsythe (New York: United Nations University Press, 2000), 52.

5. James N. Rosenau, "Pre-theories and Theories of Foreign Policy," in *Approaches to Comparative and International Politics*, ed. R. Barry Farrell (Evanston, Ill.: Northwestern University Press, 1966), 133.

6. Laura Neack, "Linking State Type with Foreign Policy Behavior," in *Foreign Policy Analysis: Continuity and Change in Its Second Generation*, ed. Laura Neack, Jeanne A. K. Hey, and Patrick J. Haney (Englewood Cliffs, N.J.: Prentice-Hall, 1995), 217.

7. Matthew S. Hirshberg, "The Self-Perpetuating National Self-Image: Cognitive Biases in Perceptions of International Interventions," *Political Psychology* 14, no. 1 (1993): 78.

8. Hirshberg, "Self-Perpetuating National Self-Image," 78.

9. J. L. Granatstein, "Peacekeeping: Did Canada Make a Difference? And What Difference Did Canada Make?" in *Making a Difference: Canada's Foreign Policy in a Changing World Order*, ed. John English and Norman Hillmer (Toronto: Lester, 1992), 223.

10. Granatstein, "Peacekeeping," 223–24.

11. The Canadian government Web site provides a detailed, comprehensive discussion of all that goes into Canada's Foreign Policy for Human Security. See "Freedom from Fear," at www.humansecurity.gc.ca (last accessed October 2001).

12. Hirshberg, "Self-Perpetuating National Self-Image," 87.

13. Hirshberg, "Self-Perpetuating National Self-Image," 96.

14. Alastair Ian Johnston, "Realism(s) and Chinese Security Policy in the Post-Cold War Period," in *Unipolar Politics: Realism and State Strategies after the Cold War*, ed. Ethan B. Kapstein and Michael Mastanduno (New York: Columbia University Press, 1999), 288.

15. Johnston, "Realism(s) and Chinese Security Policy," 289.

16. Daniel Bar-Tal and Dikla Antebi, "Beliefs about Negative Intentions of the World: A Study of Israeli Siege Mentality," *Political Psychology* 13, no. 4 (1992): 634.

17. Sergei V. Chugrov, "Russian Foreign Policy and Human Rights: Conflicted Culture and Uncertain Policy," in Forsythe, *Human Rights and Comparative Foreign Policy*, 149.

18. Peter J. Katzenstein and Nobuo Okawara, "Japan's National Security: Structures, Norms, and Policies," *International Security* 17, no. 4 (1993): 87.

19. Yozo Yokota and Chiyuki Aoi, "Japan's Foreign Policy toward Human Rights: Uncertain Changes," in Forsythe, *Human Rights and Comparative Foreign Policy*, 127.

20. Katzenstein and Okawara, "Japan's National Security," 92.

21. Katzenstein and Okawara, "Japan's National Security," 97.

22. Peter Cowhey, "Domestic Institutions and the Credibility of International Commitments: Japan and the U.S.," *International Organization* 47, no. 2 (1993): 299–326; see also Katzenstein and Okawara, "Japan's National Security"; and Yokota and Aoi, "Japan's Foreign Policy."

23. Elizabeth Kier, "Culture and Military Doctrine: France between the Wars," *International Security* 19, no. 4 (1995): 65–66.

24. Kier, "Culture and Military Doctrine," 78.

25. Kier, "Culture and Military Doctrine," 74.

26. Michael Doyle, "Kant, Liberal Legacies, and Foreign Affairs," *Philosophy and Public Affairs* 12, no. 3 (1983): 205–35. Kant's name has been the source of much creative titling in this research stream, for example: T. Clifton Morgan and Sally Howard Campbell, "Domestic Structure, Decisional Constraints, and War: So Why Kant Democracies Fight?" *Journal of Conflict Resolution* 35, no. 2 (1991): 187–211; Christopher Layne, "Kant or Cant: The Myth of the Democratic Peace," *International Security* 19, no. 2 (1994): 5–49; and Erik Gartzke, "Kant We All Just Get Along? Opportunity, Willingness, and the Origins of the Democratic Peace," *American Journal of Political Science* 42, no. 1 (1998): 1–27.

27. T. Clifton Morgan, "Democracy and War: Reflections on the Literature," *International Interactions* 18, no. 3 (1992): 198.

28. Brett Ashley Leeds and David R. Davis, "Beneath the Surface: Regime Type and International Interaction, 1953–78," *Journal of Peace Research* 36, no. 1 (1999): 7.

29. Leeds and Davis, "Beneath the Surface," 8; Morgan, "Democracy and War," 199.

30. David P. Forsythe, "Democracy, War, and Covert Action," *Journal of Peace Research* 29 (1992): 385–95; Neack, "Linking State Type with Foreign Policy Behavior," 220–21.

31. Bruce Russett, *Grasping the Democratic Peace: Principles for a Post-Cold War World* (Princeton: Princeton University Press, 1993).

32. Leeds and Davis, "Beneath the Surface," 6.

33. Edward D. Mansfield and Jack Snyder, "Democratization and the Danger of War," *International Security* 20, no. 1 (1995): 5–38.

34. Mansfield and Snyder, "Democratization and the Danger of War," 13–15.

35. Mansfield and Snyder, "Democratization and the Danger of War," 26.

36. Mansfield and Snyder, "Democratization and the Danger of War," 33.

37. Joe D. Hagan, "Domestic Political Explanations in the Analysis of Foreign Policy," in Neack, Hey, and Haney, *Foreign Policy Analysis*, 137, figure 8.1.

38. Hagan, "Domestic Political Explanations," 128.

39. Hagan, "Domestic Political Explanations," 129.

40. Edward D. Mansfield and Jack Snyder, "Democratization and War," *Foreign Affairs* 74, no. 3 (1995): 93.

41. Mansfield and Snyder, "Democratization and War," 90.

42. Neil MacFarlane, "Realism and Russian Strategy after the Collapse of the USSR," in Kapstein and Mastanduno, *Unipolar Politics*, 236.

43. Kazakhstan, Kyrgyzstan, Tajikistan, Turkmenistan, and Uzbekistan. See Rajan Menon, "In the Shadow of the Bear: Security in Post-Soviet Central Asia," *International Security* 20, no. 1 (1995): 149–81.

44. Menon, "In the Shadow of the Bear," 157.

45. Menon, "In the Shadow of the Bear," 158–59. See also Neil MacFarlane, "Realism and Russian Strategy after the Collapse of the USSR," in Kapstein and Mastanduno, *Unipolar Politics*.

46. MacFarlane, "Realism and Russian Strategy," 160.

47. Maria Persson Lofren, "Russia: Mothers for Peace Oppose Sons in War,"*Inter Press Service*, October 2, 1996, Lexis-Nexis.

48. "Putin Flies into Grozny in Fighter Bomber," *Deutsche Presse-Agentur*, March 20, 2000, Lexis-Nexis.

49. In February 2001, Sharon defeated Barak to become prime minister of Israel.

50. Ali Raiss-Tousi, "Hamas Says Palestinians Have No Choice but War," *Reuters*, October 4, 2000, Lexis-Nexis.

51. Keith B. Richburg, "Clashes Resurge at Sacred Sites, 9 Palestinians Killed in 'Day of Rage,'" *Washington Post*, October 7, 2000, A1.

52. Brandon C. Prins and Christopher Sprecher, "Institutional Constraints, Political Opposition, and Interstate Dispute Escalation: Evidence from Parliamentary Systems, 1946–89," *Journal of Peace Research* 36, no. 3 (1999): 277.

53. Prins and Christopher Sprecher, "Institutional Constraints," 274.

54. Prins and Christopher Sprecher, "Institutional Constraints," 285.

55. Juliet Kaarbo, "Power and Influence in Foreign Policy Decision-making: The Role of Junior Coalition Partners in German and Israeli Foreign Policy," *International Studies Quarterly* 40, no. 4 (1996): 503.

56. Kaarbo, "Power and Influence," 504.

57. Kaarbo, "Power and Influence," 506, 519.

58. Kaarbo, "Power and Influence," 520.

59. Kaarbo, "Power and Influence," 521–22.

60. Graham T. Allison, *The Essence of Decision: Explaining the Cuban Missile Crisis* (Boston: Little, Brown, 1971).

61. Andrew J. Pierre, "Vietnam's Contradictions," *Foreign Affairs* 79, no. 6 (2000): 69–86; quote from 73.

62. Pierre, "Vietnam's Contradictions," 73.

63. Pierre, "Vietnam's Contradictions," 74.

64. Zachary Abuza, "Institutions and Actions in Vietnamese Foreign Policymaking: A Research Note," *Contemporary Southeast Asia* 19, no. 3 (1997): 309–33.

65. Mark Sidel, "Generational and Institutional Transition in the Vietnamese Communist Party," *Asian Survey* 37, no. 5 (1997): 481–95.

66. Eric Rouleau, "Turkey's Dream of Democracy," *Foreign Affairs* 79, no. 6 (2000): 103.

67. Rouleau, "Turkey's Dream of Democracy," 102.

68. Rouleau, "Turkey's Dream of Democracy," 105–6.

69. Baehr, "Trials and Errors," 61.

70. Baehr, "Trials and Errors," 57–58.

71. Thomas Risse-Kappen, "Public Opinion, Domestic Structure, and Foreign Policy in Liberal Democracies," *World Politics* 43, no. 4 (1991): 480.

72. Risse-Kappen, "Public Opinion," 481.

73. Ole Holsti, *Public Opinion and American Foreign Policy* (Ann Arbor: University of Michigan Press, 1996), 31.

74. Holsti, *Public Opinion*, 110.

75. Shibley Telhami, "Arab Public Opinion and the Gulf War," *Political Science Quarterly* 104, no. 3 (1993): 437–52.

76. Telhami, "Arab Public Opinion," 440.

77. Telhami, "Arab Public Opinion," 445.

78. Telhami, "Arab Public Opinion," 450–51.

79. Telhami, "Arab Public Opinion," 451.

80. John F. Burns, "Mubarak Meets Arafat and Avoids Publicly Pressing Him to Meet Demands of Israel," *New York Times*, October 10, 2000, A17; "Arab Nations Stage Wave of Protests," *The Times* (London), October 9, 2000, Lexis-Nexis; and "Violence Threatens Yom Kippur," *Seattle Times*, October 9, 2000, A1.

81. Lee Hockstader, "Palestinians Suppress Coverage of Crowds Celebrating Attacks," *Washington Post*, September 16, 2001, A42.

82. Hockstader, "Palestinians Suppress Coverage"; see also "Palestinian Leaders Reject Attack Support," *Irish Times*, September 13, 2001, 12.

83. Lee Hockstader, "Palestinian Police Open Fire on Rally for Bin Laden," *Washington Post*, October 9, 2001, A1.

84. Lee Hockstader, "Palestinians' Rage Tests Arafat's Rule," *Washington Post*, October 10, 2001, A18.

85. Risse-Kappen, "Public Opinion," 510.

86. Risse-Kappen, "Public Opinion," 510.

87. Risse-Kappen, "Public Opinion," 511.

88. Risse-Kappen, "Public Opinion," 492 (table 1), 510–11.

89. Yossi Shain, "Multicultural Foreign Policy," *Foreign Policy*, Fall 1995, 69–87.

90. Shain, "Multicultural Foreign Policy," 75–76.

91. Shain, "Multicultural Foreign Policy," 78.

92. Joseph S. Nye Jr., "Redefining NATO's Mission in the Information Age," *NATO Review,* Winter 1999, 13.

93. Jonathan Mermin, "Television News and American Intervention in Somalia: The Myth of a Media-Driven Foreign Policy," *Political Science Quarterly* 112, no. 3 (1997): 387; emphasis added.

94. Mermin, "Television News," 386.

95. Mermin, "Television News," 387.

96. Mermin, "Television News," 387. Here Mermin cites Leon V. Sigal, "Sources Make the News," in *Reading the News,* ed. Robert Karl Manoof and Michael Schudson (New York: Pantheon, 1986), 16.

97. Mermin, "Television News," 387.

98. Mermin, "Television News," 387. Here Mermin refers the reader to Michael Schudson, *Discovering the News: A Social History of American Newspapers* (New York: Basic, 1978).

99. Mermin, "Television News," 388.

100. Mermin, "Television News," 388.

101. Mermin, "Television News," 389.

102. Mermin, "Television News," 392–93.

103. Mermin, "Television News," 394.

104. Patrick J. Haney, "The Submarines of September: The Nixon Administration and a Soviet Submarine Base in Cuba," Pew Case Studies in International Affairs, no. 372 (Washington, D.C.: Georgetown University School of Public Service, 1996), 3, 5.

105. Tony Shaw, "The British Popular Press and the Early Cold War," *History* 83, no. 269 (1998): 66–85.

106. Shaw, "British Popular Press," 78.

107. For a fascinating account of the life of a humanitarian aid worker who promoted the cause of human rights in Chechnya, see Scott Anderson, *The Man Who Tried to Save the World: The Dangerous Life and Mysterious Disappearance of Fred Cuny* (New York: Doubleday, 1999).

108. Warren P. Strobel, *Late-Breaking Foreign Policy: The News Media's Influence on Peace Operations* (Washington, D.C.: U.S. Institute for Peace Press, 1997), 6.

109. Strobel, *Late-Breaking Foreign Policy,* 211.

110. Strobel, *Late-Breaking Foreign Policy,* 5.

111. Strobel, *Late-Breaking Foreign Policy,* 212.

Chapter 4

1. "China, Chechnya, Cuba in U.N. Human Rights Spotlight," *Agence France Presse,* April 17, 2001, Lexis-Nexis.

2. "China Gleeful over Human Rights Victory, Slams U.S. Motives," *Agence France Presse,* April 19, 2001, Lexis-Nexis.

3. Richard Beeston and Damian Whitworth, "Washington's Enemies Deliver Snub at U.N.," *The Times* (London), May 4, 2001, Lexis-Nexis.

4. Kenneth N. Waltz, *Man, the State and War* (New York: Columbia University Press, 1959), 159.

5. Waltz, *Man, the State, and War,* 160.

6. Charles Kindleberger, "Dominance and Leadership in the International Economy: Exploitation, Public Goods, and Free Rides," *International Studies Quarterly* 25, no. 2 (1981): 249–50.

7. Robert Gilpin, *U.S. Power and the Multinational Corporation: The Political Economy of Foreign Direct Investment* (New York: Basic, 1975), 24, as quoted in James E. Dougherty and Robert L. Pfaltzgraff Jr., *Contending Theories of International Relations: A Comprehensive Survey,* 5th ed. (New York: Longman, 2001), 72.

8. One of the classic treatments of this is in Thomas C. Schelling, *Arms and Influence* (New Haven: Yale University Press, 1966).

9. For an excellent study comparing peacekeeping and peace enforcement operations in the 1990s, including those launched in Somalia, see Donald C. F. Daniel and Bradd C. Hayes with Chantal de Jonge Oudraat, *Coercive Inducement and the Containment of International Crises* (Washington, D.C.: U.S. Institute of Peace Press, 1999). Daniel, Hayes, and de Jonge Oudraat focus much of their discussion on the different rules governing the use of force in these operations.

10. Mark Bowden, *Black Hawk Down* (New York: Penguin, 1999).

11. Donald H. Rumsfeld, "A New Kind of War," *New York Times,* September 27, 2001, A21.

12. Graham Evans and Jeffrey Newnham, *The Penguin Dictionary of International Relations* (New York: Penguin Putnam, 1998), 210.

13. Evans and Newnham, *Penguin Dictionary of International Relations,* 209.

14. Edward N. Luttwak, "Where Are the Great Powers? At Home with the Kids," *Foreign Affairs* 73, no. 4 (1994): 26.

15. Luttwak, "Where Are the Great Powers," 26.

16. Luttwak, "Where Are the Great Powers," 23.

17. Luttwak, "Where Are the Great Powers," 23.

18. Charles Krauthammer, "The Unipolar Moment," *Foreign Affairs* 70, no. 1 (1990–1991): 23–33.

19. Charles Krauthammer, "Not Enough Might," *Washington Post,* October 30, 2001, A21.

20. Alan Sipress and Vernon Loeb, "U.S. Welcoming Allies' Troops: Despite Pentagon's Concerns, Taliban War Is Multi-Country," *Washington Post,* November 11, 2001, A38.

21. Jane Perlez, "The Corrupt and Brutal Reclaim Afghan Thrones, Evoking Chaos of Somalia," *New York Times,* November 19, 2001, B4; William Branigin and Keith B. Richburg, "Former Afghan Leader Returns to Kabul," *Washington Post,* November 18, 2001, A1.

22. Michael R. Gordon, "Afghans Block Britain's Plan for Big Force," *New York Times,* November 20, 2001, B1.

23. Mike Peacock, "Blair Denies Rift with U.S. over War Strategy," *Reuters,* November 21, 2001.

24. As the interim Afghan government was set to take over in Kabul, British forces were set again to be the leading country in a peacekeeping force, but a peacekeeping force under U.S. military command. As the Bush 2 administration looked to broaden the war against terrorism in late 2001, the British were suggesting that they might not be able to participate in a wider war *because* their Afghan duties would be so preoccupying. "Somalia Could Be Next: Intervention

Is Likely, but Rehabilitation Must Be the Aim," *Herald* (Glasgow), December 12, 2001, Lexis-Nexis.

25. As quoted in Ian Lustick, "The Absence of Middle Eastern Great Powers: Political 'Backwardness' in Historical Perspective," *International Organization* 51, no. 4 (1997): 659.

26. Lustick, "Absence of Middle Eastern Great Powers," 657.

27. Luttwak, "Where Are the Great Powers," 26.

28. Christopher Layne, "From Preponderance to Offshore Balancing: America's Future Grand Strategy," *International Security* 22, no. 1 (1997): 88.

29. Lustick, "Absence of Middle Eastern Great Powers," 660.

30. Mary Ann Tétreault, "Autonomy, Necessity, and the Small State: Ruling Kuwait in the Twentieth Century," *International Organization* 45, no. 4 (1991): 565–91.

31. Michael T. Klare, "The Geopolitics of War," *Nation*, November 5, 2001, 12.

32. Klare, "Geopolitics of War," 12.

33. Ken Silverstein, "Saudis and Americans: Friends in Need," *Nation*, November 3, 2001, 15.

34. Silverstein, "Saudis and Americans," 15.

35. Aram Roston, "A Royal Scandal," *Nation*, December 3, 2001, 16.

36. Fouad Ajami, "The Sentry's Solitude," *Foreign Affairs* 80, no. 6 (2001): 11.

37. Michael Mastanduno and Ethan B. Kapstein, "Realism and State Strategies after the Cold War," in *Unipolar Politics: Realism and State Strategies after the Cold War*, ed. Ethan B. Kapstein and Michael Mastanduno (New York: Columbia University Press, 1999), 4.

38. Mastanduno and Kapstein, "Realism and State Strategies," 5.

39. Mastanduno and Kapstein, "Realism and State Strategies," 5.

40. Christopher Layne, "From Preponderance to Offshore Balancing: America's Future Grand Strategy," *International Security* 22, no. 1 (1997): 86–124.

41. Benjamin Schwarz, "Why America Thinks It Has to Run the World," *Atlantic Monthly*, June 1996, 94.

42. Schwarz, "Why America Thinks," 96.

43. Schwarz, "Why America Thinks," 101.

44. Layne, "From Preponderance to Offshore Balancing," 88.

45. Schwarz, "Why America Thinks," 100. Also quoted in Benjamin Schwarz and Christopher Layne, "A New Grand Strategy," *Atlantic Monthly*, January 2002, 37.

46. In the Schwarz and Layne follow-on article cited in the previous note, they attribute the defense planning guidance report to a committee acting under the supervision of Paul Wolfowitz, the undersecretary of defense in the George W. Bush (Bush 2) administration.

47. Schwarz, "Why America Thinks," 98.

48. Schwarz and Layne, "New Grand Strategy," 36.

49. Josef Joffe, "How America Does It," *Foreign Affairs* 76, no. 5 (1997): 16.

50. Joffe, "How America Does It," 24.

51. Joffe, "How America Does It," 27.

52. Josef Joffe, "'Bismarck' or 'Britain'? Toward an American Grand Strategy after Bipolarity," *International Security* 19, no. 4 (1995): 113.

53. Thom Shanker, "Rumsfeld Asks NATO to Shift to Wide Fight against Terror," *New York Times*, December 19, 2001, B1.

54. Karen DeYoung, "Bush Seeks Power to Lift Arms Curbs," *Washington Post*, September 24, 2001, A1.

55. Rumsfeld, "A New Kind of War."

56. Layne, "From Preponderance to Offshore Balancing."

57. Schwarz and Layne, "New Grand Strategy."

58. Layne, "From Preponderance to Offshore Balancing," 117–18.

59. Layne, "From Preponderance to Offshore Balancing," 112.

60. Layne, "From Preponderance to Offshore Balancing," 112.

61. Layne, "From Preponderance to Offshore Balancing," 112.

62. David E. Sanger, "U.S. Will Drop Objections to China's Missile Buildup," *New York Times*, September 2, 2001, A1; Edward Allen, "U.S. May Soften on Chinese Weapons," *Financial Times*, September 3, 2001, 1.

63. David E. Sanger, "U.S. Restates Its Stand on Missiles in China," *New York Times*, September 5, 2001, A3.

64. Layne, "From Preponderance to Offshore Balancing," 116.

65. Schwarz and Layne, "New Grand Strategy," 42.

66. Krauthammer, "The Unipolar Moment," 24–25.

67. Samuel P. Huntington, "Why International Primacy Matters," *International Security* 17, no. 4 (1993): 68–83; Richard Bernstein and Ross H. Munro, "China: The Coming Conflict with America," *Foreign Affairs* 76, no. 2 (1997): 18–32.

68. Eric Heginbotham and Richard J. Samuels, "Mercantile Realism and Japanese Foreign Policy," *International Security* 22, no. 4 (1998): 172.

69. Richard N. Rosecrance, *The Rise of the Trading State: Commerce and Conquest in the World of Warlord States* (New York: Basic, 1985).

70. Michael Loriaux, "Realism and Reconciliation: France, Germany, and the European Union," in *Unipolar Politics: Realism and State Strategies after the Cold War*, ed. Ethan B. Kapstein and Michael Mastanduno (New York: Columbia University Press, 1999), 358.

71. Dorothy V. Jones, *Code of Peace: Ethics and Security in the World of the Warlord States* (Chicago: University of Chicago Press, 1991).

72. Neil MacFarlane, "Realism and Russian Strategy after the Collapse of the USSR," in Kapstein and Mastanduno, *Unipolar Politics*, 218–60.

73. James N. Rosenau, "Pre-theories and Theories of Foreign Policy," in *Approaches to Comparative and International Politics*, ed. R. Barry Farrell (Evanston, Ill.: Northwestern University Press, 1966), 147–48.

74. Rosenau, "Pre-theories," 147, n. 75.

75. Rosenau, "Pre-theories," 153.

76. Maria Papadakis and Harvey Starr, "Opportunity, Willingness, and Small States: The Relationship between Environment and Foreign Policy," in *New Directions in the Study of Foreign Policy*, ed. Charles F. Hermann, Charles W. Kegley, and James N. Rosenau (Winchester, Mass.: Unwin Hyman, 1987).

77. Davis B. Bobrow and Steve Chan, "Simple Labels and Complex Realities: National Security for the Third World," in *National Security in the Third World: The Management of Internal and External Threats*, ed. Edward E. Azar and Chung-in Moon (Aldershot, U.K.: Edward Elgar, 1988), 56–57.

78. Mary Ann Tétreault, "Autonomy, Necessity, and the Small State: Ruling Kuwait in the Twentieth Century," *International Organization* 45, no. 4 (1991): 565.

79. Tétreault, "Autonomy, Necessity," 572.

80. Tétreault, "Autonomy, Necessity," 567.

81. Tétreault, "Autonomy, Necessity," 588.

82. Tétreault, "Autonomy, Necessity," 573.

83. Tétreault, "Autonomy, Necessity," 577.

84. Tétreault, "Autonomy, Necessity," 579.

85. Tétreault, "Autonomy, Necessity," 582.

86. Martin W. Sampson III, "Exploiting the Seams: External Structure and Libyan Foreign Policy Changes," in *Foreign Policy Restructuring: How Governments Respond to Global Change*, ed. Jerel A. Rosati, Joe D. Hagan, and Martin W. Sampson III (Columbia: University of South Carolina Press, 1994), 93.

87. Sampson, "Exploiting the Seams," 93–94.

88. Sampson, "Exploiting the Seams," 94–95.

89. Sampson, "Exploiting the Seams," 95.

90. Sampson, "Exploiting the Seams," 99.

91. Sampson, "Exploiting the Seams," 98–99.

92. Sampson, "Exploiting the Seams," 107.

93. Michael Jansen, "Saudi Royals Risk Sharing Shah's Fate," *Irish Times*, November 10, 2001, 12.

94. Carsten Holbraad, *Middle Powers in International Politics* (New York: St. Martin's, 1984).

95. Andrew F. Cooper, Richard A. Higgott, and Kim Richard Nossal, *Relocating Middle Powers: Australia and Canada in a Changing World Order* (Vancouver: University of British Columbia Press, 1993), 19.

96. John W. Holmes, *The Shaping of Peace: Canada and the Search for World Order, 1943–1975* (Toronto: University of Toronto Press, 1982); Bernard Wood, *The Middle Powers and the General Interest* (Ottawa: North-South Institute, 1988).

97. J. L. Granatstein, "Peacekeeping: Did Canada Make a Difference? And What Difference Did Peacekeeping Make to Canada?" in *Making a Difference: Canada's Foreign Policy in a Changing World Order*, ed. John English and Norman Hillmer (Toronto: Lester, 1992), 223–24.

98. Canada is a relatively "young" country in that it did not have full autonomy over its external affairs and foreign policy until the 1930s. Before this, Canada's foreign relations were directed by Great Britain working through a very small Canadian diplomatic corps.

99. Peter R. Baehr, "Trials and Errors: The Netherlands and Human Rights," in *Human Rights and Comparative Foreign Policy*, ed. David P. Forsythe (New York: United Nations University Press, 2000), 51.

100. Granatstein, "Peacekeeping," 224–25.

101. Cooper, Higgott, and Nossal, *Relocating Middle Powers*.

102. Holbraad, *Middle Powers*, 125.

103. A short description of this conference is presented in Geoffrey Hayes, "Middle Powers in the New World Order," *Beyond the Headlines*, Winter 1993–1994.

104. James L. Dougherty and Robert L. Pfaltzgraff Jr., *Contending Theories of International Relations*, 5th ed. (New York: Longman, 2001), 167.

105. Dougherty and Pfaltzgraff, *Contending Theories*. They reference Nicholas Greenwood Onuf, *World of Our Making: Rules and Rule in Social Theory and International Relations* (Columbia: University of South Carolina Press, 1989), 35–65.

106. Alexander Wendt, "Anarchy Is What States Make of It: The Social Construction of Power Politics," *International Organization* 46, no. 2 (1992): 394.

107. Dale C. Copeland, "The Constructivist Challenge to Structural Realism," *International Security* 25, no. 2 (2000): 188.

108. Adam Chapnick, "The Canadian Middle Power Myth," *International Journal*, Spring 2000, 188.

109. Richard A. Higgott and Kim Richard Nossal, "The International Politics of Liminality: Relocating Australia in the Asia Pacific," *Australian Journal of Political Science* 32, no. 2 (1997): 169–85.

110. "Australia's Place in the World," Address by The Hon Alexander Downer, MP, Minister of Foreign Affairs, to the NSW Division of the Liberal Party, Sidney, Tuesday 26 November 1996, <http://www.dfat.gov.au/media/speeches/foreign/1996/nsw.dii.html>. See also, "Charting Australia's Regional Future: The White Paper on Foreign and Trade Policy," Speech by The Hon Alexander Downer, MP, Minister for Foreign Affairs, to the Foreign Correspondents' Association, Sydney, 29 August 1997, <http://www.dfat.gov.au/media/speeches/foreign/1997/wpaper29aug97.html>.

111. United Nations peacekeeping is, by design, a neutral undertaking that must not infringe on the sovereignty of any member state. Thus, in order for the United Nations to send observers into East Timor to prepare for the referendum, Indonesia (the ruling government) needed to consent to the deployment of foreign troops within its territory.

112. United Nations peacekeeping troops are only permitted to use their weapons in self-defense. Most missions have no authority to engage in acts that would constitute restoring law and order. The U.N. mission in East Timor was tasked with assisting the administration of the scheduled referendum in order to ensure its fairness. This mission had no broader mandate and could do nothing but stay out of the way when violence erupted.

113. James Bone, "U.N. Rejects Call for Peacekeeping Force in Timor," *The Times* (London), September 2, 1999, Lexis-Nexis.

114. Robert Burns, "U.S. May Provide Air and Other Support but Not Combat Troops," Associated Press, September 13, 1999, Lexis-Nexis; "U.S. Troops Due in Australia for Military Exercise," *Agence France Presse*, September 13, 1999, Lexis-Nexis.

115. A peace enforcement or peace support mission is tasked with the restoration of law and order. To carry out its mandate, the mission operates under liberal rules of military engagement, unlike U.N. peacekeeping operations. Peace enforcement missions became fairly routine in the 1990s. These are not U.N. missions, but U.N. approved missions led by a dominant country and joined by any interested state.

116. David E. Sanger, "Clinton Sees U.S. Playing Support Role in East Timor," *New York Times*, September 13, 1999, A7.

117. Joanne Gray, "U.S. Re-assesses Role and Follows Australia's Lead," *ABIX: Australasian Business Intelligence*, September 14, 1999, Lexis-Nexis.

118. Robert Holloway, "U.N. Will Determine Make-up of Timor Force, Annan Says," *Agence France Presse*, September 13, 1999, Lexis-Nexis.

119. Tom Raum, "President Proposes Joint Military Exercises to Speed Timor Peacekeeping," *Associated Press*, September 15, 1999, Lexis-Nexis.

120. Fred Benchley, "The Howard Defence Doctrine," *Bulletin*, September 17, 1999, as quoted in various sources over the next several weeks, including an abstract in the *ABIX: Australasian Business Intelligence*, September 28, 1999, Lexis-Nexis.

121. "Australia's Howard Unveils New Post-Timor Doctrine on Asia," *Agence France Presse*, September 22, 1999, Lexis-Nexis.

122. "Australia's Howard Unveils New Post-Timor Doctrine."

123. "Australia's Howard Unveils New Post-Timor Doctrine."

124. K. P. Waran, "Australia Insensitive to Asia in Wanting to Be Mata-Mata," *New Straits Times* (Malaysia), September 26, 1999, Lexis-Nexis.

125. Steve Connolly, "No Howard Doctrine Says PM," *AAP Newsfeed*, September 28, 1999, Lexis-Nexis.

126. "Delusions of Grandeur," editorial, *The Dominion* (Wellington), September 29, 1999, 10.

127. Higgott and Nossal, "International Politics of Liminality," 171.

128. Maria Papadakis and Harvey Starr, "Opportunity, Willingness, and Small States: The Relationship between Environment and Foreign Policy," in *New Directions in the Study of Foreign Policy*, ed. Charles F. Hermann, Charles W. Kegley Jr., and James N. Rosenau (Winchester, Mass.: Unwin Hyman, 1987).

129. Copeland, "Constructivist Challenge," 210.

Chapter 5

1. This case can be studied in detail, including issues of British, Chilean, and international law, at the following Web sites maintained by Human Rights Watch: <www.hrw.org/hrw/reports/1999/Chile/Patrick.htm> and <www.hrw.org/complaints/chile98/index.html>.

2. Marc Cooper, *Pinochet and Me: A Chilean Anti-Memoir* (London: Verso, 2001), x.

3. "Should Kissinger Be Tried for War Crimes?" *Statesman* (India), Global News Wire, March 2, 2001, Lexis-Nexis.

4. "Vatican Plea on Pinochet's Behalf Prompts Outrage," *Boston Globe*, February 20, 1999, A20.

5. Marc Cooper, "Now the U.S. Must Face Its Past on Chile," *Los Angeles Times*, December 5, 2000, B9.

6. Karen Mingst, "Uncovering the Missing Links: Linkage Actors and Their Strategies," in Laura Neack, Jeanne A. K. Hey, and Patrick J. Haney, *Foreign Policy Analysis: Continuity and Change in Its Second Generation* (Englewood Cliffs, N.J.: Prentice-Hall, 1995), 235. For more on the rights of community citizens, see the EU Web site, especially <http://europa.eu.int/abc/rights_en.htm>.

7. See the European Court of Justice Web site at <http://curia.eu.int/en/index.htm>.

8. As quoted in "When Tyrants Tremble: The Pinochet Case," Human Rights Watch online <www.hrw.org/hrw/reports/1999/chile>.

9. For an interesting teaching case on Vatican mediation between Latin American countries, see Thomas Princen, "Beagle Channel Negotiations," Pew Case Studies in International Affairs, case no. 401 (Washington, D.C.: Institute for the Study of Diplomacy, 1995).

10. Andrew Sparrow and Bruce Johnston, "Pope Backs Call to Free Pinochet," *Daily Telegraph* (London), February 19, 1999, 1. See also "Vatican Plea on Pinochet's Behalf Prompts Outrage," *Boston Globe*, February 20, 1999, A20.

11. For a time line detailing the events depicted in this tale, see "Events Leading to Hearings on Stripping Pinochet's Immunity," *Agence France Presse*, April 26, 2000, Lexis-Nexis.

12. David White, "Straw to Send Pinochet Home," *Financial Times*, January 12, 2000, 1.

13. "Events Leading to Hearings on Stripping Pinochet's Immunity."

14. This case has been followed with great attention by international media and human rights groups. For an update on the case against Pinochet, see, for example, David Graves, "Pinochet to Stand Trial but Murder Charges Dropped," *Daily Telegraph* (London), March 9, 2001, 20; and Larry Rother, "As Door Opens for Legal Actions in Chilean Coup, Kissinger Is Numbered among the Hunted," *New York Times*, March 28, 2002, A13.

15. Karl Vick, "Former Chad Dictator Faces Pinochet Test," *Washington Post*, January 27, 2000, A22.

16. John Lichfield and Jan McGirk, "Kissinger 'Too Busy' for Chile Murders Inquiry," *Independent* (London), May 30, 2001, 14.

17. Ricardo Lagos and Heraldo Muñoz, "The Pinochet Dilemma," *Foreign Policy*, Spring 1999, 27–28.

18. Lagos and Muñoz, "Pinochet Dilemma," 28.

19. Lagos and Muñoz, "Pinochet Dilemma," 27.

20. INRA News Agency, "Castro Meets Rafsanjani, Says Iran and Cuba Are Models of Resistance to USA," *BBC Worldwide Monitoring*, May 9, 2001, Lexis-Nexis.

21. R. K. Ramazani, "The Shifting Premise of Iran's Foreign Policy: Towards a Democratic Peace?" *Middle East Journal* 52, no. 2 (1998): 178.

22. Moni Basu, "Iran: Struggle Pits Theocracy vs. Democracy," *Atlanta Journal and Constitution*, December 4, 2001, 10A.

23. Ramazani, "The Shifting Premise," 179.

24. Ramazani, "The Shifting Premise," 181.

25. Ramazani, "The Shifting Premise," 183.

26. "Iran: Paper Says New Era in Iran-Saudi Ties Could Transform Region," *BBC Worldwide Monitoring*, April 26, 2001, Lexis-Nexis.

27. Oliver Knox, "US Renews Iran Sanctions, Warns Moscow over Arms Sales to Tehran," *Agence France Presse*, March 14, 2001, Lexis-Nexis.

28. Sanjoy Banerjee, "India's Human Rights Diplomacy: Crisis and Transformation," in *Human Rights and Comparative Foreign Policy*, ed. David P. Forsythe (New York: United Nations University Press, 2000), 178–205.

29. Banerjee, "India's Human Rights Diplomacy," 179.

30. Banerjee, "India's Human Rights Diplomacy," 182.

31. "Globalization Is No Excuse for States to Shirk Their Human Rights Responsibilities: Amnesty International Outlines Human Rights Violations in 149 Countries," Amnesty International news release, May 30, 2001; available online at <www.web.amnesty.org/web/news.nsf>.

32. "Globalization Is No Excuse."

33. Lagos and Muñoz, "Pinochet Dilemma," 37.

34. Lagos and Muñoz, "Pinochet Dilemma," 37.

35. Mingst, "Uncovering the Missing Link," 231.

36. Mingst, "Uncovering the Missing Link," 237, quoting Peter Haas, "Introduction: Epistemic Communities and International Policy Coordination," *International Organization* 46, no. 1 (1992): 3.

37. Karen DeYoung and Michael Dobbs, "Bin Laden: Architect of New Global Terrorism," *Washington Post,* September 16, 2001, A8.

38. Jonathan Curiel, "The Rise of Global Anger: Why They Hate the U.S. So Fiercely," *San Francisco Chronicle,* September 16, 2001, D4.

39. Barton Gellman, "Sudan's Offer to Arrest Militant Fell Through after Saudis Said No," *Washington Post,* October 3, 2001, A1.

40. Sam Dillon, "Indictment by Spanish Judge Portrays a Secret Terror Cell," *New York Times,* November 20, 2001, A1.

41. Sam Dillon with Donald G. McNeil Jr., "Spain Sets Hurdle for Extraditions," *New York Times,* November 24, 2001, A1.

Glossary

accommodation strategy   a strategy in which leaders attempt to bargain with a vocal opposition, accommodating or adopting some of its demands, in order to avoid controversy; associated with a restrained, noncontroversial foreign policy

agent-structure problem   the question of how best to understand the relationship between international actors and the international system, especially in terms of which—actor (agent) or system (structure)—is autonomous of the other

alliance   an association or formal agreement between two or more states made in order to further similar foreign policy objectives such as security

anticolonial   the sentiment that the settlement of foreign territories is illegitimate and that subordinate populations have the right of self-determination and statehood

anarchy   the general condition of the international system in which no ultimate authority (such as a world government) exists to govern relations between states and other international actors

autocratic   a form of government in which a leader (or an autocrat) wields unlimited power

belief set   an organized, relatively integrated, and persistent set of perceptions that an individual, group, or state holds about a particular universe

bilateral   state to state; refers to a relationship or policy between two states

bipolar system   an international system in which power is fairly evenly distributed between two significant powers (states) or two power blocs (groups of states)

centre   also known as the **core;** a term derived from the Marxist, dependency, or structuralist worldviews; the world's wealthiest, most powerful states that work together to construct international institutions which serve to maintain their mutual interests and predominance over the majority of the world's states (which together compose the periphery)

civil society   the public realm "located" between households and government in which interest groups of all sorts protect individuals from the government (and from the free market)

cliency relationship   a reciprocal and strategic relationship between a strong state and a weak one (or between a great power and a small power)

225

CNN effect   an explanation of the media's role in foreign policy making which posits that media broadcasts of unsettling international images incite the public to demand foreign policy action by the government; foreign policy makers, then, must take under consideration issues that they may not have otherwise considered and/or they must make foreign policy decisions without full and appropriate deliberation

coalition building   the bringing together of diverse actors and groups who share an interest in a common policy outcome; because the coalition is loosely built on a narrow issue-base, it requires constant maintenance and rebuilding by coalition leaders

coalition government   in a parliamentary system, an arrangement to govern between two or more political parties that together control sufficient votes to be the majority group in parliament; the leader of the party with the greatest number of seats in parliament is the head of the government formed

cognition   the study of the mental process or faculty of knowing

cognitive consistency   the idea that the images in a belief set must be logically connected and fairly well integrated

cognitive miser   the idea that individuals are assumed to be limited cognitive managers who rely on shortcuts to interpret and understand new information

constructive engagement   a policy of long-term involvement meant to change or influence the policy and behavior of a target state through offering incentives rather than threats and punishments

constructivism   a view that proposes that our understanding of (the world) world politics is a social creation (construction); for instance, constructivism holds that the international system is not anarchic but is understood to be anarchic

crisis   a circumstance in which a threat exists that requires immediate action by decision makers

democracy   a type of government in which power is exercised by the people through freely contested, open, and regularly held elections in which representatives are selected for government office

democratic peace   the theory that democracies are less likely to go to war with other democracies

democratization   the process in which constitutional limits are placed on the exercise of power by central authorities while free and openly contested elections for political office, with universal suffrage, are regularized as the norm

deterrence   a situation in which one's enemy is stopped from initiating a military attack because of the threat of disproportionate retaliation and/or punishment

elite   individuals who exercise great influence in the policy-making process (or individuals who have greater access to decision makers)

escalation-deescalation strategy   a strategy in which (1) an actor plans a series of moves that are contingent on the reactions/moves of an opponent, (2) each move is undertaken in order to maximize relative gains, and (3) the actor intends to back away before incurring any significant loss at the hands of the opponent

EU (European Union)   formed by the 1992 Maastricht Treaty; most recent integration of the European community along political, economic, and foreign policy lines

failed state   a country in which no central government exists that can exercise effective control over the entire national territory; generally characterized by a stalemated civil war and the lack of international recognition for any group of would-be national leaders

game theory   a mathematically based method for evaluating interactive choices which assumes that each player in the "game" (1) operates under the same assumptions and rules for interaction, (2) is aware of the payoff system, and (3) holds a clear understanding of "winning"

global free trade system   a system in which all or a significant majority of the world's states engage in unrestricted trade with one another

globalization   the growing internationalization of culture and economics, accompanied by increased interdependence between individuals and international actors

governance   the act, process, or power of governing

grand strategy   a global vision and set of operating principles that frame the foreign policy of a major power

grassroots mobilization   a linkage actor strategy in which public education and publicity efforts create widespread public engagement in favor of a cause or policy outcome

humanitarian intervention   military involvement in the internal affairs of a state by another state, group of states, or international organization for the purpose of stopping massive human rights violations and/or preventing a humanitarian disaster such as widespread famine

ICC (International Criminal Court)   an international tribunal formally created in July 2002 for prosecuting individuals charged with crimes against humanity and/or war crimes; based in The Hague

insulation strategy   a strategy in which leaders deflect attention from and otherwise protect their foreign policy through suppressing, overriding, or coopting the opposition

INTERFET   The International Force in East Timor, a multinational force under Australian command launched in September 1999 to restore peace and security in East Timor

international organization   a formal organization created by an agreement among states in order to facilitate cooperation on matters of mutual concern; may be regionally based or global

international political economy   the study of the relationship between international politics and economics, or study that proceeds from the assumption that politics and economics are indivisible in the international system

international system   as a descriptive term (rather than as a level of analysis), refers to the totality of international actors, distribution of resources, and the (written and unwritten) rules and (formal and informal) institutions that govern relations among the actors

internationalism   a foreign policy orientation that favors cooperation and mutual empowerment over the narrow pursuit of immediate national interests

IO   *see* **international organization**

isolationism, isolationist   a foreign policy orientation that attempts to disconnect the state from international obligations and entanglements in order to "go it alone" and pursue near-total self-reliance

leader   a person, usually the head of a government, who makes policy choices affecting the international and domestic environments

leadership   the top decision makers in a national government

legitimacy   the recognition or acceptance by citizens and/or international actors, including other states, that a regime or government has the right to exercise power and make decisions on behalf of a state or country

leverage   the use of a group's or state's unique circumstances to strengthen its position relative to another group or state

liberal economic regime   the international agreements and institutions that together construct, protect, and maintain a global free trade system

liberal economic theory   a theory which posits that free trade between countries will increase overall wealth and make conflict between those countries less likely

linkage   the direct or indirect interconnectedness of two policies, groups, ideas, and so on, originating in one system and reacted to in another

linkage actors   individuals, government representatives, and nonstate actors who work across national boundaries to influence public policy

MAD (mutual assured destruction)   the idea that because both the Americans and Soviets possessed nuclear second-strike capability (the ability to sustain a first attack and retaliate in kind), any war between the two initiated by either side would destroy both

methodology   the approaches and practices used in the study of a subject

MFN (most favored nation)   refers to the extension of beneficial trade terms (usually in the form of lowered tariffs) to a country that reflect the best terms extended to third parties in the past or in the future

MNC (multinational corporation)   a business nonstate actor whose production and/or service operations (not just marketing and sales) can be found in many countries

mobilization strategy   a strategy in which leaders use assertive and sometimes risky foreign policy behaviors and calls to nationalism to assert their government's legitimacy against a vocal opposition

multilateralism, multilateralist   acting in cooperation with other states to achieve a common international objective

multinational force   a coercive military group composed of troops from three or more states whose purpose is to create orderly, secure conditions within a conflict zone; often deployed with U.N. approval, but not under U.N. command and control

multipolar system   an international system in which power is fairly evenly distributed among four or five major powers (states)

nation   a sociocultural group with a common language, common cultural institutions, and sometimes a common religion; a group whose members have a sense of a common history and destiny as a "people"

nation building   within a state, refers to efforts by the national government to facilitate political and economic development; also refers to international efforts to facilitate political and economic development within a target state

national interest   the interest(s) of a state that are of primary importance for protection and enhancement

national self-image   the concept or image of the country that is shared among a country's elite and mass public and guides the country's foreign and domestic policies and behaviors

nationalism   strong, positive feelings about a group that are shared among its members and lead the members to want to preserve the group at all costs

NATO (North Atlantic Treaty Organization)   an international organization (alliance) established for the mutual defense of its member states—the United States, Canada, and initially the countries of Western Europe; originally designed to counter the military threat of the Soviet Union and its allies in Central and Eastern Europe; today its members include many of the former Soviet allies and Russia (in a special relationship); now an organization designed to offer peace support operations

negotiation   the process through which international actors interact with and engage one another in order to achieve common objectives

neoimperial   describes the idea that the Western, or advanced industrialized states, use indirect means—usually with some moral justification—to impose their political and economic structures on less developed countries

nested game   *see* **two-level game**

NGO (nongovernmental organization)   a nonstate international actor whose members are not states, and whose membership and interests transcend national boundaries

nonstate actor   an international actor that is not a state or a representative of a state

nuclear deterrence   the condition in which opposing nuclear-weapons states refrain from using such weapons against one another because of the mutual threat of unacceptable damage

PA (Palestinian [National] Authority)   the semi-autonomous governing body of the Palestinian people in the West Bank and Gaza led by Yasser Arafat; intended to be the precursor to the government of the independent country Palestine

partisanship   devotion or commitment to a political party, group, or cause

peace enforcement   the use of military power for the purpose of compelling an end to hostilities and the restoration of order; often used to establish conditions for peacekeeping

peacekeeping   the use of a neutral, noncombatant multinational armed force for the purpose of enforcing a cease-fire, maintaining a demilitarized zone, and/or overseeing the return to normal politics, generally under the command and control of the United Nations

periphery   the states that are economically and politically dependent on the centre or core; also called the developing world

pluralist model   the theory that public policy results from bargaining, negotiating, and politicking among many distinct and autonomous interests within a society

policy coalition   a group composed of diverse interests formed by political leaders in order to get a certain policy program accepted and executed

political opening   within domestic politics, the lifting of barriers on political participation at all levels; associated with democratization

positivism/positivist   an approach to studying social phenomena that is founded on science-based ways of knowing

power approach   a linkage actor strategy in which the highest diplomatic circles or ultimate power resources are tapped in order to influence a policy outcome

preponderance   a condition in which one state possesses disproportionate political, military, and economic power, thereby giving that state a disproportionate voice in international affairs

public opinion   the general views of the majority of individuals about some idea, person, policy, or action

rational choice an approach to studying the behavior of actors in the international system which assumes that all actors will select the course of action that they perceive as most likely to bring about the preferred outcome while maximizing benefits and minimizing costs

regime the central, primary decision makers within a national government

security the absence of threat to acquired core values or national interests

security dilemma a cyclic situation in which actions undertaken by a state to increase its security ultimately decrease overall security because other states (mis)perceive the defensive actions to be hostile and threatening and so they respond in kind

self-determination the right of a group, generally a nation, to govern itself and determine the nature of its own political system

siege mentality when members of a group, nation, or state share the belief that the outside world holds hostile behavioral intentions toward the group

soft power the ability to persuade others to pursue common goals; also understood as the "pull" of an attractive culture

sovereignty the ultimate decision-making and decision-enforcing authority within a defined territory; only states are said to be sovereign in the international system

state a legal-political concept denoting a sovereign actor in the international system with a recognized territory, a population, and an effective government

state building the historical process whereby the institutions of government are constructed and the authority of the government is extended over territory and population

structuralism an approach to the study of international politics and economics that focuses on the structure of the world system—especially the world economic system—and how that structure influences the distribution of power and resources and state behavior

technocratic approach a linkage actor strategy in which expert knowledge is utilized to influence a policy outcome

terrorism the focused use of violence for the purpose of intimidating the victims and achieving certain political objectives

transnational actors individuals or organizations in the international system that conduct activities across national borders

two-level game a concept that national leaders must divide their attention between the domestic and international environments, sometimes using one arena to further agendas in the other; also known as a **nested game**

UN (United Nations) global international organization created in 1945; designed to prevent war and maintain international peace primarily through collective security but secondarily through a wide range of activities

unilateralism, unilateralist when a state acts alone in its pursuit of its own narrowly defined foreign policy goals

unipolar system an international system in which one state holds a preponderance of political, military, and economic power

Index

About the Author

Laura Neack is the Paul Rejai Professor of Political Science at Miami University, Oxford, Ohio. She teaches courses in world politics, comparative foreign policy, and international security. She is the coeditor of two books, *Global Society in Transition* (2002) and *Foreign Policy Analysis: Continuity and Change in Its Second Generation* (1995), and the author of journal articles and book chapters on foreign policy behavior and peacekeeping. She is the editor of the quarterly journal *International Politics* and sits on the editorial boards of the *Bulletin of the Atomic Scientists* and Rowman & Littlefield's New Millennium Books in International Studies. She received her doctorate in political science in 1991 from the University of Kentucky.

ABOUT THE AUTHOR

NEW MILLENNIUM BOOKS
IN INTERNATIONAL STUDIES
Deborah J. Gerner, Series Editor

NEW MILLENNIUM BOOKS issue out of the unique position of the global system at the end of the Cold War, the end of the twentieth century, and the beginning of a new millennium in which our understandings about war, peace, identity, sovereignty, security, and sustainability—whether economic, environmental, or ethical—are likely to be challenged. In the new millennium of international relations, new theories, new actors, and new policies and processes are all bound to be engaged. Books in the series are of three types: compact core texts, supplementary texts, and readers.

Editorial Board

Mark Boyer
University of Connecticut

Maryann Cusimano Love
Catholic University
of America

John Freeman
University of Minnesota

Nils Petter Gleditsch
International Peace
Research Institute

Joshua Goldstein
American University

Vicki Golich
California State
University, San Marcos

Ted Robert Gurr
University of Maryland

Ole Holsti
Duke University

Barry Hughes
University of Denver

Christopher Joyner
Georgetown University

Margaret Karns
University of Dayton

Audie Klotz
University of Illinois,
Chicago

Marc Levy
Columbia University

Laura Neack
Miami University

Anne Sisson Runyan
University of Cincinnati

Gerald Schneider
University of Konstanz,
Germany

Philip Schrodt
University of Kansas

Eric Selbin
Southwestern University

Timothy M. Shaw
University of London

Thomas Weiss
City University of
New York
Graduate Center

Eugene Wittkopf
Louisiana State
University

Michael Zuern
Bremen University

Titles in the Series

The New Foreign Policy: U.S. and Comparative Foreign Policy
in the 21st Century
Laura Neack

Global Backlash: Citizen Initiatives for a Just World Economy
Edited by Robin Broad

Negotiating a Complex World: An Introduction to
International Negotiation
Brigid Starkey, Mark A. Boyer, and Jonathan Wilkenfeld

Military–Civilian Interactions: Intervening in Humanitarian Crises
Thomas G. Weiss

Forthcoming in the Series

Globalization and Belonging: The Politics of Identity in a Changing World
Sheila Croucher

The Global New Deal: Economic and Social Human Rights in World Politics
William F. Felice

Liberals and Criminals: IPE in the New Millennium
H. Richard Friman

International Law in the 21st Century
Christopher C. Joyner

Global Politics as If People Mattered: World Political Economy
from the Ground Up
Ronnie D. Lipschutz and Mary Ann Tetreault

The Peace Puzzle: Ending Violent Conflict in the 21st Century
George A. Lopez

Political Violence
Philip A. Schrodt